TRADE, GROWTH, AND THE BALANCE OF PAYMENTS

Essays in Honor of Gottfried Haberler
on the occasion of his 65th birthday

TRADE, GROWTH, AND THE BALANCE OF PAYMENTS

ESSAYS IN HONOR OF GOTTFRIED HABERLER

by

Robert E. Baldwin
Jagdish Bhagwati
Richard E. Caves
Harry G. Johnson
Reinhard Kamitz
Peter B. Kenen
Charles P. Kindleberger

Fritz Machlup
Jürg Niehans
Bertil Ohlin
Paul A. Samuelson
Egon Sohmen
Wolfgang F. Stolper
Jan Tinbergen

1965

RAND M^C NALLY & COMPANY – CHICAGO

NORTH-HOLLAND PUBLISHING COMPANY

AMSTERDAM

Library of Congress Catalog Card Number 65:18588

Published by:

RAND Mᶜ NALLY AND COMPANY – CHICAGO

Sole distributors outside the United States and Canada:

NORTH-HOLLAND PUBLISHING COMPANY – AMSTERDAM

PRINTED IN THE NETHERLANDS

PREFACE

Few scholars have contributed more to the development of international economics in the twentieth century than Gottfried Haberler. The application to trade theory of the doctrine of opportunity cost, the synthesis of the "second best" aspects of trade policy – without such contributions as these we would be much the poorer. In his teaching and writing, Professor Haberler has always stressed the structure of international economic theory and the relations among its shards and fragments. By leading his students to a full understanding of the architecture of trade theory, he has saved them from giddy flights into ill-conceived theoretical novelty and headlong plunges into analytical error. He has taken a sternly unsentimental approach to questions of public policy that never neglects their analytical underpinnings, and those who have disagreed with him in the forum of policy have often gone away with a better understanding of the logical implications and weaknesses of their own positions.

While Professor Haberler's broad professional interests have always included the fields of business cycles and economic theory, international economics has occupied most of his attention in recent years. As his associates and former students in this field, we have chosen to honor him with a collection of essays on this subject that, we hope, will reflect the range and diversity of his own interests. Professor Haberler once wrote: "International trade theory has never been satisfied merely with explaining, but has always aimed at *evaluation* and policy recommendation. Quite frequently concern with problems of economic policy has given rise to innovation and improvement in the theory itself." The following essays reflect that interrelation of theory and policy. We have grouped them into three major areas of policy problems: trade and resource allocation; trade, growth, and development; and money, prices, and the balance of payments.

Richard E. Caves
Harry G. Johnson
Peter B. Kenen

November, 1964

TABLE OF CONTENTS

Preface

PART THREE   *Money, prices, and the balance of payments*

PART ONE

Trade and resource allocation

OPTIMAL TRADE INTERVENTION
IN THE PRESENCE OF DOMESTIC DISTORTIONS[1]

Harry G. Johnson

I Introduction

In the period since the war, the concern of economists with the problems of the underdeveloped countries and the formulation of policies to stimulate economic development has led to renewed interest in the economic arguments for protection. I use the description "economic arguments" to distinguish arguments that recommend protection as a means of increasing real income or economic welfare from arguments that recommend protection as a means of achieving such essentially noneconomic objectives as increasing self-sufficiency for political and military reasons, diversifying the economy to provide a richer way of life for the citizenry and so strengthening national identity, or preserving a valued traditional way of life. In the first place, writers on economic development have taken over

[1] This paper originated as a guest lecture at the Claremont Colleges, California, delivered in March, 1963. It was originally scheduled for publication in the *Indian Economic Review*, but the editors of that journal have graciously released it for inclusion in this volume on the grounds that its contents bear witness to the depth and durability of Gottfried Haberler's contribution to the pure theory of international trade and economic welfare.

The paper represents a condensation of analysis developed in lectures and writings over a period of years. The organization of the argument around the two central propositions of the paper, however, is derived from discussion with Jagdish Bhagwati, and particularly from an early reading of his brilliant joint article with V. K. Ramaswami, "Domestic Distortions, Tariffs and the Theory of Optimum Subsidy", *Journal of Political Economy*, LXXI, No. 1 (February, 1963), 44-50. To these two authors belongs the credit for reducing a mass of *ad hoc* arguments concerning tariffs to a simple application of second-best welfare theory. The present paper extends their analysis to some arguments for protection not considered by them, elaborates more fully on the infant industry argument, and adds to their results two propositions about noneconomic arguments for protection. I should like also to acknowledge a debt to Erling Olsen, whose comments on an earlier draft prompted improvements in the presentation of the factor-price rigidity case.

and made considerable use of the theory of the optimum tariff, originated by Bickerdike and revived in the 1940's and early 1950's as a by-product of the contemporary debate over the legitimacy of welfare propositions in economics. Secondly, writers in the economic development area have laid considerable stress on the traditional "external economies" and "infant industry" arguments for protection; in recent years they have also developed new, or at least heretofore not much emphasized, arguments for protection based on the alleged fact that in underdeveloped countries wages in manufacturing exceed the opportunity cost of labor in the economy – the marginal productivity of labor in the agricultural sector. Two distinct reasons for the alleged discrepancy between industrial wage rates and the opportunity costs of labor are advanced, it not always being recognized that they are distinct. One, which can be associated with the name of Arthur Lewis,[2] is that industrial wages are related to earnings in the agricultural sector, and that these earnings are determined by the average product of labor, which exceeds the marginal product of labor because agricultural labor has familial or traditional claims on the rent of land. The other reason, associated with the name of Everett Hagen[3] but equally attributable to Lewis,[4] is that the industrial wage rate exceeds the agricultural wage rate by a margin larger than can be explained by the economic costs of urban life;[5] this difference Hagen associates with the dynamic need for a growing economy to transfer labor from agriculture to industry, although it can also be explained by social influences on industrial wage determination.

The theory of the optimum tariff rests on the proposition that if a country possesses monopolistic or monopsonistic power in world markets, world market prices for its exports and imports will not correspond to the marginal national revenue from exports or marginal national cost of its

---

[2]   W. Arthur Lewis, "Economic Development with Unlimited Supplies of Labour", *Manchester School of Economic and Social Studies*, XXII, No. 2 (May, 1954), 139-91, and "Unlimited Labour: Further Notes", *Manchester School of Economic and Social Studies*, XXVI, No. 1 (January, 1958), 1-32.

[3]   Everett E. Hagen, "An Economic Justification of Protectionism", *Quarterly Journal of Economics*, LXXII, No. 4 (November, 1958), 496-514.

[4]   "Economic Development...", pp. 150-51.

[5]   Hagen (*op. cit.*, p. 496, n. 2) traces the origins of the argument to Jacob Viner's review of M. Manoilesco's *The Theory of Protection and International Trade* (London: P. S. King, 1931), in the *Journal of Political Economy*, XL, No. 1 (February, 1932), 121-25.

imports, and asserts that by appropriately chosen export and import duties – taxes on trade – the country can equate the relative prices of goods to domestic producers and consumers with their relative opportunity costs in international trade. In other words, the theory of the optimum tariff rests on the existence of a distortion in international markets, viewed from the national standpoint, such that market prices diverge from opportunity costs; and the optimum tariff is recommended as a means of offsetting this distortion. The other economic arguments for protection, with which this paper is concerned, rest on the presence of distortions in the domestic economy, which create a divergence between domestic prices and domestic opportunity costs; in these arguments, protection is recommended as a means of offsetting the distortions that prevent domestic prices from reflecting domestic opportunity costs.

The purpose of this paper is to explain and elaborate on two propositions concerning arguments for protection derived from the existence or alleged existence of domestic distortions. The first proposition is that such distortions do not logically lead to the recommendation of protection, in the sense of taxes on international trade; instead, they lead to the recommendation of other forms of government intervention which do not discriminate between domestic and international trade and which differ according to the nature of the distortion they are intended to correct. The second proposition is that if protection is adopted as a means of correcting domestic distortions, not only will the result be that economic welfare will fall short of the maximum obtainable, but economic welfare may even be reduced below what it would be under a policy of free trade. These two propositions can be combined in the proposition that the only valid argument for protection as a means of maximizing economic welfare is the optimum tariff argument; all other arguments for protection of this kind are in principle arguments for some form of government intervention in the domestic economy, and lead to the recommendation of protection only when supported both by practical considerations that render the appropriate form of intervention infeasible, and empirical evidence that protection will in fact increase economic welfare.

II Definitions and assumptions

As a preliminary to the development of the main theme, it is necessary to comment briefly on certain aspects of the setting of the problem and the definition of terms.

In the first place, it is necessary to define the word "protection". Economists generally use this word in a very loose sense, which carries the connotation of a tariff on imports but also lends itself to extension to any policy that raises the price received by domestic producers of an importable commodity above the world market price. Not only can the effect of a tariff be achieved in the modern world by other devices, such as import restrictions, exchange controls, and multiple exchange rates – devices which may achieve the effect of raising the domestic relative price of importable goods above their relative price in the world market by operating to restrict exports as well as to restrict imports – but the domestic relative price received by producers of importable goods can be raised above the world price by two quite different means – by raising the domestic price to both producers and consumers above the world price, through tariffs or equivalent devices, and by raising the domestic price to producers only above the world price, while leaving consumers free to buy at world prices, through subsidies on production or equivalent taxation of production of alternative products. These two means of raising prices to domestic producers above world prices differ sharply in their economic implications, as will appear from what follows, and the confusion of them in the loose usage of the term "protection" has been responsible for serious analytical errors in the literature. In this paper, I confine the term "protection" to policies that create a divergence between the relative prices of commodities to domestic consumers and producers, and their relative prices in world markets. This usage does not preclude anyone who wishes to describe policies of subsidizing domestic production by one means or another as protection from doing so, and interpreting my analysis as showing that protection by subsidies is economically desirable in certain cases of domestic distortion, provided that he clearly distinguishes protection by subsidy from protection by tariff. It is perhaps worth noting in passing – though this is not part of the subject of this paper – that the identification of protection with the tariff is a potent source of confusion in other contexts than the relation of protection to economic welfare; for example, the degree of protection afforded to a particular industry by a tariff structure depends not only on the tariff rate on its product but on the tariffs and other taxes levied or subsidies paid both on its inputs and on the other goods that could be produced by the resources it uses;[6] and these complications include the effects of over-valuation or undervaluation of the exchange rate.

Secondly, it is necessary to be precise about the meaning attached to an improvement or deterioration in economic welfare. Disagreement on this question was the foundation of the classic debate between Gottfried Haberler and Thomas Balogh that followed on Haberler's attempt to analyze the issues discussed in this paper with the assistance of a criterion of improvement in welfare that has subsequently been shown to be objectionable.[7] This paper employs the concept of welfare in the modern sense of potential welfare, and regards a change in the economic environment as producing a potential improvement in economic welfare if, in the new environment, everyone could be made better off – in the usual sense of enjoying a higher consumption of goods and services – than in the old environment, if income were distributed in accordance with any social welfare function applied consistently in the new and the old environment. This approach permits the use of community indifference curves to represent the potential welfare of the community. One might indeed go further and maintain that the assumption that some social welfare function exists and is implemented is essential to any rational discussion of national economic policy.

Thirdly, it is assumed in this paper, in accordance with the conventions of theoretical analysis of these problems, that government intervention is a costless operation: in other words, there is no cost attached to the choice between a tax and a subsidy. This assumption ignores the empirical consideration, frequently introduced into arguments about protection, that poor countries have considerably greater difficulty in levying taxes to finance subsidies than they have in levying tariffs on imports. This consideration is of practical rather than theoretical consequence, and to constitute a case for tariffs requires supplementation by empirical measurement of both the relative administrative costs and the economic effects of

---

[6] For an analysis of the protective incidence of a particular tariff structure, see my "The Bladen Plan for Increased Protection of the Canadian Automotive Industry", *Canadian Journal of Economics and Political Science*, XXIX, No. 2 (May, 1963), 212-38.

[7] Haberler, "Some Problems in the Pure Theory of International Trade", *Economic Journal*, LX, No. 2 (June, 1950), 223-40; Balogh, "Welfare and Freer Trade – A Reply", *Economic Journal*, LXI, No. 241 (March, 1951), 72-82; Haberler, "Welfare and Freer Trade – A Rejoinder", *Economic Journal*, LXI, No. 244 (December, 1951), 777-84.

the alternative methods of promoting favored industries – as has already
been mentioned. Its relevance to practical policy-making is probably less
than is frequently assumed, since on the one hand the intent of a protective
tariff is not to yield revenue, and on the other hand the effect of a subsidy
on one type of production can be achieved by taxes levied on alternative
lines of production. The assumption also ignores the possibility that the
income or other taxes levied to finance subsidies to production may have a
distorting effect on the supply or allocation of resources. Abandonment of
this assumption would also lead to the necessity of empirical assessment
of the relative economic costs of alternative methods of promoting
favored industries.

Finally, something should be said about the bearing of theoretical
analysis of the arguments for protection on practical policy-making and
the assessment of actual tariff systems. The demonstration that in certain
carefully defined circumstances a tariff levied at a theoretically specified
rate would make a country better off than it would be under free trade is
not – contrary to the implication of many economic writings on protection – equivalent to a demonstration that past or present tariffs have in
fact made the nations imposing them better off than they would have been
under free trade, or a justification of whatever tariffs legislators might
choose to adopt. Modern economic analysis of the cases in which a tariff
or other governmental intervention in the price system would improve
economic welfare, in other words, does not constitute a defense of indiscriminate protectionism and a rejection of the market mechanism;
rather, it points to a number of respects in which the market mechanism
fails to work as it should, and indicates remedies designed to make the
market function properly. The usefulness of the exercise depends precisely
on the assumption that legislators do not normally know what makes for
improvement of economic welfare, and would be prepared to act on better
information if it could be provided. If economists did not customarily
accept this assumption, their work on economic policy would have to be
oriented entirely differently; in particular, research on commercial policy
would – depending on the theory of government adopted – be concerned
with inferring from actual tariff structures either the divergences between
social and private costs and benefits discovered by the collective wisdom
of the legislators to exist in the economy, or the political power of various
economic groups in the community, as measured by their capacity to
extort transfers of income from their fellow-citizens.

III   The two propositions

With the preliminary definitions, assumptions, and observations established, I turn to the main theme of the paper, the two propositions concerning optimal government intervention in the presence of domestic distortions. The first proposition, that the correction of such distortions does not require intervention in the form of taxes on international trade (taxes here include negative taxes or subsidies), follows directly from the well-known first-order marginal conditions of Pareto optimality. These conditions specify that the marginal rate of substitution between goods in consumption should be equal to the marginal rate of transformation between goods in production, and in an open economy include transformation through international exchange as well as transformation through domestic production. It follows that any distortion that prevents market prices from corresponding to marginal social rates of substitution or transformation should be corrected by a tax, a subsidy, or a combination of taxes and subsidies that restores the necessary marginal equalities; for simplicity, it is convenient to consider the simplest remedy, a tax or subsidy imposed at the point where the distortion occurs. Where there is a distortion in foreign markets, owing to imperfectly elastic foreign demand or supply, Pareto optimality requires the imposition of taxes on trade designed to equate the domestic price ratios facing producers and consumers with the marginal rates of transformation between commodities in international trade – that is, the imposition of the optimum tariff structure.[8] In the case of domestic distortions, Pareto optimality requires the imposition of taxes or subsidies on consumption, production, or factor supply, as the situation requires.

Where externalities in consumption make social marginal rates of substitution diverge from private, taxes or subsidies on consumption are required; where external economies in production exist, or where monopolistic influences raise prices above marginal costs, marginal subsidies on

---

[8]   It should perhaps be emphasized that the welfare being maximized is the national welfare, and the distortions in question are distortions only from the national point of view. Also, tariff retaliation by other countries does not necessarily prevent a country from gaining by the imposition of an optimum tariff structure; see my "Optimum Tariffs and Retaliation", *Review of Economic Studies*, XXII (2), No. 55 (1953-54), 142-53, reprinted in H. G. Johnson, *International Trade and Economic Growth* (London: George Allen & Unwin, 1958), chap. ii.

production are required, and where external diseconomies are present, marginal taxes on production are required; and where the price of a factor in a particular occupation exceeds its price in other occupations by more than can be accounted for by the nonpecuniary disadvantages of that occupation, a subsidy on the use of that factor in that occupation is required. The point of central importance is that the correction of domestic distortions requires a tax or subsidy on either domestic consumption or domestic production or domestic factor use, not on international trade.

The imposition of any tax or subsidy on international trade, other than what is indicated by the optimum tariff analysis, for the purpose of correcting a domestic distortion, itself introduces an inequality between either the marginal rate of substitution in domestic consumption or the marginal rate of transformation in domestic production and the marginal rate of transformation in foreign trade, and so constitutes a violation of Pareto optimality. A tax on luxury imports, for example, designed to discourage an undesirable demonstration effect and therefore to correct an external diseconomy of consumption, permits the marginal rate of transformation of domestic resources into the importable good in question to exceed the marginal rate of transformation through foreign trade. A tax on imports or subsidy to exports of goods subject to external economies or monopolistic pricing in domestic production, designed to offset these distortions, makes the relative marginal cost of these goods to consumers higher than their marginal cost to the economy. Since the offsetting of domestic distortions by taxes or subsidies on trade necessarily removes one distortion at the expense of introducing another, interventions in international trade introduced for this purpose cannot lead to a situation of Pareto optimality. Consequently, tariffs and other trade interventions justified on grounds of the existence of domestic distortions cannot lead to the maximization of real income. The only forms of intervention that can do so are interventions that offset the existing distortions without introducing new distortions; such interventions are confined to taxes and subsidies on domestic consumption, production, or factor use.

The second proposition, that taxes or subsidies on international trade designed to offset domestic distortions will not necessarily increase economic welfare by comparison with the free trade situation, is a direct application of the theory of second best developed by Meade, Lipsey and

Lancaster, and others.[9] One implication of that theory is that it is impossible to predict on *a priori* grounds – that is, without comprehensive empirical information on the tastes and technology of the economy – whether the substitution of one violation of the Pareto optimality conditions for another will worsen or improve economic welfare. Since the use of intervention in trade to offset domestic distortions necessarily involves precisely this kind of substitution, it is impossible to say whether the result will be an improvement in welfare or not. For example, in the consumption externality case mentioned above, free trade produces the result $MRT_d = MRT_f > MRS$; and an import tariff produces the result $MRT_d > MRT_f = MRS$. In the case of external economies in production or monopolistic pricing, free trade produces the result $MRT_d < MRT_f = MRS$, and an import tariff produces the result $MRT_d = MRT_f < MRS$. In the case of a distortion in the market for factors, there are additional violations of the Pareto optimality conditions in the factor markets under both free trade and protection.[10]

The remainder of the paper is concerned with illustrating these propositions by reference to various arguments for protection. For this purpose, it is convenient to follow the general outline of Haberler's classic article,[11] modified to include fuller treatment of the arguments emphasized in the recent literature on underdeveloped countries, and to divide the arguments for protection into four groups. These are: arguments derived from immobility of factors and downward rigidity of factor prices; arguments derived from distortions in commodity markets; arguments derived from distortions in factor markets; and the infant industry argument. The first class of argument, to which Haberler devoted considerable space, grew out of the unemployment problem of the 1930's and the associated revival of protectionism. The second includes both the classical problems of external economies and diseconomies, and the problem of monopolistic distortions to which considerable attention was

---

[9] See J. E. Meade, *Trade and Welfare* (London: Oxford University Press, 1955), and R. G. Lipsey and K. Lancaster, "The General Theory of the Second Best", *Review of Economic Studies*, XXIV, No. 63 (1956-57), 11-32.

[10] *MRS* symbolizes marginal rate of substitution in domestic consumption, MRT_d marginal rate of transformation in domestic production, MRT_t marginal rate of transformation in foreign trade; all of these are defined in terms of the amount of the export good given up in exchange for a unit increment of the import good.

[11] "Some Problems...", pp. 223-40.

devoted in the 1930's following the development of the theory of monopolistic (imperfect) competition. The third involves the essential elements
of the new case for protection developed on the basis of the disequilibrium
in the labor market alleged to be characteristic of underdeveloped
countries. The fourth is, of course, the orthodox accepted exception to the
case for free trade.

IV   The standard trade model

To provide a frame of reference for the analysis of these arguments, it is
convenient to use the standard model of international trade. This model
simplifies the problem by assuming that the economy produces two
commodities only, by employing only two factors of production, the
available quantities of which are assumed to be given; the production
functions for the two commodities are assumed to be subject to constant
returns to scale, an assumption which eliminates externalities in production; and perfect competition is assumed in the commodity and factor
markets, which assumption includes perfect flexibility of prices and
mobility of factors between industries. These assumptions permit the
production conditions of the economy to be summarized in a community
transformation curve between the two commodities, such that at any exchange ratio between the commodities production will be represented by
the point on the transformation curve at which the slope of that curve is
equal to the exchange ratio. On the demand side, factor owners are
assumed to be indifferent between occupations – utility depends only on
the quantities of goods consumed – and consumers' welfare is assumed to
depend only on personal consumption, which assumption eliminates
externalities in consumption. (Such consumption externalities are ignored
in the remainder of this paper, since they have not been advanced as an
important argument for protection, and the relevant analysis follows
directly from the proposition already presented, and from analogy with
the cases of production distortion dealt with below.) The individual tastes
and distribution of income that determine the demand for the two
commodities are assumed to be summarizable in a set of community
indifference curves, such that for any given income and exchange ratio the
consumption of the two commodities will be that which places the
community on the highest attainable indifference curve. Since in a

competitive economy the distribution of income depends on the distribution of factor ownership and varies with factor prices, the set of community indifference curves has to be interpreted as embodying either the concept of potential welfare employed in modern welfare economics, or the expression of a particular social welfare function in a particular invariant distribution of income among the members of the community. The conclusions concerning the effects of alternative types of government intervention on economic welfare derived below are to be interpreted as referring to welfare in either of these two senses. Since the concern of the paper is with government intervention in the presence of domestic distortions, it is convenient to exclude distortions in foreign markets by

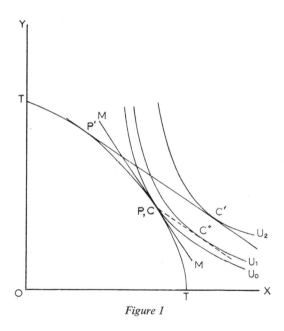

Figure 1

assuming that the opportunity to trade internationally consists in the opportunity to exchange goods in the world market at an exchange ratio different from that which would rule in the economy in the absence of the opportunity to trade, which international exchange ratio is assumed to be independent of the direction or magnitude of the trade of the country under analysis. The two commodities will be referred to as X and Y, and it is assumed throughout that the country's true comparative advantage lies in Y, in the sense that the comparative cost of Y in the absence of the opportunity to trade is lower than the comparative cost of Y embodied in the international exchange ratio.

This standard model of international trade is represented in the accompanying Figure 1, where TT is the transformation curve and U_0, U_1, U_2 are the community indifference curves. In the absence of the opportunity to trade, the community would produce and consume at P, C, the closed-economy exchange ratio between the goods being represented by the slope of the common tangent MM to the transformation and indifference curves at that point. The opportunity to trade (represented by the slope $P'C'$) allows the economy to increase its welfare from U_0 to U_2, by shifting from production and consumption at P, C to production at P' and consumption at C'. The gain in welfare resulting from trade can be divided into two components: the increase in welfare from U_0 to U_1 resulting from the opportunity to exchange the goods produced in the absence of trade for the more attractive consumption combination C'' – the consumption or exchange gain; and the increase in welfare from U_1 to U_2 resulting from the opportunity to produce a combination of goods more valuable at the international price ratio than the closed economy output – the production or specialization gain. The adjustment to the higher international price of Y necessarily involves an increase in the relative price of the factor used relatively intensively in producing that commodity, and a reduction in the relative price of the factor used relatively intensively in producing the importable commodity X.

V   Factor immobility and price rigidity

For the analysis of arguments for protection derived from immobility of factors and downward rigidity of factor prices, it is convenient to pose the problem in terms of whether the opening of the opportunity to trade makes a country worse off when these conditions exist, so that a prohibitive tariff would secure a higher level of welfare than could be attained under free trade, even though in reality the argument for protection on these grounds usually arises when trade is already established and the international price of imports suddenly falls. The difference of assumptions merely simplifies the problem without altering the conclusions.

As Haberler has shown, there is a fundamental difference between the effects of immobility of factors, combined with flexibility of factor prices, and of downward rigidity of factor prices, whether combined with immobility or not. As the analysis of the standard model of trade shows, the country would enjoy a consumption or exchange gain from trade even if production remained at the closed-economy equilibrium point. Production would remain at that point if factors were completely immobile but their prices were perfectly flexible; if factors were partially mobile, production would shift to some point within the transformation curve but necessarily entailing a higher value of production at world market prices, that is, yielding some production or specialization gain. It follows that so long as factor prices are flexible, immobility of factors cannot prevent the country from being better off under free trade than with protection. The fundamental reason for this is that immobility does not by itself entail a distortion of the first-order conditions of Pareto optimality. So long as factor prices are flexible, and immobility is taken as an immutable fact of life (more is said on this point below), factor prices will reflect the alternative opportunity costs of factors to the economy; hence there is no domestic distortion to be offset by protection, and protection will simply introduce a distortion of the marginal conditions for optimality in foreign trade.

Downward rigidity of factor prices does introduce a distortion, if (as Haberler has carefully pointed out) such rigidity does not reflect a perfectly elastic supply of the factor in question (derived, for example, from an infinite elasticity of substitution between leisure and consumption) but instead reflects institutional limitations on voluntary choice (imposed, for example, by conventional pricing of labor services or collective bargaining).[12] Analysis of the effects of downward rigidity of factor prices requires definition of the terms in which factor prices are rigid downwards, since factor prices may be rigid in terms of one commodity or the other or of the utility level enjoyed, and consideration of various possible combinations of downward price rigidity and immobility.

If factor prices are rigid in terms of X and both factors are immobile,

---

[12] It should be noted that, for analysis with the techniques of trade theory, factor prices must be assumed to be rigid in real terms; if factor prices are rigid in money terms ("money illusion" of the Keynesian type is present), full employment can always be secured by devaluation coupled with an appropriate domestic fiscal-monetary policy. This point is not made explicit in Haberler's analysis; cf. "Some Problems...", pp. 227-31.

production will remain where it was in the absence of trade (at point P in Figure 2). The result will be the same as with factor price flexibility, since the marginal productivities of the factors in the X industry in terms of X are unchanged, while the marginal productivities of the factors in the Y industry are unchanged in terms of Y but greater in terms of X, because

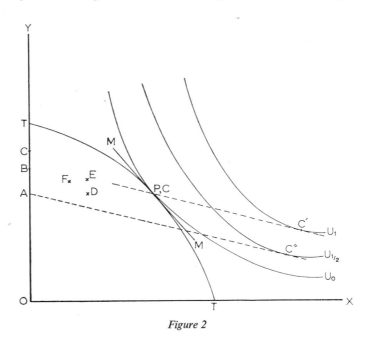

Figure 2

the price of X in terms of Y has fallen as a result of trade. If both factor prices are rigid in terms of Y or of constant-utility combinations of X and Y, and both factors are immobile, production of X will cease, and both factors used in producing X will become wholly unemployed (the economy will produce at point A in Figure 2, level with P, C). This result follows from the fact that the marginal productivities of the factors in the X industry will be unchanged in terms of X but lower in terms of Y or any combination of X and Y, because the price of X in terms of Y has decreased as a result of trade. Since the value of each factor's marginal product is now below its price when the factors are combined in the ratio optimal at these factor prices, and since neither factor price can fall to induce factor substitution and raise the marginal productivity of the other factor, the cost of production of X must exceed its price at any positive level of output.

If both factor prices are rigid (in terms of X or of Y or of a constant-utility combination of X and Y), and both factors are perfectly mobile, production of X will cease and factors will be transferred into production of Y. Some of the factor used intensively in producing X must, however, become unemployed, so that production of Y will be less than the maximum possible production shown by the transformation curve, since full employment of both factors necessitates a reduction of the price of that factor in terms of both commodities, according to the well-known Stolper-Samuelson analysis.[13] The amount of unemployment of the factor in question will be greater, and the increase in production of Y less, if factor prices are rigid in terms of Y than if they are rigid in terms of X, since a given factor price expressed in Y now buys more X, and the marginal productivity of the surplus factor in the Y industry can fall if factor prices are rigid in terms of X but not if they are rigid in terms of Y. (The extremes are represented for illustrative purposes by points B and C in Figure 2: if factor prices are rigid in terms of utility, production of Y will fall somewhere between these points.)

If both factors are immobile but the price of one of them is flexible, whereas the price of the other is rigid in terms of Y or of a constant-utility combination of X and Y, production of X will not cease altogether; instead, enough of the rigid-priced factor in that industry will become unemployed to lower its ratio to the other factor to what is consistent with its rigid price. Obviously, the unemployment of that factor and the decrease in production of X will be greater if that factor's price is rigid in terms of Y than if it is rigid in terms of a constant-utility combination of X and Y, and in the latter case will be less the less important is Y in the factor's consumption. (This case is represented in Figure 2 by the single point D, in the same horizontal line as A and P, C.) If one of the factors is mobile, and its price is rigid in terms of X or of a constant-utility combination of X and Y, whereas the other factor is immobile and flexible-priced, some of the rigid-priced factor will transfer to the Y industry, increasing output there. The transfer will proceed to the point

---

[13]   W. F. Stolper and P. A. Samuelson, "Protection and Real Wages", *Review of Economic Studies*, IX (November, 1941), 58-73, reprinted in *Readings in the Theory of International Trade* (Philadelphia: The Blakiston Co., 1949).

where its effect in raising the ratio of the mobile factor to the other in the Y industry lowers the marginal productivity of the mobile factor in the Y industry to the level set by its price-rigidity. (This case is represented by point E in Figure 2; E may be vertically above D as in the diagram or to the left of it, and must correspond to a higher value of output at world prices than D.) If one of the factors is mobile and flexible-priced, whereas the other factor is immobile and its price is rigid in terms of X or of Y or of a constant-utility combination of X and Y, production of Y will increase and of X decrease as compared with the case of immobility of both factors; production of X may or may not cease entirely depending on the elasticities of substitution between the factors in the two industries and on the terms in which the immobile factor's price is rigid. (This case is represented by point F in the diagram, and may or may not correspond to a higher value of output than at D.)

Whatever the combination of factor immobility and factor price rigidity assumed, production will be altered to some point in the interior of the transformation curve corresponding to production of less X and possibly no more Y than in the closed-economy equilibrium (except for the extreme case of complete immobility and factor price rigidity in terms of X already noted). This does not, however, necessarily imply that free trade makes the country worse off than it would be under the self-sufficiency obtainable by a prohibitive tariff. It may, or it may not. Figure 2 illustrates the possibility of the country's being better off with free trade than with a prohibitive tariff even in the extreme case in which production of X ceases altogether, with no consequent increase in the production of Y, owing to a combination of complete factor immobility with factor price rigidity. In this case, as the diagram shows, the country could be made still better off than under free trade by subsidizing production of the initial output of X sufficiently to permit the factors being paid the minimum prices they demand, but trading at the international exchange ratio. In the less extreme cases, more complex forms of subsidy may be necessary to achieve the output combination that has the highest value at the international exchange ratio attainable under the relevant restrictions on factor mobility.

VI Distortions in the commodity market

The second group of arguments for protection to be discussed comprises arguments derived from the existence of distortions in the markets for commodities that have the effect of raising the market price of the commodity in which the country has a comparative advantage above its alternative opportunity cost. One possibility is the presence of monopoly or oligopoly conditions in the production of the good, which have the effect of raising the price to consumers above the marginal cost of production. Another is the presence of external economies or diseconomies, which make marginal cost as it appears to producers higher than marginal social cost. The marginal social cost of increased output of a particular commodity may be lower than the marginal private cost because expansion of the industry producing it yields economies of scale external to the individual firm, or because contraction of the industry from which this industry draws its factors of production lowers costs of production in the former because that industry is subject to diseconomies of scale, or because expansion of the one industry lowers the cost of production of the other through any one of a variety of effects.

The result of either type of distortion, in terms of the simple model of

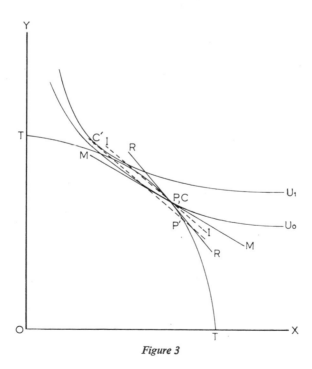

Figure 3

international trade, is that the market price ratio at which a particular combination of *X* and *Y* will be produced will be less steep than the slope of the transformation curve, reflecting the assumption that the relative price of *Y* (the good in which the country is assumed to have a comparative advantage) exceeds its social opportunity cost. In the absence of the opportunity to trade, the country will therefore in equilibrium produce more *X* and less *Y* than would be socially optimal; the closed-economy equilibrium is represented in Figure 3 by the point *P*, *C*, the slope of *MM* corresponding to the market price ratio and that of *RR* to the true comparative cost ratio. The opening of the opportunity to trade at an international price ratio at which the country's true comparative advantage lies in *Y* has two alternative possible results, according to the relation between the international price ratio and the closed-economy market price ratio: this relation may indicate either an apparent comparative advantage in *X*, in which case the country specializes in the wrong direction, or an apparent comparative advantage in *Y* corresponding to the country's true comparative advantage, in which case the country specializes in the right direction but to a suboptimal extent.

The first case is represented in Figure 3 by the international price ratio *II*, which leads the country to the production equilibrium *P'* and the consumption equilibrium *C'*, involving the export of *X*, in which the country is at a true comparative disadvantage. The point *P'* necessarily represents a lower value of output at the international price ratio than the closed-economy production point *P*; but *C'* may lie on either a lower indifference curve than the closed-economy consumption point *C*, or a higher one, the latter possibility being illustrated in the diagram. In other words, trade leads to a production loss and a consumption gain, and the latter may or may not offset the former.

The argument for protection in this case is that the country will gain by imposing a tariff on imports to raise their price to consumers above the world price, compensating for the distortion that makes the apparent cost of domestically produced importables exceed their true social cost. (Alternatively, the country could levy a tax on exports to compensate for the distortion that makes their true social cost exceed their apparent cost.) Since the country's true comparative advantage lies in the good it imports, the imposition of an import tariff (or an export duty) at a rate just sufficient to compensate for the distortion would effect a return to self-sufficiency at the production and consumption equilibrium *P*, *C*, since a tax on trade cannot reverse the direction of trade. The effect of the tariff would be to increase the value of the country's output at the international price ratio; but, as the diagram exemplifies, the resulting pattern of consumption might yield a lower level of economic welfare than would be attained in the absence of protection. In short, the imposition of the tariff to correct the distortion of domestic prices from opportunity costs achieves a production gain at the expense of a consumption loss, and the

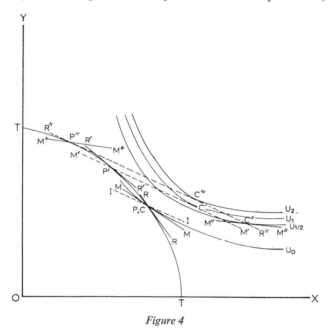

Figure 4

net effect may be a gain or a loss, by comparison with free trade. Thus free trade in the wrong direction may be superior to protection designed to correct a distortion of domestic market prices; which policy is actually superior depends on the magnitudes of the distortion of domestic prices from opportunity costs and the difference between the closed-economy exchange ratio and the international exchange ratio, and the shape of the community's preference system.[14]

[14] Bhagwati and Ramaswami (*op. cit.*, p. 49) use this demonstration to show that Hagen's analysis errs in concluding that self-sufficiency is necessarily better than free trade in this case.

The second case is illustrated in Figure 4, where at the international price ratio *II* the country's apparent comparative advantage lies in the commodity in which it has a true comparative advantage, and the opportunity to trade leads to the production equilibrium P' and consumption equilibrium C', involving the export of commodity *Y*. P' necessarily represents a higher value of national output at the international exchange ratio than the closed-economy production point *P*, so that the country enjoys both a consumption gain and a production gain from trade; but the volume of international trade falls short of the optimum level, owing to the excess of the price of *Y* over its comparative cost.

In this case, the arguments for intervention in international trade to correct the distortion of domestic prices would indicate an export subsidy on *Y* (or import subsidy on *X*). The same policy might be recommended to overcome the inability of the tariff to promote exports in the circumstances of the case previously considered. (In either case, to be effectively a subsidy on trade rather than on production, the export subsidy would have to be accompanied by measures preventing reimportation.) The introduction of such a subsidy at a rate just sufficient to offset the distortion would lead to the production equilibrium P'' and consumption equilibrium C'' shown in Figure 4, the new domestic price ratio being represented by $M''M''$. The subsidy would necessarily raise the value of output at the international exchange ratio above what it would be under free trade, but, as the diagram illustrates, it might nevertheless lead to a consumption pattern yielding a lower level of welfare than that enjoyed under free trade, owing to the consumption loss induced by the effect of the subsidy in raising the domestic relative price of the exported good *Y* above the world market price. In order to achieve the maximum attainable economic welfare (C''' in Figure 4), the country should subsidize production of *Y* (or tax production of *X*) at a rate sufficient to compensate for the domestic distortion, without discriminating between domestic and foreign consumers by a tax (in the first case) or subsidy (in the second case) on international trade.[15]

One further comment on arguments for governmental intervention derived from distortions in domestic commodity markets is worth making. The foregoing analysis lumps together distortions originating in

---

[15]   Bhagwati and Ramaswami (*op. cit.*, p. 47) use this demonstration to show that Haberler was wrong to recommend an export or import subsidy in this case.

external economies and diseconomies, and distortions originating in imperfectly competitive market organization; and it assumes that the distortions are independent of the governmental intervention, so that intervention can be designed to offset them. This assumption is legitimate for the first type of distortion, but of doubtful validity for the second. Monopolistic practices are generally intimately interrelated with commercial policy, and there is reason to believe that producers often collude to exploit the profit opportunities created by protection. Where this is so, the attempt to offset monopolistic distortions by protective interventions in trade (taxes or subsidies on trade) may well be offset by increased distortions, so that intervention generates a consumption loss without a countervailing production gain; the same reaction could render nugatory the attempt to employ optimal intervention in the form of production taxes or subsidies. In these circumstances, the only effective means of achieving maximum economic welfare would be a direct attack on the source of the distortion, through trust-busting policies, although it is worth noting that genuine free trade may be the most effective policy for controlling monopoly.

VII   Distortions in the factor market

The third group of arguments for protection comprises arguments derived from the existence of distortions in the markets for factors that, by raising the price of a factor used in producing the commodity in which the country has a comparative advantage above the factor's marginal productivity in the rest of the economy, raises the private cost of production of the commodity above its alternative opportunity cost. As mentioned, two reasons for such a distortion are commonly advanced in the literature on economic development, both of which pertain to a distortion in the labor market and are used to favor protection of industry – that earnings of labor in agriculture exceed the marginal productivity of labor there, so that the industrial wage must exceed the alternative opportunity cost of labor, and that industrial wages exceed wages in agriculture by a margin greater than can be accounted for by the disutility or higher cost of urban life.

The effect of such distortions in factor markets is twofold: first, they make the allocation of factors between industries inefficient, so that production is below the maximum attainable – in terms of the model of international trade, the transformation curve is pulled in toward the origin, except at the extreme points of specialization on one or the other commodity. Second, they will normally cause the market exchange ratio between the commodities to differ from the social opportunity cost ratio, the only exception occurring when a distortion in the market for one factor is exactly offset by an opposite distortion in the market for the others. In particular, if the marginal productivity of one particular factor in one industry must exceed its marginal productivity in the other, the price of the commodity produced by the former industry must exceed its opportunity cost. Consequently, in this case the country's economic welfare will be below the maximum attainable, both in the absence of the opportunity to trade and under free trade, for two reasons: first, the country will be on a transformation curve inferior to the transformation curve that would be available to it in the absence of the distortion in the factor market; and second, owing to the discrepancy between private costs of production and social costs in the commodity market resulting from the distortion in the factor market, the country will choose a suboptimal position on the restricted transformation curve available to it.

Given the existence of a distortion in the market for a factor requiring its marginal productivity to be higher in the industry in which the country has a comparative advantage, the opportunity to trade may have either of the two consequences analyzed in connection with distortions in the commodity markets; and, as demonstrated in that analysis, the protectionist policy of remedying the effects of the distortion by an export or import duty (if the country specializes on the commodity in which it has a comparative disadvantage) or an export or import subsidy (if the country specializes on the commodity in which it has a comparative advantage) may make the country either worse off or better off than it would be under free trade. A policy of subsidization of production of the commodity overpriced by the distortion, or of taxation of production of the other commodity, would maximize the economic welfare attainable from the restricted transformation curve. The important point, however, is that all of these policies aimed at offsetting the distortion by operating on the prices received by producers of commodities would leave the country on a transformation curve restricted by the inefficiency of factor use induced by the factor market distortion. This particular cause of suboptimal economic welfare could be eliminated in four different ways – by a tax on the use in one industry or subsidy on the use in the other of either factor, the rate of tax or subsidy being chosen to exactly offset the distortion. But only two of these – a subsidy on the use of the factor subject to distortion in the industry in which its marginal productivity is required/to be higher, or a tax on its use in the other industry – would simultaneously eliminate the associated distortion of commodity prices from opportunity costs, the other two accentuating the distortion in the commodity market. Thus the attainment of maximum economic welfare in this case requires subsidization or taxation of the use of the factor subject to distortion; taxation or subsidization of commodity production can maximize welfare subject to the inefficiency of factor use but cannot correct that inefficiency; taxation or subsidization of commodity trade not only fails to eliminate inefficiency in factor allocation but may even reduce welfare, given the inefficiency of factor allocation, below what it would be under free trade.

The foregoing argument has accepted the validity of the contention that in underdeveloped countries there is a distortion in the labor market such that the marginal productivity of labor in industry must be higher than the marginal productivity of labor in agriculture (the alternative opportunity cost of labor). Before leaving this group of arguments for protection, it is appropriate to express some doubts about the validity of this contention and its implications for economic policy. As already mentioned, there are two separate arguments supporting this contention – that industrial wages exceed agricultural wages, and that industrial wages are comparable to agricultural earnings but that the latter exceed the marginal productivity of labor in agriculture because agricultural workers claim a share of agricultural rent.

So far as the first argument is concerned, the mere fact that industrial wages exceed agricultural wages is not sufficient to prove a distortion, since the difference may be accounted for by the higher costs or disutility of urban living, the greater skill or stamina required of urban industrial labor, or the economic cost of migration, factors which necessitate compensation in the form of a higher industrial than agricultural wage if allocation of the labor force is to be efficient. An attempt to iron out wage differences due to these factors would involve misallocation of labor. There are, however, two plausible reasons for believing that observed industrial-agricultural wage differences may entail a genuine distortion.[16]

---

[16] Bhagwati and Ramaswami (*ibid.*) list eight reasons for the existence of a wage differential between the rural and urban sectors, of which four are economic and four

The first is that frequently in underdeveloped countries either trade union organization or social legislation and popular sentiment impose industrial wage levels well above the alternative opportunity cost of labor; this possibility is substantiated by the evidence of persistent large-scale urban unemployment, and by the fact that wage levels tend to increase with size of establishment. Insofar as trade union organization or political pressure forces industry to pay wages above the alternative opportunity cost of labor, however, any attempt to remedy the distortion by subsidization of the use of labor or by protection might be frustrated by the exaction of still higher wages. The second reason is suggested by an interpretation of migration from rural to urban employment as an investment in the formation of human capital, the investment involving both a transportation and an education cost; insofar as the market for capital to finance investment in human beings is imperfect, the marginal rate of return on such investment may be far higher than the social opportunity cost of capital to the economy.

So far as the second reason for distortion is concerned – the excess of agricultural earnings over the marginal productivity of agricultural labor – since this implies that the private return on capital invested in agriculture is less than the social return, the distortion in the labor market may be more than offset by an opposite distortion in the capital market, so that rather than indicating the desirability of subsidization of the use of labor in industry, this argument may in fact indicate the desirability of subsidization of the use of capital in agriculture.

VIII The infant industry argument

The fourth type of argument for protection to be considered is the infant

---

(one of which is Hagen's) may involve genuine distortions. They agree with the earlier analysis of A. Fishlow and P. David ("Optimal Resource Allocation in an Imperfect Market Setting", *Journal of Political Economy*, LXIX, No. 6 [December, 1961], 529-46) in regarding Hagen's "dynamic" argument for the existence of a distortion as an illegitimate superimposition of dynamic considerations on static analysis. The same point has been made by P. B. Kenen ("Development, Mobility, and the Case for Tariffs", *Kyklos*, XVI, No. 2 [1963], 321-24). Fishlow and David's other reasons correspond approximately with those discussed here, although they introduce the interesting case of factory legislation preventing the younger members of the family from working; they do not, however, raise the possibility that there may be a distortion of investment in migration of human capital.

industry argument. Although this argument is frequently confused, at least in description, with the "external economies" argument, the two are logically distinct. The external economies argument is static, in the sense that the assumed distortion due to external economies or diseconomies is by implication a permanent characteristic of the technology of production that would require correction by government intervention of a permanent kind. The infant industry argument, by contrast, is explicitly dynamic, or more accurately an argument for temporary intervention to correct a transient distortion, the justification for protection being assumed to disappear with the passage of time.

The infant industry argument bases the case for temporary protection on the assertion that the industry in question (or, more commonly in the literature on economic development, manufacturing in general) would eventually be able to compete on equal terms with foreign producers in the domestic or world market if it were given temporary tariff protection to enable it to establish itself, but would be unable to establish itself against free competition from established foreign producers owing to the temporary excessive costs it would have to incur in the initial stages. Since the incurring of costs for a limited period in return for future benefits is a type of investment, the infant industry argument is essentially an assertion that free competition would produce a socially inefficient allocation of investment resources. For the argument to be valid, it is not sufficient to demonstrate that present costs, in the form of losses on production in the infancy of the industry, must be incurred for the sake of future benefits in the form of higher income than would otherwise be earned. For if the higher income accrues to those who incur the costs, and the capital market functions efficiently, the investment will be privately undertaken unless the rate of return on it is below the rate of return available on alternative investments, in which case the investment would be socially as well as privately unprofitable. To provide an argument for government intervention, it must be demonstrated either that the social rate of return exceeds the private rate of return on the investment, or that the private rate of return necessary to induce the investment exceeds the private and social rates of return available on alternative investment, by a wide enough margin to make a socially profitable investment privately unprofitable.

The social rate of return on investment in an infant industry may exceed the private rate of return for a variety of reasons, of which two may be of particular relevance to the problems of underdeveloped countries.[17] One relates to the fact that, once created, the product of investment in the acquisition of knowledge, unlike the product of material investments, can be enjoyed by additional users without additional cost of production. In other words, once knowledge of production technique is acquired, it can be applied by others than those who have assumed the cost of acquiring it; the social benefit at least potentially exceeds the private benefit of investment in learning industrial production techniques, and the social use of the results of such learning may even reduce the private reward for undertaking the investment. Where the social benefits of the learning process exceed the private benefits, the most appropriate governmental policy would be to subsidize the learning process itself, through such techniques as financing or sponsoring pilot enterprises on condition that the experience acquired and techniques developed be made available to all would-be producers. The other reason why the social benefit may exceed the private hinges on the facts that much of the technique of production is embodied in the skill of the labor force, and that the institutions of the labor market give the worker the property rights in any skills he acquires at the employer's expense. Consequently, the private rate of return to the employer on the investment in on-the-job training may be lower than the social rate of return, because the trained worker may be hired away by a competitor. The appropriate policy in this case would entail the government either financing on-the-job training or establishing institutions enabling labor to finance its own training out of the higher future income resulting from training.[18] In either of the two cases just described, a subsidy on production or on investment in the infant industry would in principle be economically inefficient, since neither type of subsidy would necessarily stimulate the type of investment in knowledge subject to an excess of social over private return.

The private rate of return necessary to induce investment in infant industries may also exceed the private and social rates of return on alterna-

---

[17] M. C. Kemp, "The Mill-Bastable Infant Industry Dogma", *Journal of Politica Economy*, LXVIII, No. 1 (February, 1960), 65-67.

[18] The analysis here is incomplete, since in certain circumstances competition would lead to the workers bearing the cost of the nonspecific part of the training received on the job through lower initial wages. On this point see Gary S. Becker, "Investment in Human Capital: A Theoretical Analysis", *Journal of Political Economy*, LXX, No. 5, Part II, Supplement (October, 1962), 9-49, esp. 10-25.

tive investments for a variety of reasons. Entrepreneurs may be excessively pessimistic about the prospects of success, or unwilling to take chances; in this case the most appropriate policy would involve publication of expert estimates of the prospects for the industries in question. Alternatively, imperfections in the capital market may make the cost of finance for investment in new industries excessively high, especially if these industries require an initially large scale for economical production by the firm; in this case, subsidization of provision of capital would be the appropriate policy.

Whatever the distortion in the allocation of investment capital used to support the infant industry argument for protection, it is apparent from the general principles governing optimal governmental intervention in the presence of domestic distortions that the optimal policy entails some sort of subsidy to the infant industries, rather than protection. Where infant industry distortions exist, protection justified by their presence may have the effect of reducing economic welfare rather than raising it. The reason is that protection increases the social cost of the investment in the learning process of the infant industry, by adding to the cost of a transitional subsidy the consumption cost of protection; the additional cost may be sufficient to reduce the social rate of return on the investment below the social rate of return on alternative investments.

It has been mentioned above that, for the infant industry argument to justify government intervention, investment in the learning process of the infant industry must be socially profitable. This requirement implies that the customary formulations of both the infant industry argument and the most potent argument used against it are seriously defective. The customary formulation argues that there is a case for protection on infant industry grounds if the industry could eventually compete in the domestic or world market without protection. This argument is invalid because protection involves a present cost which can only be justified economically by an increase in future income above what it would otherwise be; and a necessary condition for this is that the infant industries should eventually be able to compete while paying higher returns to the factors they employ than those factors would have enjoyed if the infant industries had not been assisted to maturity by protection. The most potent argument against infant industry protection is that the infant industries in fact never grow up, but instead continue to require protection. The argument overlooks the possibility that, although the continuance of protection is a political fact, it is not always an economic necessity: protection may be continued even though intramarginal firms or units of production do not require it, and the country may gain from infant industry protection even though such protection continues indefinitely. The possibility of such a gain is illustrated in Figure 5, where as a result of infant industry protection the transformation curve shifts outwards from TT to TT', and the community

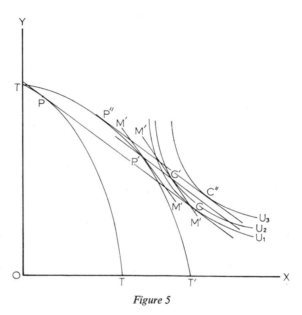

Figure 5

as a consequence enjoys the welfare level U_2 in place of the welfare level U_1 in the long run. If the cost of protection, in terms of a lower welfare level in the period of transition from TT to TT', is low enough, the increase in welfare from U_1 to U_2 great enough, and the social rate of return required to justify the investment low enough, the eventual welfare level U_2 may be superior to the eventual welfare level U_1, even though U_2 is inferior to the welfare level U_3 that could be enjoyed if the infant industry tariff were removed once it had served it purpose.

IX   Conclusion: noneconomic arguments for protection

This paper has been concerned with elaborating on two propositions concerning arguments for protection based on the alleged existence of domestic distortions creating a divergence between marginal private and marginal social benefits or costs. These are that welfare maximization requires a correction of the relevant domestic distortion by an appropriate tax or subsidy on production, consumption, or factor use, and not a tax or subsidy on international trade; and that, given the presence of a domestic distortion, protection designed to offset it may decrease welfare rather than increase it. In conclusion, it is appropriate to comment on two further matters, the reasons why economists who admit the need for correction of domestic distortions are so prone to concede the argument for tariffs in these cases, and the bearing of the analysis on noneconomic arguments for protection.

The explanation for the propensity of economists to concede the argument for protection rather than present the case for more appropriate and theoretically reliable remedies seems to lie in two factors – the tendency of economists when confronted with policy problems to ignore the rather elusive principle of consumers' sovereignty and to adopt the apparently but illusively firmer welfare criterion of an increase in the value of production, and the historical emphasis of the theory of international trade on the real cost approach to economic welfare as contrasted with the opportunity cost approach, an emphasis ultimately derived from the labor theory of value. The latter emphasis has been a major source of weakness in the theoretical analysis of contemporary international trade problems, both in connection with the theory of tariffs and in connection with the more recently evolved theory of customs unions and discriminatory tariff reduction.

While this paper has concentrated on the economic arguments for protection – specifically, on arguments for protection as a means of correcting domestic distortions leading to inequalities between marginal social and marginal private costs or benefits – the analysis does have some important implications for what have been described in the introduction as noneconomic arguments for protection.[19] Such arguments stress the noneconomic value of changes in production and consumption or

---

[19] This paragraph was prompted by the existence of an apparent conflict in the literature on protection. W. M. Corden ("Tariffs, Subsidies and the Terms of Trade", *Economica*, XXIV, No. 3 [August, 1957], 235-42) shows that the most efficient (least-cost) method of protection is by a subsidy (when the terms of trade are fixed) or by an

resource allocation patterns achieved by protection. Conceptually, they can be divided into arguments that stress the noneconomic value of increased *domestic production* of, and arguments that stress the noneconomic value of increased *self-sufficiency* in (a reduced volume of imports of) certain types of commodities that under free trade would be imported. The argument of this paper has shown that where domestic distortions make the production of a commodity lower than it should be, optimal government intervention entails subsidization of production rather than interferences with international trade. The same conclusion can be shown to hold for noneconomic arguments based on the desirability of larger domestic production, such as the national identity and way-of-life arguments mentioned above. On the other hand, it can be shown that for noneconomic arguments based on the desirability of a smaller volume of imports, the method of tariff protection is superior to the method of subsidization. The reason is that in the first case an increase of domestic production achieved by protection, as contrasted with an increase achieved by subsidization, involves an additional cost in the form of a consumption loss. In the second case, however, the reduction in consumption achieved by the tariff is to be regarded as a gain, since it also contributes to the reduction of imports; and since at the margin the production loss from subsidizing production is proportional to the rate of subsidy, and the consumption loss from taxing consumption is proportional to the rate of tax, it follows that a given reduction in imports can be achieved more efficiently by means of the tariff, which subsidizes production and taxes consumption at the same rate, than by means of a production subsidy alone, which subsidy would necessarily be at a higher rate than the required tariff rate.

These propositions are illustrated in Figure 6, where P' represents the production point and C' the consumption point achieved by the imposition of a tariff that distorts the domestic exchange ratio and transformaton ratio from the international exchange ratio $P'C'$ to $M'M'$. It is obvious that the country could reach the consumption point C and the associated

---

optimum tariff and a production subsidy (when the terms of trade are variable). J. H. Young (*Canadian Commercial Policy* [Ottawa: Royal Commission on Canada's Economic Prospects, 1957]) shows that protection by tariff costs less than protection by subsidy. As shown below, both are right. The explanation is that Corden takes the object of protection to be to increase domestic production, whereas Young takes the object to be to replace imports by domestic production.

higher welfare level U_2, while keeping domestic production at the same level P', by replacing the tariff by a subsidy on production of X (or a tax on production of Y). If, however, the object of policy is not the domestic production pattern shown by P' but the restriction of international trade to the level represented by the distance $P'C'$, achievement of this object by means of subsidization of domestic production necessarily involves a greater loss of welfare than achievement of it by means of tariff protection.

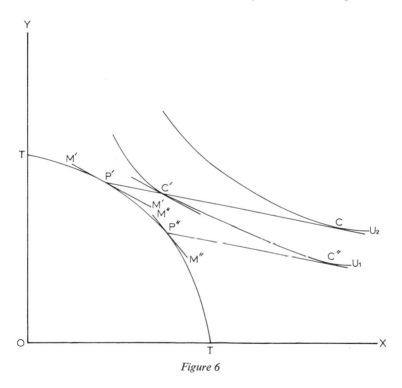

Figure 6

To appreciate this, consider the production subsidy represented by the domestic price ratio $M''M''$, which combined with free trade places the country on the indifference curve U_1 reached with the tariff. It follows from the tangencies of the transformation curve and the indifference curve U_1 to the tariff-distorted domestic exchange ratio at P' and C' that the distance between the production point P'' and consumption point C'' achieved with a subsidy welfare-indifferent to the tariff is greater than that between the production point P' and consumption point C' achieved with the tariff.

In short, for a given welfare loss, trade is restricted less by a production subsidy than by a tariff; therefore, the achievement of a given restriction of trade requires a smaller welfare loss if trade is restricted by a tariff than if trade is restricted by a production subsidy.

EQUALIZATION BY TRADE
OF THE INTEREST RATE ALONG
WITH THE REAL WAGE[1]

Paul A. Samuelson

My friend and former student, Professor Jagdish Bhagwati of Delhi, wrote me the following interesting lines, and with his permission I venture to quote from them here:

> I have a puzzle for you. In your papers on factor price equalization, if one admits capital as a factor of production (let it take the shape of a machine), then what your theorem proves is that the *rental* on the machines is equalized between countries. However, this seems *not* the same as saying that the rate of interest has been equalized. For the rate of interest in the economy is given by [capitalizing the rental and] it seems to me perfectly possible for the rentals to be equal and yet for the interest rates to be different, depending on the time-preferences of the people in the two countries.... can we incorporate growth into this system in a rigorous way unless we really begin by scrapping the Swedish-Samuelson model?

This is indeed an interesting question. Nor was it accidental that in my own work on factor-price equalization I quietly replaced the venerable pair labor and capital by labor and land, hoping thereby to sidestep some of the intricacies involved in any discussion of capital. However, the time

---

[1] This was written in early 1960 and privately circulated. It is reference 54 in the valuable bibliography of Jagdish Bhagwati, "The Pure Theory of International Trade: A Survey", *Economic Journal*, LXXIV (March, 1964), 1-84, a masterly and invaluable survey. Except for the final parts, which are new, I have made no substantive changes. Since this was written, other scholars, such as Mr. V. K. Ramaswami and Professors Jaroslav Vanek, Peter Kenen, and Murray Kemp, have carried on related researches. I wish to acknowledge thanks to the Carnegie Corporation for research aids and to F. H. Skidmore for assistance.

has come to put forward some of my tentative researches that do face up to the capital problem.

At the beginning let it be stressed that I have no desire to persuade anyone into believing that the following simple models leading to factor-price equalization are realistic. Nor do I think that such simple capital models as are represented here say the last word about growth theory. My simple purpose is to examine the interesting problem posed by Bhagwati and to show that there do exist a variety of rigorous capital models in which the interest rates among countries are indeed equalized by free trade among international goods.[2]

I Assumptions

I shall make the assumptions usual for this kind of analysis. Flows of food and clothing, x_1 and x_2, are respectively produced by stocks of labor and homogeneous physical capital, (L_1, K_1) and (L_2, K_2), where capital cannot move in international trade and can be supposed to be like a flexible machine. If capital goods are to be strictly homogeneous, then an old and a new machine must have exactly the same properties, which requires us to use the depreciation assumptions I employed in my Corfu paper[3] on capital: namely, depreciation must be a constant percentage per unit time regardless of age, although possibly varying between industries to which the capital is applied. Thus, a life table involving exponential decay must hold for capital goods used in each industry, with the average length of life in the ith industry being a prescribed technological constant, $1/m_i$.

A new element added to the picture is the fact that there is an additional industry that produces a flow of gross capital formation, x_0, by using

---

    [2]   There certainly do exist models in which rents get equalized but interest does not. Think only of a labor-land model, where one country has a 5 per cent time preference rate and the other a 10 per cent. Land will be twice as valuable in the first country, even when rentals are equalized. See Murray C. Kemp, *The Pure Theory of International Trade* (Englewood Cliffs, N.J.: Prentice-Hall, 1964), p. 49. But if land can be produced, it becomes like my K.

    [3]   "The Evaluation of 'Social Income': Capital Formation and Wealth", *The Theory of Capital*, ed. F. A. Lutz and D. C. Hague (London: Macmillan and Co., 1961), chap. iii.

labor and capital (L_0, K_0). As is usually assumed, all neoclassical production functions are the same between countries and show constant
returns to scale and smoothly substitutable diminishing marginal productivities. (The assumption of smooth substitutability could be lightened
without affecting most results.)

Relative factor endowments of total labor and capital need not be the
same in different countries. Either endowments can be assumed to differ
by a little or, if certain strong factor-intensity differences for food and
clothing are assumed to hold everywhere, the relative factor endowments
can differ widely between countries. The usual assumption is made that
something of food and clothing (and of gross capital formation) is being
produced in both countries. Note that tastes for food, clothing, and
saving-investment are not assumed to be the same in both countries; in
particular, net capital formation, dK/dt, could be negative in one or both
countries, provided its magnitude fell short of capital consumption or
depreciation – which simply means that time preference need only be
such that some positive gross capital formation goes on in all countries.

Finally, the absence of impediments to trade implies a common international price ratio for food and clothing. (The case of more than two
internationally traded goods can be handled easily by my later general
mathematical analysis.)

All the above assumptions and the implied equilibrium conditions can
be written down symbolically:

homogeneous production functions:

$$x_i = F_i(L_i, K_i) > 0 \qquad (i = 0, 1, 2), \tag{a}$$

physical depreciation:

$$D = D_0 + D_1 + D_2 = m_0 K_0 + m_1 K_1 + m_2 K_2, \tag{b}$$

net (physical) capital formation:

$$\frac{dK}{dt} = \frac{d(K_0 + K_1 + K_2)}{dt} = x_0 - D = x_0 - \sum_0^2 m_i K_i, \tag{c}$$

uniform money wage:

$$w = p_0 \frac{\partial F_0(L_0, K_0)}{\partial L_0} = p_1 \frac{\partial F_1(L_1, K_1)}{\partial L_1} = p_2 \frac{\partial F_2(L_2, K_2)}{\partial L_2}, \tag{d}$$

gross rentals of capital:

$$R_0 = p_0 \frac{\partial F_0(L_0, K_0)}{\partial K_0}, \quad R_1 = p_1 \frac{\partial F_1(L_1, K_1)}{\partial K_1}, \quad R_2 = p_2 \frac{\partial F_2(L_2, K_2)}{\partial K_2}, \quad \text{(e)}$$

uniform net rental (after depreciation allowance):

$$R = R_0 - m_0 p_0 = R_1 - m_1 p_0 = R_2 - m_2 p_0, \tag{f}$$

uniform interest rate:

$$r = \frac{R}{p_0} = \frac{\partial F_0(L_0, K_0)}{\partial K_0} - m_0 = \frac{RK_i}{p_0 K_i}, \tag{g}$$

given (clothing-food) international price ratio:

$$\frac{p_2}{p_1} = \pi_2. \tag{h}$$

No description of demand conditions in either country has been given, for the reason that these turn out to register all their pricing effects through π_2 alone. Whatever the level of this international price ratio, I shall show that it alone determines a unique wage and interest imputation that must be the same for all countries satisfying our nonspecialization and factor-intensity assumptions. Before demonstrating this fact mathematically or graphically, a brief literary explanation of the model's properties is in order.

In this model, food and clothing production require direct labor in their F_1 and F_2 production functions. Their competitive unit costs involve a direct payment to labor in the form of direct wages. Since capital goods are also used, there is a direct capital cost equal to the interest on the value of the capital goods directly tied up. But these direct "value added" terms are not the whole of it. Some of the capital goods are used up in the act of production, and this depreciation also involves a cost. Even if the firm pays a gross rental that frees it from worrying about capital used up, the competitive owners of the capital goods will be able to include in their gross rentals a charge sufficient to compensate for depreciation. And if depreciation (user cost, so to speak) is different in food and clothing, we will expect the gross rental to be that much higher in the industry with high depreciation or m_i.

All of the above remarks apply also to the production and costing of the gross flow of production of capital goods, x_0. From $F_0(L_0, K_0)$ there are incurred *direct* wage and interest costs; and in addition there are indirect depreciation costs whose magnitude depends on the decay factor m_0.

II Factor costs and equilibrium commodity prices

These relations can be summarized conveniently in the following table of gross and net national product (Table 1).

Table 1

	Money output	Value added		Depreciation
		Direct labor costs	Direct interest costs	
Capital goods industry	$p_0 x_0$	$=$ wL_0	$+$ $rp_0 K_0$	$+$ $m_0 p_0 K_0$
Food industry	$p_1 x_1$	$=$ wL_1	$+$ $rp_0 K_1$	$+$ $m_1 p_0 K_1$
Clothing industry	$p_2 x_2$	$=$ wL_2	$+$ $rp_0 K_2$	$+$ $m_2 p_0 K_2$
Total	$\sum_0^2 p_i x_i$	$=$ $w \sum_0^2 L_i$	$+$ $rp_0 \sum_0^2 K_i$	$+$ $p_0 \sum_0^2 m_i K_i$
or	GNP	$=$ NNP		$+$ Depreciation

Since we are interested in commodity unit costs, we will want to divide each industry row by the industry physical output. The result for each industry will be

$$p_i = \left(\frac{L_i}{x_i}\right) w + \left(\frac{K_i}{x_i}\right) rp_0 + m\left(\frac{K_i}{x_i}\right) p_0$$

$$= a_i w + b_i r p_0 + m_i b_i p_0, \quad (i = 1, 2, 3),$$

where the a's and b's are respectively the *direct* labor and capital coefficients of production for each industry, connected by the production relation along the unit isoquant

$$F_i(a_i, b_i) = 1.$$

This is plotted in Figure 1. Note that the Cassel-Leontief fixed coefficient case, as shown by the broken-line L-shaped isoquant, is perfectly admissable. In the more neoclassical case of smooth substitutability, the production coefficients are variable; but in equilibrium they are determinate functions of the ratio of w to the gross capital rental, being determined so as to minimize unit costs; and if the price of capital goods were known, so that depreciation charges were known, these coefficients would be determinate functions of the ratio of the wage to the net capital rental or to the interest rate, they again being selected so as to minimize food and clothing unit costs.

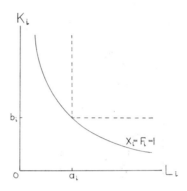

Figure 1

The unit isoquant of an industry's production function gives us its direct coefficients of production.

Nevertheless, the unit cost and price of capital goods, p_0, is not yet known; it is one of the unknowns of our simultaneous equations, which are written out below

$$p_0 = a_0 w + b_0 r p_0 + b_0 m_0 p_0,$$
$$p_1 = a_1 w + b_1 r p_0 + b_1 m_1 p_0, \tag{1}$$
$$p_2 = a_2 w + b_2 r p_0 + b_2 m_2 p_0.$$

Let us first consider the simpler Cassel-Leontief case where the a's and b's are fixed technological coefficients. Given the technical constants and prescribed interest rate and money wage, we have three simultaneous equations for the three unknown money prices (p_0, p_1, p_2). Can they always be solved for prices? Yes: for every system capable of generating a positive interest rate,[4] the commodity costs and prices are uniquely

---

[4]   In my model, the familiar Hawkins-Simon condition for this is merely that $1 - b_0 m_0 > 0$. This says no more than the following: the indirect amount of physical

determined by factor prices *regardless of factor intensities of food and clothing.*

To see this, and also to deepen our insight into capital theory, it is useful to rewrite (1) in its equivalent form involving the net rental of capital goods R rather than the interest rate r. (Recall that the net rental excludes from the nonuniform gross rentals the nonuniform charges for depreciation incurred as a result of using the capital good in the respective industries.) The definitional capitalization equation relating a capital good's dollar net rental per unit time R to the interest rate per unit time is of course $p_0 = R/r$ or $rp_0 = R$, as shown in (g) of our equilibrium equations. So our (1) becomes

$$p_0 = a_0 w + b_0 R + b_0 m_0 p_0,$$
$$p_1 = a_1 w + b_1 R + b_1 m_1 p_0, \qquad (2)$$
$$p_2 = a_2 w + b_2 R + b_2 m_2 p_0.$$

It is no accident that the first equation involves only the unknown p_0: we have merely for simplicity refused to follow Leontief's whirlpool assumption which would require food and clothing as inputs, along with labor and machine inputs, to produce machine output. Solving the first equation for p_0 gives

$$p_0 = \frac{a_0}{1 - b_0 m_0} w + \frac{b_0}{1 - b_0 m_0} R = A_0 w + B_0 R. \qquad (3)$$

The positive A_0 and B_0 coefficients can be interpreted as total (direct plus indirect to allow for depreciation) labor and machine requirements to produce a unit of x_0. Substituting this result directly into the remaining price equations gives

$$p_1 = A_1 w + B_1 R,$$
$$p_2 = A_2 w + B_2 R, \qquad (3')$$

where the new positive *total* coefficients of production have come from adding to the direct coefficients the indirect factor requirements needed to make good the physical depreciation,

$$A_i = a_i + b_i m_i A_0,$$
$$B_i = b_i + b_i m_i B_0, \qquad (i = 0, 1, 2). \qquad (4)$$

capital needed as a result of depreciation of capital goods used to make one more unit of physical capital goods must itself be less than one unit; for otherwise the stock of capital goods would have to run down even if *no* food and clothing were being produced!

All this proves that money factor prices do determine money goods prices in the fixed-coefficient case. What about the case where there is more than one technical factor combination by which goods can be produced? It is not hard to see that in such a case A_0 and B_0 will be functions of w/R and nothing else, being chosen so as to minimize p_0 for given w and R. Also, with optimal p_0 having been determined, A_i and B_i in the remaining industries become determinate functions of the ratios of (w, R, p_0) or for that matter of the simple ratio w/R, being chosen to minimize independently the unit costs of production p_i. So specifying w and R on the righthand side of (3) does indeed determine the commodity p's on the lefthand side in the most general case.[5]

III   Graphical summary

All of my results can be summarized by the kind of diagram I introduced in my 1949 *Economic Journal* paper on factor-price equalization (see

---

[5]   The marginal productivity conditions of (d)-(g) guarantee all the minimizations in the postulated smooth neoclassical case. In all other cases, general inequalities of nonlinear programming will achieve the same results. Note too that the fixed depreciation constants, m_i, might just as well be permitted to be technologically variable, but determinate, functions of w/R to minimize unit costs all around. Mathematically, by the methods given in my "Prices of Factors and Goods in General Equilibrium", *Review of Economic Studies*, XXI, No. 1 (1953-54), 1-20, it can be shown that the (3″) equations

$$p_i = A_i (w/R)\, w + B_i (w/R)\, R \qquad (i = 1, 2)$$

have for their Jacobian $\partial (p_1, p_2) / \partial (w, R) = A_1 (w/R) B_2 (w/R) - A_2 (w/R) B_1 (w/R)$; and to be able to solve backward for w and R in terms of (p_1, p_2), or what is the same thing for w/R and r in terms of $p_2/p_1 = \pi_2$, it is sufficient that this Jacobian satisfy the strong factor-intensity assumption of being one-signed for all w/R. A similar result holds if we add more domestically produced and traded goods to food and clothing and more factors (such as land) to labor and machines. Then the crucial Jacobian matrix

$$[\partial (p_1, p_2, p_3, \ldots)/\partial (w, R, \text{land rent}, \ldots)] \text{ becomes more}$$

$$\begin{bmatrix} A_1 (w, R, \ldots) & B_1 (w, R, \ldots) & C_1 (w, R, \ldots) & \ldots \\ A_2 (w, R, \ldots) & \ldots & \ldots & \ldots \\ A_3 (w, R, \ldots) & \ldots & \ldots & \ldots \\ \ldots & \ldots & \ldots & \ldots \end{bmatrix}$$

and, in a correction of my theorem on determinateness (*"Prices of Factors and Goods..."*,

Figure 2). The new righthand curves are appended to show that the interest rate and the real wage (expressed in *either* food or clothing) are equalized.[6] Since it is not my intention to propagandize for factor-price

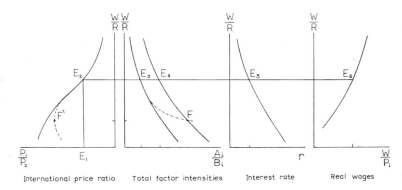

Figure 2

Factor-price and interest rate equalization. At any internationally given clothing-food price ratio, we run up from E_1 to E_2 to read off the wage-net rent ratio, and across to E_3 and E_4, and to E_5 and E_6, which show the resulting interest rate and real wage. (Note that if factor intensities reverse, as in the broken-line curves, that two countries with *quite different* factor endowments will *not* have the same factor prices.)

equalization, I have indicated with the broken curves how changing factor intensities could introduce multiple solutions for factor prices. Note though, whatever the factor intensities in a region, in the absence of technical change a rising interest rate always implies a falling real wage and a cheapening of the good that happens to be labor intensive at the

---

p. 9), Gale and Nikaido have shown (in an as-yet unpublished work) that it is sufficient for factor-price equalization that this matrix have all its principal minors everywhere one-signed. In the *Economic Journal*, LXIX (December, 1959), 725-32, I. F. Pearce seems to suggest that nonsingularity alone will suffice, but Professor McKenzie has provided a counter-example to this conjecture.

[6] Here is but a brief demonstration that r is inversely related and the real wages directly related to w/R.

By definition $r = R/p_0 = R [A_0 (w/R) w + B_0 (w/R) R]^{-1} = r (w/R)$.

Necessarily $r' (w/R) < 0$ since $\partial \log r/\partial \log R = 1 - B_0 R (A_0 w + B_0 R)^{-1} > 0$.

Also $w/p_i = w [A_i (w/R) w + B_i (w/R) R]^{-1} = f_i (w/R)$ with $f_i' (w/R) > 0$ because $\partial \log (w/p_i)/\partial \log w = 1 - A_i w (A_i w + B_i R)^{-1} > 0$.

expense of the good that happens to be capital intensive – in accordance with commonsense expectations.[7]

For those students of economic development who are enamored of the over-all capital output ratio $p_0(K_0+K_1+K_2)/(p_0x_0+p_1x_1+p_2x_2)$, it may be mentioned that this probably will be greater for the country with the higher $(K_0+K_1+K_2)/(L_0+L_1+L_2)$ endowment ratio, even though the capital output ratios for *every* industry, p_0K_i/p_ix_i, are *exactly* the same between countries. The difference, of course, comes from the fact that the country generously endowed with capital will give greater production weight to goods that are more capital intensive, and it will export food and import the labor-intensive clothing.[8]

IV The "local" factor-price equalization theorem

Now that capital has been admitted in a rigorous way into an international trade model, let me revert to the conclusion I originally had in mind when writing my first 1948 *Economic Journal* paper on the subject.[9]

---

[7] If factor endowments in two regions are very far apart, then the total labor and capital available for direct and indirect food and clothing production after net capital formation has been taken care of are likely to be so different in proportion as to make it impossible to find a common pair of points like E_3 and E_4 which bracket these available domestic factor-supply ratios. In such a case, we know that at least one of the countries will produce nothing of one of the traded goods, and we cannot expect factor-price equalization. Along with this familiar possibility, our capital model introduces a new possibility: suppose in one or both countries gross capital formation is zero because time preference makes desired net capital formation be more negative than depreciation; then w/R may still be equalized between countries, but r may exceed the equalized values of $R(A_0w + B_0R)^{-1}$ and by different degrees in the two countries depending upon their different time preferences – in complete agreement with Mr. Bhagwati's quoted passage. The case becomes like that of unproducible land, mentioned earlier.

[8] The result is "probable" rather than "certain" because if x_0 production were itself especially labor intensive (capital intensive) and if the country had an especially strong (weak) demand for this domestic good's production, the presumption about aggregate capital output ratios might be reversed. As always, we must take note of demand differences between countries.

[9] "International Trade and the Equalisation of Factor Prices", *Economic Journal*, LVIII (June, 1948), 163-84.

Commodity movement is almost certainly a substitute for factor movements in this sense: if trade does not originally equalize factor prices and this causes factors to migrate so as to wipe out the difference, none the less *before* migration has proceeded far enough to equalize factor proportions, factor migration will come to a stop as commodity trade either will have equalized factor returns or will have so reduced the differential as to make the cost of transporting another unit of the factor greater than the present discounted value of the higher earnings it can hope to secure abroad.

This point does not, like the complete factor-price equalization theorem, require that the two goods be *everywhere* of the same factor intensity. It requires only that the complete migration of factors would lead to a situation in which the goods will not be of *exactly* the same factor intensities, even though they might exchange factor intensities elsewhere. (*I.e.*, the local theorem holds everywhere in Figure 2 except at point *F.*) Properly stated, this "local" factor-price equalization theorem holds wherever there are as many traded goods as factors, even if that number be much greater than two.[10]

Even if the over-all factor-price equalization theorem were inapplicable because of changing factor intensities, this local theorem may be of more economic interest than has been brought out in the literature. To take a fantastic case, suppose two factors could explain the trade pattern of the world. Now Arrow, Chenery, Minhas, and Solow[11] have done geographical studies of production of the same goods in different countries and have come up with the interesting finding that production functions involving constant fractional elasticities of substitution are suggested by the cross-sectional statistics. As they point out, the fact that these constants differ by industry means that relative factor intensities of goods are likely to become reversed in different geographical regions – a phenomenon that would be quite impossible in the case of two goods obeying

---

[10] If free factor mobility would lead to a position where the Jacobian matrix $[\partial (P_1, ..., P_n)/\partial (W, R, ...)]$ is nonsingular, factor migration will stop *before* endowment ratios are equalized, because goods mobility will provide an adequate substitute for the *final* movement of factors.

[11] K. J. Arrow, H. B. Chenery, B. Minhas, and R. M. Solow, "Capital-Labor Substitution and Economic Efficiency", *Review of Economics and Statistics*, XLIII (August, 1961), 225-50.

different Cobb-Douglas production functions. Although the authors are modest in their claims as to the applicability of their research, their result is interesting in itself, and they have for once offered a cross-sectional study of production functions which is not internally contradictory and nonsensical. Moreover, despite all the theoretical discussion of the possibility of factor-intensity reversal, this is the first instance I have heard about that goes beyond the speculative and anecdotal stage.

For the sake of the argument, let us suppose that this finding implies that India and Australia will *not* be able to achieve factor-price equalization through trade alone because their factor endowments are so far apart as to put them on different branches of the curve in Figure 2, one being above and the other below F.[12] Then we must face up to the fact that the world will not end up with a single pattern of factor prices. The failure of this global theorem must not distract us from noting what may still be true: trade might still equalize factor prices for Australia, New Zealand, Canada, the United States, and other countries falling on the same branch of the functions; and it might equalize factor prices for all the labor-rich countries such as India, China, Pakistan, and so forth, which fall on another branch. In short, the "local" version of the factor-price equalization theorem says that, in the absence of complete specialization and other specifiable phenomena, there will be only as many factor price patterns as there are distinct branches of the curve and not as many as there are countries.[13]

V Case of any number of heterogeneous capital goods [14]

The previous analysis rests on the Non-Substitution Theorem involving

---

[12] To say nothing of the fact that assuming the same two-variable production functions for such countries might seem a naive and fruitless hypothesis.

[13] If factor-intensity curves coincide over a finite range, there could result an infinity of different factor-price patterns for certain π_2 ratios, and the chances of keeping food *and* clothing production going in all countries might become very slim. If we include under "complete specialization" the concept of "incipient specialization", which is the case where the two goods have identical two-factor intensities and hence straight-line transformation curves, the singular cases (like F) are swept under the carpet and the theorem can be stated more easily.

[14] A brief fragment on the Leontief Paradox has been omitted to make room for this extension.

the interest rate, which, as developed in my articles on Marx and Ricardo, and subsequently in the Johann Akerman *Festschrift*, generalizes the 1949 Non-Substitution Theorem of Georgescu-Roegen and Samuelson.[15] Non-substitution theorems of this type generally rest on the assumption of Leontief and neoclassical writers that there be *no joint production* (*e.g.*, it takes demand conditions to determine relative wool and mutton prices even in a timeless world where labor is the sole input). Simple circulating capital models fit in well with nonjointness of production. But durable capital, such as K in the previous models, intrinsically involves the joint production by labor and machines of current consumption goods *and* of older machines.

Fortunately, as indicated in my Ricardo papers, jointness of production of nonfinal goods can be tolerated in some models that still obey non-substitution theorems. This we have in effect just seen in the previous discussion of interest-rate equalization with durable K. Here I shall show how one can handle the case of n heterogeneous durable capital goods $(K_1, ..., K_n)$ which, with one primary (labor) factor, L, can produce their own net capital formations $(\dot{K}_1, ..., \dot{K}_n)$ and r consumption goods $(C_1, ..., C_r)$, by the neoclassical production functions:

$$\dot{K}_j = F_j(L_j, K_{1j}, ..., K_{nj}) - m_j K_j \qquad (j = 1, ..., n),$$
$$C_j = F_{n+j}(L_{n+j}, K_{1,n+j}, ..., K_{n,n+j}) \qquad (j = 1, ..., r). \tag{5}$$

where $K_{ij} =$ the amount of the ith machine used in the jth industry and m_j is the depreciation coefficient for the jth K (and not, as before, for the jth industry, since now m_j is assumed independent of industry use). Note, too, that what was previously p_1 and p_2 will now be P_{c_1} and P_{c_2}.

---

[15] P. A. Samuelson, "Wages and Interest: A Modern Dissection of Marxian, Economic Models", *American Economic Review*, XLVII (December, 1957), 884-912; *idem*, "A Modern Treatment of the Ricardian Economy: I. The Pricing of Goods and of Labor and Land Services", *Quarterly Journal of Economics*, LXXIII (February, 1959), 1-35; *idem*, "A Modern Treatment of the Ricardian Economy: II. Capital and Interest Aspects of the Pricing Process", *Quarterly Journal of Economics*, LXXIII (May, 1959), 217-31. On the 1949 theorem, see T. C. Koopmans (ed.), *Activity Analysis of Production and Allocation* (New York: John Wiley & Sons, 1951), chaps. vii and x by P. A. Samuelson and Nicholas Georgescu-Roegen, respectively, and chaps. viii and ix by T. C. Koopmans and Kenneth J. Arrow, respectively; P. A. Samuelson, "A New Theorem on Non-Substitution", *Money, Growth and Methodology*, published in honor of Johann Akerman (Lund Social Science Studies, Vol. XX [Lund: CWK Gleerup, 1961]), pp. 407-23.

Define $a_{0j} = L_j/F_j$, $a_{ij} = K_{ij}/F_j$. Then

$$F_j(a_{0j}, a_{1j}, ..., a_{nj}) = 1 \qquad (j = 1, ..., n, n+1, ..., n+r), \qquad (6)$$

and the least-cost a_{ij} will depend on money rental rates for labor (*i.e.*, the money wage W_0) and money (gross) rentals for all capital goods ($W_1, ..., W_n$). Or

$$a_{ij} = a_{ij}(W_0, W_1, ..., W_n) = a_{ij}(1, w_1, ..., w_n), \qquad (7)$$

where $w_j = W_j/W_0$, the (gross) rental of the jth machine relative to the labor wage.

The cost-of-production price for each machine is equal to the sum of the costs of the per-unit requirements of each input:

$$
\begin{aligned}
P_1 &= W_0 a_{01} + W_1 a_{12} + ... + W_n a_{n1} \\
&\vdots \qquad \vdots \qquad \vdots \qquad \vdots \qquad \vdots \\
P_n &= W_0 a_{0n} + W_1 a_{1n} + ... + W_n a_{nn}.
\end{aligned}
\qquad (8)
$$

For simplicity, I have made exponential-decay depreciation independent of the use to which any K_j is put. Hence, the gross rental of the jth good has been made the same W_j to every user. And this rental is merely equal to interest on capitalized value plus value of capital depreciated:

$$W_j = (r + m_j)P_j \qquad (j = 1, ..., n). \qquad (9)$$

But now we can substitute (9) into (8) and get implicit equations to determine $(W_1/W_0, ..., W_n/W_0) = (w_1, ..., w_n)$:

$$w_j - \sum_{i=1}^{n} w_i \bar{a}_{ij}(1, w_1, ..., w_n) = \bar{a}_{0j}(1, w_1, ..., w_n) \qquad (j = 1, 2, ..., n). \quad (10)$$

Evidently the $(r+m_j)\bar{a}_{ij}$ are to be treated just like new $\bar{a}_{ij}$ in a timeless Walras-Leontief system, and r must be small enough relative to (m_j, a_{ij}) that

$$
\begin{bmatrix} 1 & 0 & ... & 0 \\ \vdots & \vdots & \vdots & \vdots \\ 0 & ... & ... & 1 \end{bmatrix} - \begin{bmatrix} (r + m_j)a_{ij} \end{bmatrix}
$$

have a nonnegative inverse, which is the Hawkins-Simon set of conditions for a viable system. If we rule out uninteresting decomposable cases, equations (10) will determine positive unique $(w_1^*, ..., w_n^*)$ and optimal $a_{i,j}^*$ corresponding to them. And then we find for each consumption industry

$$\frac{P_{cj}}{W_0} = a_{0,n+j}^* + \sum_{i=1}^{n} w_i^* a_{i,n+j} = p_j(r),\qquad(11)$$

with $p_j'(r) > 0$, so that the higher the interest rate the lower will be *every* real wage.

Now suppose there are uniform differences in factor intensity, so that for some two goods that are simultaneously produced in both countries, say goods 1 and 2, $p_1(r)/p_2(r) = p_{12}(r)$ is a monotone, strictly increasing (or decreasing) function of r. *Then, the interest rate will be equalized by positive trade in those goods alone.*

To put the matter as strongly as I have elsewhere, (a) if effective knowledge of production were the same everywhere (so that the same F_j functions prevailed), (b) if the real rate of interest were the same everywhere, (c) if the only primary factor is labor, which in its "raw" untrained state is the same everywhere, then the real wages and *all* real price ratios would be the same everywhere and there would be no need for any trade at all; or, more accurately, there would be need only for that amount of intramarginal trade required to keep interest rates equalized.

Suppose, for once, we let capital goods or loan funds move internationally along with consumption goods. Then we find that only differences in (a) effective knowledge, (b) endowments of *primary* factors, and (c) differences in interest rates can permit differences in living standards and productivities. Anticlimactically, the curse of the poor is their poverty – their poverty in knowledge (as distinct from training, unless knowledge of how to train is lacking), their poverty in primary factors, and their poverty in having access to low-interest capital funds (and all that that implies for real machinery and training in an equilibrium model).

Of course, all the above refers to long-enough-run equilibrium of constant-returns-to-scale systems and presupposes enough time for the system to have utilized its access to low-interest resources over time. If a developing economy can import machines themselves, it will be able, starting from a capital stock appropriate to a higher interest rate, to speed up the pace at which it achieves the new long-run equilibrium appropriate to a lower interest rate.

VI   Handling all kinds of intermediate goods: a sweeping theorem

Professors L. W. McKenzie, Jaroslav Vanek, and I have discussed how intermediate goods influence factor-price equalization problems.[16] The case considered here, where machines that work with primary factors must themselves be produced by primary factors and machines, is merely a durable-goods instance of this. The whole problem can be handled by a beautifully simple device, which enables one to sweep all the intermediate-goods relations under the carpet.

So long as *all* the F_j functions involve no jointness of production – and even if they involve intermediate flows with positive coefficients of the form $(a_{n+j,1}, ..., a_{n+j,n+r})$ – we can always define new net production functions which give the maximum amount of any net final product (be it an investment dK_j/dt or a consumption C_K) in terms of the primary factors devoted to its net production alone (which means all the primary factors needed to produce *all* the gross outputs needed to provide the intermediate inputs that such net output of the one good requires).

To help understand this somewhat complicated description, consider an economy which produces food and clothing and other final goods by means of primary factors like labor and land. By definition of what we mean by a primary factor, labor and land cannot themselves be produced within the system. But suppose that the final good like food also requires for its production a certain amount of intermediate clothing and food itself; and suppose it requires machines, which can themselves be reproduced out of primary factors and intermediate flows and machines themselves.

Imagine putting this economy inside a black box. We observe only primary factors going into the box as inputs. And we observe only final net products coming out of the box as outputs. We do not see the intermediate inputs and gross flows within the box itself. Call final outputs $X_1, X_2, ...$ whether they be consumption goods or net capital formations. Call primary inputs $Y_1, Y_2, ...$ whether they be many kinds of raw labor

---

[16]   Jaroslav Vanek, "Variable Factor Proportions and Interindustry Flows in the Theory of International Trade", *Quarterly Journal of Economics*, LXXVII (February, 1963), 129-42; L. W. McKenzie, "Specialization and Efficiency in World Production", *Review of Economic Studies*, XXI (June, 1954), 165-80; *idem*, "Specialization in Production and the Production Possibility Locus", *Review of Economic Studies*, XXIII (1955-56), 56-64; *idem*, "Equality of Factor Prices in World Trade", *Econometrica*, XXIII (July, 1955), 239-57.

or land. There still results a production-possibility frontier relating these ultimate outputs and inputs of the form:

$$0 \equiv T(X_1, X_2, \ldots; Y_1, Y_2, \ldots) \equiv T(\lambda X_1, \lambda X_2, \ldots; \lambda Y_1, \lambda Y_2, \ldots), \quad (12)$$

where λ can be any positive scalar because of our assumption of constant returns to scale.

So far nothing remarkable has been said. But suppose that every production function inside the box has the $F_j(\ldots)$ property of *never involving joint production of any outputs*. (Joint use of inputs is, of course, to be expected.) Then, by concentrating on one X_i alone, setting all others equal to zero, we can define the net production function of X_i producible from given totals of all primary inputs. Call this

$$X_i = N_i(Y_1, Y_2, \ldots) \quad \text{or} \quad T(0, \ldots, 0, X_i, 0, \ldots; Y_1, Y_2, \ldots) = 0, \quad (13)$$

and note that it is equivalent to putting all other X's equal to zero in (12) above and solving explicitly for X_i. This production function will have all the homogeneity and concavity properties of any gross F_j function met anywhere in neoclassical theory. That is what the present theorem asserts. But it asserts more than that.

If society actually wants something positive of both X_1 and X_2, *it cannot do better* than to produce all the X_1 by its independent N_1 function and X_2 by its independent N_2 function. So to speak, we could organize the X_1 food industry so that in its corner of the black box it produces *for itself* all the unseen intermediate clothing, machine, and food flows needed to enable it to produce the *net* food output to come out of the box. The same goes for the X_2 industry given the task of producing net clothing. I realize this sounds as if the division of labor is being abrogated; but remember, what Adam Smith insisted on, that much of the division of labor is required only because of *divergences* from the constant-returns-to-scale assumptions of neoclassical analysis.

Perhaps the theorem will seem obvious. But at one time, to me, it seemed wrong. I feared that there might inevitably be interactions between the X_1 and X_2 productions. But further reflection on the strong nonjointness assumptions reveals that this apprehension is misguided.[17] In equilibrium, primary factor prices and all other prices will be uniform

---

[17] Conversation with Professors Vanek and McKenzie helped clarify my mind on these points.

within the black box, and there can never be any inefficiency or penalty if one industry "integrates" itself to produce *all* its nonprimary requirements. (Needless to say, turnover taxes or other impediments between sectors would require modification of these statements.)

The conclusion from this last analysis can now be drawn. To discuss the role of intermediate goods and durable machinery in factor-price equalization, we can often employ the net production function giving each final good in terms of *total* primary inputs needed for it alone. We thus sweep all complications into the background and concern ourselves only with the crucial factor intensities (and generalized Jacobian matrixes) of these standard net functions.

VII   A trading world without geography

We are now in a position to uncover a striking idealized case. Suppose natural resources are not limiting factors and that (raw, untrained) labor is the only primary factor. Of course, in some general Austrian sense, "time" is also a bottleneck factor, since it is technically feasible for an economy to go from one high-interest (or profit) state to another, more productive, low-interest state only by *consuming* less final outputs than the system is capable of producing permanently in each intermediate state.

But now suppose that the rate of interest does get equalized by free trade in some two goods that are being produced simultaneously. (Warning: this is not an innocent assumption.) Then with r the same everywhere, the net production functions involve only raw labor. And on the assumption that "a man's genetically a man, for a' that", these identical net functions are the simple linear ones of the Ricardian, labor-theory-of-value, constant-cost case. This is a case of equal absolute advantage everywhere! Enough trade must take place to keep r equalized, but no further trade need take place. As the world saves and invests, it matters not where the capital goods are placed, just so long as every worker has access to enough credit and the implied $(K_1, ..., K_n)$ to enable him to produce something worth producing at the common interest rate.

Ironically, when I push the Heckscher-Ohlin axioms all the way, we come full circle back to a *uniform* Ricardian world. To break the circle and return to the real world, which does involve geography, we must, as Bertil Ohlin long ago insisted, study the uneven endowment of primary factors that does characterize the only globe we yet know.

ON THE EQUIVALENCE OF TARIFFS
AND QUOTAS

Jagdish Bhagwati

The notion that tariffs and quotas are equivalent – in the sense that a tariff rate will produce an import level which, if alternatively set as a quota, will produce an identical discrepancy between foreign and domestic prices – is fairly widespread in the literature on trade theory.[1] It is to be found not merely in textbooks, but also in much of the technical literature (*e.g.*, in balance-of-payments analysis). For instance, it is customary to argue that the use of quantitative restrictions is identical with the use of some *equivalent* tariff, that the use of (further) tariffs is justified only insofar as the country is below the optimum tariff level, and that the use of quantitative restrictions to reduce an external deficit is therefore justified, from the welfare viewpoint, only when the country does not already have optimal restrictions.[2]

Equivalence in the sense defined obtains as a logically true proposition, however, only in a limited class of situations. Indeed, it is easy to construct

---

[1] C. P. Kindleberger's *International Economics* (Homewood, Ill.: Richard D. Irwin, 1958), however, does explicitly analyze a case of nonequivalence. Kindleberger (pp. 621-23) concentrates on showing how a quota can create a domestic monopoly, and hence does not generalize the argument concerning nonequivalence in the way attempted here. Earlier, J. E. Meade analyzed various possibilities of monopoly arising from the administration of quota systems (see *The Theory of International Economic Policy*, Volume I: *The Balance of Payments* [London: Oxford University Press, 1951], chap. xxi, esp. pp. 282-85), but in most of his analysis of balance-of-payments adjustment he assumes equivalence. The problem, as posed and analyzed here, is mentioned in my earlier paper on "Quantitative Restrictions and Quotas in International Trade", to be published in the *International Encyclopaedia of the Social Sciences*.

[2] This type of argument, for example, can be found in H. G. Johnson's *International Trade and Economic Growth* (London: George Allen & Unwin, 1958), chap. vi. It also plays a prominent role in J. M. Fleming's "On Making the Best of Balance of Payments Restrictions on Imports", *Economic Journal*, LI (March, 1951), 48-71.

53

several possible situations where the equivalence breaks down. This paper demonstrates some of these possibilities and then proceeds, in the light of this analysis, to correct some of the current misconceptions about tariffs and quotas which have their origin in the equivalence proposition.

I Alternative possibilities

The traditional equivalence proposition is deduced in the context of a model which assumes (a) competitive foreign supply, (b) perfect competition in domestic production, and (c) a quota which is allocated so as to ensure perfect competition among the quota-holders, one consequence of which is that all quotas are used. This *universal* assumption of competitiveness ensures the equivalence which, as we shall soon see, generally breaks down with the introduction of monopoly elements in any one or more of the three listed areas.

We will begin the analysis with the case of universal perfect competition and then examine the following alternative cases: (a) perfect competition in (domestic) production replaced by pure monopoly in production; (b) perfect competition among quota-holders replaced by monopolist holding of quota; and (c) simultaneous presence of monopoly in quota-holding and in domestic production.[3]

Throughout the analysis, we use the following notation:

P_F = foreign price

P_D = domestic price

t = tariff rate

S_D = domestic supply (production) of the commodity

S_F = foreign supply (production) of the commodity

D = total domestic demand for (consumption of) the commodity

D_D = net domestic demand for the commodity, available to the domestic suppliers

C = total cost of domestic production of the commodity

---

[3] We are thus not taking up any case involving monopolistic sale from foreign sources. This may well be an important possibility, but the analysis could easily be extended to cover it, if considered desirable in any specific context.

Case I   Competitive supply from abroad, perfect competition in domestic production, and perfect competition among quota-
holders.

We first set out the model for the case when a tariff, rather than a
quota, is imposed.

$$S_D = S_D(P_D) \tag{1}$$

$$S_F = S_F(P_F) \tag{2}$$

$$P_F(1 + t) = P_D \tag{3}$$

$$S_D + S_F = D \tag{4}$$

$$D = D(P_D). \tag{5}$$

Equation (1) states that the domestic supply is a function of domestic

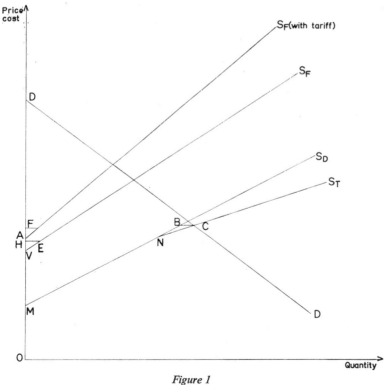

Figure 1

price; equation (2) that the foreign supply is a function of foreign price; equation (3) that the domestic price exceeds the foreign price by the amount of the tariff; equation (4) that aggregate supply must equal domestic demand; and equation (5) that domestic demand is a function of domestic price.

We thus have five equations and six unknowns: S_D, S_F, D, P_D, P_F, and t. Thus, if t is given, the remaining unknowns are determined. Corresponding to every tariff rate (t), therefore, there will be some import level (S_F).

In the case where an import quota is set, the system is identical to that for the tariff case. Corresponding to every import level (S_F) chosen as the quota, therefore, there will be some (implicit) tariff rate, *i.e.*, discrepancy between P_D and P_F. Moreover, the systems being identical, a tariff will generate an import level which, set alternatively as a quota, will generate the *same* tariff rate.

Figure 1 shows graphically the equilibrium in this system. The tariff rate AV/VO shifts the S_F schedule upwards. The resulting total supply schedule S_T (aggregating S_F and S_D) cuts the D schedule to give the import level $BC (=EH)$, foreign price OH, and domestic price OF. Conversely, with a quota of BC, the domestic price will turn out to be OF, the foreign price to be OH, and the (implicit) tariff rate therefore to be $(FH/OH=) AV/VO$. Equivalence thus obtains in this case.

Case II   Competitive supply from abroad, monopoly in domestic production, and perfect competition among quota-holders.

Starting again with the case of tariffs, we find that the economic system is the following:

$$S_F = S_F(P_F) \tag{1}$$

$$D = D(P_D) \tag{2}$$

$$D_D = D(P_D) - S_F(P_F) \tag{3}$$

$$D_D = S_D \tag{4}$$

$$C = C(S_D) \tag{5}$$

$$\frac{d(P_D S_D)}{dS_D} = \frac{dC}{dS_D} \tag{6}$$

$$_F(1 + t) = P_D. \tag{7}$$

Equation (1) states that the foreign supply is a function of foreign price; equation (2) that total domestic demand is a function of domestic price; equation (3) that the net demand available to the domestic monopolist is the difference between total demand and foreign supply; equation (4) that net domestic demand equals domestic supply; equation (5) that total cost of domestic production (supply) is a function of the level of production; equation (6) that marginal revenue in domestic production is equated by the monopolist with his marginal cost; and equation (7) that the domestic price is higher than the foreign price by the amount of the tariff.

We have here seven equations and eight unknowns: D, D_D, S_F, S_D, P_D, P_F, C, and t. By choosing the tariff rate, t, therefore, we can determine the remaining values. Consequently, corresponding to every t there will be some level of imports, S_F.

But in contrast to Case I, the present system shows nonequivalence. For a quota, the system is the following:

$$D = D(P_D) \tag{1}$$

$$S_F = S_F(P_F) \tag{2}$$

$$D_D = D(P_D) - S_F(P_F) \tag{3}$$

$$D_D = S_D \tag{4}$$

$$C = C(S_D) \tag{5}$$

$$\frac{d(P_D S_D)}{dS_D} = \frac{dC}{dS_D} \tag{6}$$

$$\frac{P_D}{P_F} = 1 + t. \tag{7}$$

The system looks identical with that for a tariff.[4] However, the two systems are *not* identical, because the lefthand sides of equations (6), representing marginal revenue, are actually different. Under a tariff,

$$\frac{d(P_D S_D)}{dS_D} = P_D \frac{dD}{dS_D} + D \frac{dP_D}{dS_D} - P_D \frac{dS_F}{dS_D} - S_F \frac{dP_D}{dS_D};$$

---

[4] Of course, equations (2) and (7) are now to be understood differently. In the present, quota case, equation (2) gives the foreign price corresponding to the import quota set; whereas in equation (7), t is the *implicit* tariff rate, obtained merely as $(P_D/P_F - 1)$. Neither of these differences, however, affects the equivalence proposition.

whereas under a quota,

$$\frac{d(P_D S_D)}{dS_D} = P_D \frac{dD}{dS_D} + D \frac{dP_D}{dS_D} - S_F \frac{dP_D}{dS_D}.$$

The difference of $-P_D (dS_F/dS_D)$ crucially divides the two systems, accounting for the nonequivalence of tariffs and quotas in this case. For, with this difference, a tariff rate will correspond to an import level which, if alternatively set as a quota, will not generate an identical (implicit) tariff rate. Indeed, the implicit tariff rate must be higher than the explicit one.

The difference is due to the fact that, with a tariff, the reduction in domestic price due to an increase in domestic output reduces the quantity of imports supplied, so that increased sales are effected partly by reducing imports, whereas with a quota imports are not reduced and the whole

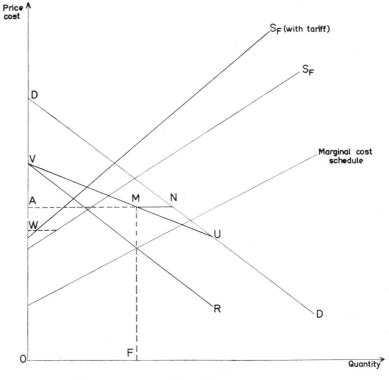

Figure 2

increase in sales must come from an increase in quantity demanded. Marginal revenue at any given output is therefore higher with the tariff than with a quota $(-P_D (dS_F/dS_D)$ is positive because (dS_F/dS_D) is negative). Hence output will be higher, and domestic price lower, under a tariff than it would be under a quota, for the same level of imports. This nonequivalence is easily illustrated graphically: Figures 2 and 3 show respectively the tariff and quota systems, two figures being employed instead of one to avoid confusion. In Figure 2, we set a tariff rate which generates an import level; in Figure 3, we set the *same* import level as a quota and show that a *different* (and higher) implicit tariff rate is generated.

In Figure 2, the tariff rate $(=AW/WO)$ shifts the supply schedule S_F upwards. The net demand schedule for the domestic monopolist then is VUD, while VR is the marginal revenue schedule for the monopolist. Equilibrium exists where the latter cuts the marginal cost schedule for

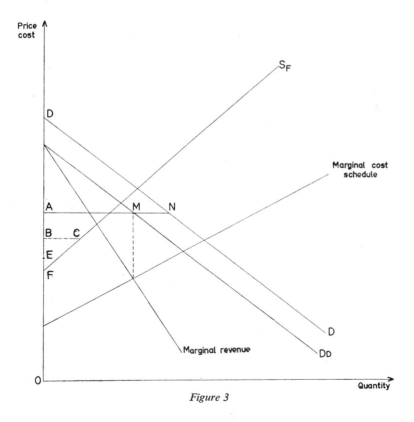

Figure 3

the monopolist, so that the monopolist's production (S_D) is at OF, the domestic price at OA, the foreign price at OW, and the import level (S_F) at MN.

We then use the *same* import level MN as the quota in Figure 3. The *net* demand schedule for the domestic monopolist is now D_D; it is steeper than the net demand schedule segment VU in the previous diagram. The corresponding marginal revenue schedule must lie farther below M (in Figure 2) than the previous marginal revenue schedule VR; it therefore cuts the monopolist's marginal cost schedule at a lower output than under the tariff, to yield OA as the domestic price and OB as the foreign price, the implicit tariff rate being AB/OB. Since OB in Figure 3 is equal to OW in Figure 2 (imports being the same in both cases), and OA in Figure 3 must be greater than OA in Figure 2, the implicit tariff rate under the quota must exceed the explicit tariff rate that would produce the same volume of imports. This demonstrates the nonequivalence between tariffs and quotas when there is monopoly in domestic production.

Case III   Competitive supply from abroad, perfect competition in domestic production, and monopolist-holding of quotas.

The analysis of a tariff in this case is identical with that in Case I. With a quota, however, the system is now different. Since the quota-holder may be assumed to maximize his profits, he will vary his imports (within the quota set) so as to achieve this goal. The system then becomes the following:

$$D = D(P_D) \tag{1}$$

$$S_F = D(P_D) - S_D(P_D) \tag{2}$$

$$S_D = S_D(P_D) \tag{3}$$

$$S_F = S_F(P_F) \tag{4}$$

$$\frac{P_D}{P_F} = (1 + t) \tag{5}$$

$$\frac{d(P_D - P_F)S_F}{dS_F} \gtreqless 0. \tag{6}$$

The first five equations are already familiar. The last merely states the first-order, maximizing (equilibrium) condition for the monopolist quota-holder; the equality sign holds if the monopolist uses less than his full quota, the inequality if he uses all of his quota. There are thus six equations and six unknowns: P_F, P_D, S_F, S_D, D, and t. The import level which will maximize the quota-holder's profits is thus determinate;[5] and it is obvious that if this import volume is less than would occur under the tariff, the implicit tariff rate must exceed the explicit tariff rate. Since the tariff system and the quota system are different in this case, the equivalence

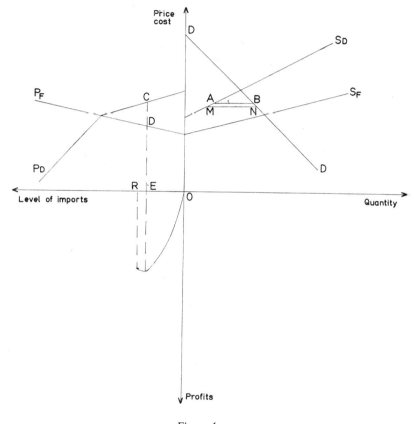

Figure 4

proposition breaks down. It will hold only in the special case when the shapes of the various schedules make it most profitable for the monopolist to use his full quota.

Equilibrium in the quota system is easily illustrated in the three-quadrant Figure 4. The righthand quadrant contains the usual S_D, S_F, and

---

[5]   This import level will, however, be subject to an *upper bound* set by the quota.

D schedules. The upper-lefthand quadrant contains two schedules, one depicting the domestic price and the other the foreign price, corresponding to different levels of utilization of the quota $MN (=OR)$ by the quota-holder. The lower-lefthand quadrant shows the level of profits corresponding to every level of utilization of the quota. $AB (=OE)$ then represents the level of quota utilization at which the profits of the quota-holder are at a maximum; and the corresponding (implicit) tariff rate is CD/DE.[6] This is necessarily greater than, or at least equal to, the tariff rate that would produce the level of imports OR.

Case IV   Competitive supply from abroad, monopoly in domestic production, and monopolist holding of quotas.

The tariff system in this case is identical to that in Case II (and Figure 2). The quota system, however, will now differ – unless, of course, it is assumed that the quota-holder acts as a perfect competitor and fails to maximize his profits. Since the quota-holder may also be expected to maximize his profits, the problem becomes that of duopoly, and, as with that general class of problems, there are as many solutions as the behavioral assumptions one cares to make. We take only two simple cases here; they are sufficient for underlining the nonequivalence possibility.

Case A   Assume that the producer maximizes his profits at every level of imports chosen by the quota-holder, and that the quota-holder then chooses that level of imports which, given this assumption about the producer's behavior, yields him the maximum profit.

In this case, the system is the following:

$$D = D(P_D) \tag{1}$$

---

[6]   The equilibrium value of S_F can easily be shown to be:

$$\frac{P_D - P_F}{P'_F - (1/D' - S'_D)},$$

where

$$P'_F = \frac{dP_F}{dS_F}, \qquad D' = \frac{dD}{dP_D},$$

and

$$S'_D = \frac{dS_D}{dP_D}.$$

$$S_F = S_F(P_F) \tag{2}$$

$$S_F + S_D = D \tag{3}$$

$$C = C(S_D) \tag{4}$$

$$\frac{P_D}{P_F} = (1 + t) \tag{5}$$

$$\frac{d(P_D - P_F)S_F}{dS_F} \gtreqqless 0 \tag{6}$$

$$\frac{d(S_D P_D)}{dS_D} = \frac{dC}{dS_D}. \tag{7}$$

The first five equations are familiar. Equation (6) is the profit-maximizing, equilibrium condition for the monopolist quota-holder, and equation (7) the corresponding condition for the monopolist producer. There are thus seven equations and seven unknowns: D, D_F, S_D, P_F, P_D, t, and C. The (implicit) tariff rate and the (actual) import level are thus determined simultaneously. Note further that the tariff and quota systems are again different, so that nonequivalence will obtain,[7] except where conditions lead the monopolist quota-holder to use all his quota. Where the quota is not entirely utilized, the implicit tariff rate must be higher than the explicit tariff rate.

Case B   Assume instead that the quota is allotted to the producer-monopolist himself.[8]

In this case, the producer becomes a pure monopolist, with two sources of supply – domestic and foreign. He will then use them in such a way as to maximize his profits. The system of equations is then the following:

$$D = D(P_D) \tag{1}$$

$$S_F + S_D = D \tag{2}$$

$$S_F = S_F(P_F) \tag{3}$$

---

[7]   This case could also be illustrated by adapting the three-quadrant diagram in Figure 4 so as to introduce monopoly instead of competition in domestic production.

[8]   This is not as fanciful an assumption as it appears. In countries such as India, considerable concentration of ownership and control obtains in economic activity, owing to a variety of reasons such as strictly controlled entry and economies of scale combined with limited markets. It is thus not merely possible, but also probable, for the case described in the text to obtain in practice.

$$C = C(S_D) \qquad\qquad (4)$$

$$\frac{P_D}{P_F} = 1 + t \qquad\qquad (5)$$

$$\frac{d(P_F S_F)}{dS_F} \lesseqgtr \frac{dC}{dS_D} = \frac{d(P_D D)}{dD}. \qquad (6) \text{ and } (7)$$

We thus have seven equations (all familiar by now) and seven unknowns D, S_F, S_D, C, P_F, P_D and t. Thus, both the (implicit) tariff rate and the rate of quota utilization are determined. Note again the differences in the tariff and quota systems in this case, implying nonequivalence.

This case is easily illustrated in Figure 5, where MC is the marginal cost schedule for imports, and the aggregate marginal cost schedule, for both sources of supply, is SRA_{mc}. The latter's intersection with the marginal

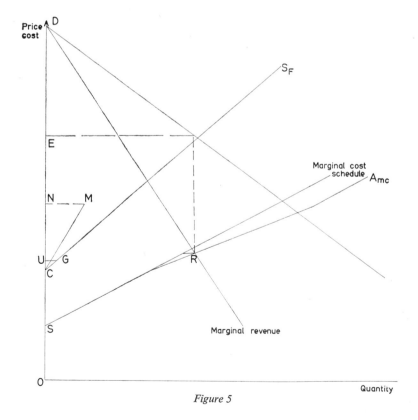

Figure 5

revenue schedule at R yields the domestic price as EO, the foreign price as UO, the (implicit) tariff rate as EU/UO, and the level of imports as GU.[9]

II Implications of nonequivalence

The demonstration that the equivalence of tariffs and quotas can break down, once we move away from the universally competitive model, is not merely interesting in itself but also has important implications in several areas of analysis.

1. It is often stated that quotas are preferred to tariffs because their import-restricting effect, although in principle equivalent to that of tariffs, is *certain*, whereas that of tariffs is not. The reason cited is the difficulty of estimating the supply and demand schedules, both domestic and foreign. In point of fact, the possible differences in market structure (at the level of foreign supply and domestic production) under the two systems have also to be assessed accurately – and these, as well as their effects, can be far more difficult to judge.

Moreover, the impression that quotas necessarily produce *certain* predictions about the level of actual imports is incorrect. They frequently set only an *upper bound* to the level of imports – not merely because foreign or domestic supply and/or demand schedules have changed or because of administrative delays in allocations of exchange, but also because the market structure may depart from the universally competitive model (as in Case IV, for example).[10]

2. Yet another inference from the equivalence proposition has been that when *both* tariffs and quotas are applied to an industry, and the discrepancy between the foreign and domestic prices *exceeds* the tariff rate, the tariff is redundant (except insofar as it cuts into the profits of the quota-holders and yields corresponding revenue to the state). This inference is invalid, of course, when nonequivalence obtains, and it is

---

[9] The reader who wishes to illustrate nonequivalence in a simple fashion can use the (derived) tariff rate EU/UO and the same S_F, D, and marginal cost schedules to show how, if this tariff rate is actually imposed, the import level resulting can differ from GU.

[10] Nonutilization due to administrative delays and changed supply or demand conditions is, of course, quite important. The time profile of utilization *within* the time horizon specified also can be interesting to analyze and would involve an intertemporal, profit-maximizing solution.

important to note this in view of the widespread, simultaneous use of tariffs and quotas in many developing countries.[11]

The imposition of a tariff, even when the equilibrium solution with this tariff plus a specific quota shows a greater difference between P_F and P_D than the tariff would have produced, may still have a *net* supplementary protective effect, in the sense of increasing domestic production above what it would otherwise be. This can readily be illustrated in the framework of Case IV, assumption B, in which the domestic monopolist also has a monopoly of the quota. A tariff on imports (at less than the implicit tariff rate) would raise their marginal cost to the monopolist, inducing him to shift toward more domestic production while at the same time curtailing total sales. Similar interactions of quotas and tariffs could be demonstrated in other frameworks as well.

Before concluding, we may spell out briefly two other propositions, relating to quotas per se rather than to the equivalence proposition, which seem to be of some interest.

1. It is frequently thought that import-quota auctions would be equivalent to ordinary quotas, while the profits made by quota-holders would accrue to the state as auction premiums. On the other hand, it is clear from the preceding analysis that the issue depends on *how* the auctions are conducted. For example, if quotas are allocated to a "large" number of holders under the ordinary system, whereas the auction permits one buyer to bid highest, the latter will bid *until* the *monopolist*-profit is exhausted by way of premium, so that the resulting situation will become one of monopoly quota-holding instead of the original competition among quota-holders.[12] In this case, therefore, the auction would convert

---

[11] Firms frequently ask for tariff protection for their industries, even when the tariff may in fact be "redundant" (in the sense of the text) by virtue of import control, because import control is subject to frequent revision – semiannually in India – and hence its protective effect is "uncertain", whereas tariffs are revised in practice only after several years and hence can be "relied upon". Frequently also, there are built-in leakages, even in import control, which introduce uncertainty. Thus, for example, many countries now experiment with export-incentive schemes involving "import-replacement" licenses. Under these schemes, imports of a commodity earning a higher premium could well increase, thereby reducing the "protective" effect of import control for the domestic producers of this commodity. A tariff could then be very useful indeed in reducing such a leakage!

[12] This argument, of course, presumes that the monopolistic buying-up occurs under auctions but that no monopoly is obtained by purchasing from the quota-

the situation from one system to another – from Case I to Case III (if we assume competition in domestic production). The equivalence of auctions and ordinary quotas would thus break down.

2. Another interesting policy proposition relates to the widely observed association of quantitative import restrictions with monopoly (or oligopoly) in domestic production and its consequently deleterious effects on *both* the level of output and the level of efficiency (with respect to minimizing the cost of producing a specified output).[13]

The restrictive effect on the level of output is implicit in the analysis of Case II. The effect on efficiency, however, is perhaps far more significant – and has been the concern of planners, using import control regimes, in many developing countries.

It is pertinent, therefore, to consider seriously whether the import control regime should not be modified so as to build into the system a threat of "liberalization" of imports when there is evidence of quality deterioration, inefficiency, or restrictive output policies. (This is, of course, similar to the traditional prescription with respect to removal of tariff protection.)

This prescription, however, runs counter to the present indiscriminate resort to quantitative restrictions and the tendency to ignore the economic costs of import control analyzed here. But there is little doubt that it is imperative to experiment with this idea in practice if a way out of the current widespread "featherbedding" and inefficiency in sheltered markets is to be reduced to less gigantic proportions.[14]

---

holders under the nonauction system of allocation. These assumptions, however, may be realistic.

[13] The absence of foreign competition, combined with a planning setup which rules out new entry and the driving out of inefficient producers, has resulted in considerable inefficiency in countries such as India. It is enough to be a consumer (or a producer using domestic intermediates) in India to see the force of this observation!

[14] Under balance-of-payments pressures, more countries may be expected to slide into such economic regimes. During a consulting assignment in Turkey in the summer of 1964, I found Turkey gradually moving into such a setup. There, as soon as a domestic industry is established, the imports of that commodity are practically automatically "deliberalized". Aside from the adverse effects on quality and costs which may confidently be expected from this policy, its operation has led to interesting destabilization in the short term. Thus, as soon as the industry comes into operation, there is an excessive import of the commodity in the expectation that it will be deliberalized: this happened with rubber tires, for example. No solution has yet been found to this problem.

TARIFF-CUTTING TECHNIQUES IN THE KENNEDY ROUND

Robert E. Baldwin

I An across-the-board approach

In recent tariff negotiations under the General Agreement on Tariffs and Trade, it became evident that the traditional item-by-item technique of bargaining no longer was adequate for achieving a significant liberalization of world trade. This method tended to limit both the scope of the negotiations and the depth of the average cut. Domestic pressures within each country were successful in excluding many items from the negotiations on the basis of particular reasons that would not have been accepted if an across-the-board approach had been followed.[1] Furthermore, when one country excluded important items in a particular industry, other participants tended, for bargaining reasons, to exclude their significant import items in the same industry. The outcome was that the recent negotiations tended to be confined to those items about which there was no significant import-competition problem in any country and, therefore, in which no one was especially interested. The negotiators also tended to become more concerned with giving up as little as possible in return for as much as possible than with seeking a mutually beneficial tariff reduction.

---

[1] Under an across-the-board technique, there is a presumption that the duty on every item is to be reduced. Opponents to a cut on a particular item must show why a cut should not be made. With the item-by-item technique, on the other hand, the burden tends to be on the proponents of a duty reduction for a particular item to show why any reduction at all should be made. The same distinction holds with respect to the depth of the cut. Reductions under a linear approach are either equal for all items or else follow some simple rule. There is no presumption under the item-by-item technique, however, that the depth of the cut will be, for example, the maximum permitted by law. It would be necessary, in this case, for the proponents of such a duty cut to show why the cut should not be less.

The drawbacks to the traditional negotiating procedure became very clear during the Dillon Round of 1961. Although in 1958 the President was granted the authority to reduce almost all duties by another 20 per cent, the actual United States cut was only about 8 per cent on only 14 per cent of dutiable trade. It also took over three years to prepare for and complete this round of tariff negotiations. On technical grounds alone, it was obvious that a broad, deep tariff-cutting exercise would be severely handicapped by the item-by-item technique.

In asking for the 50 per cent cutting authority of the Trade Expansion Act, the administration made clear to Congress that it intended to abandon this old approach and use a broader tariff-reducing technique in future negotiations. Since the European Economic Community actually had suggested a 20 per cent, across-the-board cut at the outset of the Dillon Round, it was thought that the Six would accept a United States proposal for an equal percentage cut on almost all protected items. This view was reinforced by the fact that the Community was following this procedure in eliminating duties among its own members. It was also believed that the other major trading nations would strongly support an across-the-board technique, since many of them had previously expressed a desire to use this approach.

In preliminary discussions with the EEC on the Kennedy Round, United States negotiators discovered that the Community did not favor a 50 per cent, across-the-board cut. It proposed instead a plan based on the concept of *écrêtement, i.e.,* "depeaking". Under the plan, duties on manufactured goods were to be reduced by 50 per cent of the *difference* between their existing levels and 10 per cent. Duties on semimanufactures and raw materials were to be cut 50 per cent of the difference between the existing rate and 5 per cent and zero, respectively.[2]

The United States strongly opposed the *écrêtement* notion on the grounds that it would not produce a significant average reduction in tariffs. Even before taking into consideration any exceptions, the formula gives an average reduction for the main trading countries of only around 15 per cent. Furthermore, the average United States cut would be substantially greater than the Community's average reduction. This is be-

---

[2]   Agricultural products, incidentally, were not covered by the formula. The EEC maintained that some means other than an across-the-board cutting procedure would have to be found for achieving trade liberalization in agriculture.

cause the Common External Tariff of the EEC was formed by averaging member countries' rates, a procedure that resulted in a concentration of tariffs in the 10 to 15 per cent range. These tariffs would be reduced very little under the *écrêtement* rule. In view of the desire to achieve a duty reduction averaging as close to 50 per cent as possible and the obvious unacceptability of any plan that reduced United States duties more than those of the Six, the EEC proposal was regarded by the United States as a nonstarter. All the other major trading members of GATT also opposed the EEC scheme.

With the direct approval of President Kennedy, United States negotiators took a hard line when the ministers met in May, 1963, for the purpose of establishing rules and procedures for the Kennedy Round. The United States delegation insisted that a linear rule be followed in the negotiations, and a serious crisis occurred at the ministerial meeting. However, the outcome appeared to be a general acceptance of the United States goal. The Ministerial Resolution issued stated: "That ... the tariff negotiations ... shall be based upon a plan of substantial linear tariff reductions with a bare minimum of exceptions which shall be subject to confrontation and justification. The linear reductions shall be equal".[3]

Immediately following this statement, however, was an important qualification: "In those cases where there are significant disparities in tariff levels, the tariff reductions will be based upon special rules of general and automatic application".[4] The chairman elaborated somewhat upon this vague sentence by establishing two interpretations for the record. The first was that the term "significant" meant "meaningful in trade terms", and the second that the purpose of the special rules was "to reduce such disparities".

II The disparities issue

The existence of so-called tariff disparities was the main basis for the EEC's *écrêtement* proposal. Disparities refer to differences in the rates of duty on particular items between any two countries. Under the EEC's

[3] The text of this agreement was published in the Department of State *Bulletin*, June 24, 1963.
[4] *Ibid.*

harmonization scheme, the percentage duty cut on any item is greater, the higher the duty on the item. Consequently, the relative difference in rates on any item between two countries is reduced under this formula. On the other hand, under the United States linear proposal, the same percentage cut in duties is made on all items. Tariff differences are still reduced in absolute terms, however. The ministers arrived at a compromise by stating that, in the case of "significant" disparities, the percentage cuts on the item involved would be unequal among the participants. They placed the statement concerning disparities in such a way, however, as to imply that "significant" disparities were in fact not very numerous.

The EEC contended that the existence of large numbers of high-duty items in the United States tariff schedule was the major cause of tariff disparities.[5] There are, for example, over 900 items with rates of at least 30 per cent, compared to only a handful of such rates in the EEC tariff schedule, even though the average United States and EEC tariffs are roughly the same. According to the Community, these high duties raise three major difficulties for a linear reduction rule:[6]

1. An equal cut in high United States and middle-level EEC rates would increase United States exports to the Community much more than EEC exports to the United States. (It is simultaneously argued that cuts in the larger number of low-duty United States items are not worth much in terms of increased exports for the EEC, because those low duties are already only a minor obstacle to trade.)

2. An equal cut would increase imports into the EEC from third countries more than such imports into the United States. In other words, exports from third countries would be diverted (in relative terms) from the United States to the EEC.

3. The United States would end up with many more high rates than the Six and thus with greater bargaining power for future trade negotiations with the EEC.

The nub of these arguments is that the over-all elasticity of import demand is less in the United States than in the EEC, because of the relative inelasticity of import demand for the comparatively large number of high- and low-duty items in the United States tariff schedule. In sup-

---

[5] For an analysis of the level and dispersion of the United States and EEC tariffs, see *Trade Negotiations for a Better Free World Economy* (New York: Committee for Economic Development, 1964), Appendix B.

[6] See *ibid.*, pp. 46-49 and S26-S28 for a discussion of some of these arguments.

porting this contention, the only substantive point EEC officials make about the high United States duties is that they are in effect prohibitive and will remain so even after a 50 per cent reduction. There is, in other words, considerable "water" in the United States tariff.

It is difficult to take this argument very seriously. Previous item-by-item negotiations have eliminated almost all of this form of "excessive" protection. For example, the Tariff Commission in recent tariff rounds determined for each item of interest its "peril point", the rate below which it believed a further cut would seriously injure the industry producing the item. Since this level is far below any which could be considered excessively protectionist, and since the reductions actually offered foreigners in the past brought most high duties at least to these levels, it is very unlikely that there is any appreciable degree of "water" in the United States tariff structure. United States negotiators long ago utilized it in bargaining with other countries.[7] There are reasons for believing, on the contrary, that there is a certain amount of "water" in the Common External Tariff.[8]

It is also difficult to see much force in the Community's contention concerning the elasticity of import demand for low-duty United States items. Most low-duty items are primary products or semimanufactures. On these products, which tend to be homogeneous, a low duty can be fully as protective as a higher duty on a differentiated manufactured good. However, quite aside from this point, the argument as presented by EEC spokesmen seems to confuse the effect of a given percentage tariff cut on the price of the product and the concept of price sensitivity. A 50 per cent cut on a 10 per cent duty item, for example, will decrease the product's price relatively less – all other things being equal – than a 50 per cent reduction in a 50 per cent tariff.[9] Under the *ceteris paribus* assumption, the increase in imports of the product will, therefore, be less. But this has

[7] Sometimes the existence of nonperformance items in the United States tariff schedule is pointed to as evidence of "water" in these duties. Actually, these items almost always turn out to be obsolete products.

[8] Walter S. Salant and Others, *The United States Balance of Payments in 1968* (Washington, D.C.: The Brookings Institution, 1963), pp. 101-2.

[9] Suppose the price at which a product can be purchased from foreigners is $1.00 per unit of the product. A 10 per cent duty will raise its domestic price to $1.10, whereas a 50 per cent tariff will increase the internal price to $1.50. Cutting the duty in half in both of these cases will reduce the $1.10 price to $1.05, or by 4.5 per cent, and the $1.50 price to $1.25, or by 16.7 per cent.

nothing to do with differences in elasticities. Since the average EEC and United States duties are about the same, as are the volumes of dutiable imports for the two areas, the smaller increase in imports on low-duty United States items would probably be balanced by the larger import increase on the high-duty United States items.

On general grounds, there is reason to believe that the elasticity of import demand for nonagricultural goods actually is higher for the United States than for the EEC. The ratio of imports to domestic production is lower in the former than in the Community. This tends to enable foreign exports to increase their market in the United States relatively more with a given tariff cut than United States importers increase their sales to the EEC with the same duty reduction. Moreover, consumer goods make up a somewhat larger fraction of total nonagricultural imports in the United States than in the EEC. Since the market elasticity of demand for consumer goods is generally considered greater than that for capital goods or raw materials, this relationship also operates to increase the United States import demand elasticity relative to that in the EEC.

Of course, the elasticity of demand for imports is but one factor determining the effect of a linear tariff cut on a country's import volume. As Richard Cooper has demonstrated in a recent article,[10] such factors as the average tariff level, the average volume of trade, and the degree of dispersion of these variables also affect the trade impact of a duty cut. Using data compiled by Frances Topping,[11] Cooper estimated the effect of a 50 per cent linear cut on the volume of United States and EEC import trade. He concluded that, if agricultural items are excluded from the calculations, United States imports would increase substantially more than those of the EEC, even if import demand elasticities are assumed to be the same.[12] In short, not only did the EEC fail to make a convincing analytical case for the existence of a higher elasticity of import demand

---

[10]   Richard N. Cooper, "Tariff Dispersion and Trade Negotiations", *Journal of Political Economy*, LXXII (December, 1964), 597-603.

[11]   Frances K. Topping, *Comparative Tariffs and Trade* (New York: Committee for Economic Development, 1963).

[12]   The main reason for this result is that the average level of tariffs on industrial items is actually somewhat higher in the United States than in the EEC. Consequently, the average reduction in prices (and thus, *ceteris paribus*, the increase in imports) tends to be greater in the United States than in the Community.

in the Community than in the United States, but also available empirical evidence relating to certain other important factors affecting the volume of trade after a tariff cut fails to support the EEC's claims.

III   The EEC proposal on disparities

Even though United States negotiators fully appreciated the weaknesses of the EEC contentions, they reluctantly accepted the language of the Ministerial Resolution on disparities in order to prevent a collapse of the negotiations. The United States also believed that the magnitude of the issue would be kept small under the language of the resolution. However, the EEC used the disparity issue to slow down the pace of the preparatory negotiations. Although the ministers had instructed their negotiators to reach final agreement on disparities by August 1, 1963, the Community did not propose a disparities rule until January, 1964.

The EEC proposal consisted of two parts: an arithmetic criterion for identifying disparate items and certain qualitative criteria that modified the arithmetic formula. Arithmetically, a disparity was defined as existing if the duty on a manufactured or raw-material item in one or more of the reference countries (United States, EEC, and United Kingdom) was at least twice as high as the duty on the same item in a linear participant country, and at the same time exceeded this latter duty by 10 percentage points or more. In the case of semimanufactured products, the requirement of a 10-percentage-point spread was dropped.

The Community's rationale for treating semimanufactures differently from manufactured commodities under their disparities proposal (as well as under their harmonization scheme proposed earlier) relates to differences in the domestic value-added component of these two classes of commodities. Suppose, for example, that the value of a particular semimanufactured item is made up one-half of duty-free raw materials that must be imported and one-half of processing activities that are carried out domestically. Under these circumstances, a 10 per cent duty on the semimanufactured product would afford effective protection of 20 per cent to domestic producers of the item. Since other processing countries will have to incur the same raw-material costs, the country with the 10 per cent duty can possess costs on the processing component of the product that are 20 per cent higher (*i.e.*, the ad valorem duty multiplied by the reciprocal of the proportion of domestically added value) than those in other processing countries and still match the domestic price of imports from these countries. However, as the proportion of imported materials to the total value of the product declines through additional processing, the magnification in domestic protection given by the 10 per cent duty becomes lower. If one assumes that the proportion of imported materials is higher for semimanufactures than for manufactured goods and that duties on raw materials are zero, it follows that a small difference in rates between two countries on semimanufactures will represent the same difference in effective domestic protection as a larger difference on manufactured commodities.[13] Since duties on semimanufactured commodities generally are low, EEC officials felt that the 10-point-spread requirement would exclude many meaningful disparities among this class of commodities.

It is true, of course, that the degree of effective protection on a particular domestic processing activity for a product depends upon the proportion that the value added by this activity bears to the total value of the product, the rate of duty levied on the processed item, and the duty levied on the product up to the particular activity being considered. But the domestic protection provided by a certain rate of duty may be much greater for any particular manufactured product than for any particular semimanufactured commodity simply because the domestic value-added component of *all* manufactured goods is not larger than that for *all* semimanufactures. Furthermore, the domestic value-added share in a particular product varies considerably from country to country, as does the list of manufactured and semimanufactured products. In view of these specific objections and the general objection that the whole disparity notion is too vague to attempt to be very precise in identifying disparate items arithmetically, one wonders whether the Community's proposal on semimanufactures was not tailored to protect certain industries in the EEC.

Once a disparity was identified, the EEC proposed that the high-duty reference country involved cut 50 per cent, but a low-duty country claiming

---

13   To be more precise, the effective degree of protection for a particular item can be expressed as equal (in percentage terms) to: $(tp - t'p')/(p - p')$ 100, where t is the ad valorem duty on the product; t' is the ad valorem duty on the imported components of the product; p' is the import price of these components, and p the import price of the processed product.

the disparity reduce by a percentage that – depending on the width of the disparity – averaged only about 25 per cent. This procedure ensured that the depth of the linear cut could still be 50 per cent, and yet disparities could also be reduced by a special unequal tariff-reducing rule.[14] Although accomplishing this important objective, the proposed reducing procedure led to another serious difficulty.

This was the so-called third-country problem. Take the example of watches. The duty in the United States on many types of watches is over 50 per cent, whereas the duty on comparable items in the EEC is generally below 15 per cent. Moreover, Switzerland, which is the main exporter of watches to both the EEC and the United States, has a duty rate of only about 5 per cent on these items. Therefore, both the EEC (15 per cent) and the Swiss (5 per cent) can claim a disparity against the United States (50 per cent) on watches, and thus reduce their duties by only about 25 per cent instead of the suggested linear figure of 50 per cent. But this smaller cut by Switzerland and the EEC would not hurt the United States, since the latter does not export watches in any significant quantities. However, the 25 per cent (rather than 50 per cent) cut by the EEC would harm the Swiss, who are major exporters to the Community. The Swiss wish to obtain a 50 per cent duty cut in their export markets, and yet, simply because the United States has a high duty on the item, they are faced with only a 25 per cent duty cut in one of their major export markets.

This illustration of a third country paying the penalty for the existence of a disparity was not an isolated case. In 60 per cent of the cases where the EEC could claim a disparity under its proposal, some country other than the high-duty reference country was the principal supplier of the product to the Six. This is no accident. The country with the high duty usually does not export a substantial quantity of the product. The main reason it has a high duty is to protect domestic producers who are faced with import competition. In other words, the EEC formula tends to

---

14   There are two ways of treating disparities: either the high countries reduce on their disparate items by more than the general linear figure, or else the low countries reduce by less than this figure on the disparities they claim. Since the United States is limited by law to a 50 per cent reduction, the first procedure would require the linear reduction figure to be less than 50 per cent. It would bring about a lower average cut among the participants than the second method, since the number of disparate items is considerably less than the number of linear items.

select those very products for which some third, low-duty country is the major supplier to the disparity claimers.

United States negotiators argued that this was nonsense. They claimed that the ministerial statement that disparities must be "meaningful in trade terms" required the exclusion of such cases where some third country was the principal supplier to the low-duty disparity claimer. As one of the qualitative criteria determining disparities, the Community did agree to deal, on a bilateral item-by-item basis, with European countries who were adversely affected by this third-country problem, but the EEC refused to exclude automatically all cases where the high-duty reference country was not a major supplier of the item.

The Community did, however, express a willingness to consider excluding cases satisfying the arithmetic criterion, but where there were already substantial imports from the EEC into the high-duty country.[15] By "substantial" the EEC meant imports that represented an important fraction of the domestic consumption of the item in the high-duty country. Finally, as another of the qualitative criteria for determining disparities, the EEC also agreed to drop cases meeting the arithmetic formula where either there was no production in the low-duty country or total imports of the product into this country were insignificant in size.

The United States was prepared to go along with the EEC proposal, provided there were certain modifications in it. The major point in the United States counterproposal was that there must be some rule that automatically excluded the possibility of third countries being seriously hurt by tariff cuts in their major export markets that were less than the linear figure. The reason for this position was the fear of a snowballing effect that would seriously erode the depth of the average cut. United States negotiators knew that only the EEC was really interested in initiating disparity claims, although other nations would insist upon their right to restore the balance of reciprocity on any disparities invoked against them. Indeed, several of the European Free Trade Association countries had indicated a willingness to wait until the end-of-the-day balancing process before considering the possibility of invoking disparities themselves, provided initial disparity claims by others did not adversely

---

[15] The United States negotiators, who were instrumental in inserting the term "meaningful in trade terms" into the 1963 Ministerial Resolution, apparently had in mind the exclusion of such cases when they proposed the phrase.

affect their trade prospects to a significant extent. The United States believed that this qualification was not likely to hold under the Community proposal, however. Instead, the smaller EFTA countries and Japan very likely would find many of their important EEC markets much less open than would be the case under a 50 per cent cut. These countries not only had threatened to invoke immediately the very large number of disparities they could claim, but even to exclude certain items from the cutting process in order to counter the restrictive effects of the Community's actions, if in fact the initial EEC claims hurt them seriously. The United States feared that the Six then would use this action as an excuse to pull back even further from an across-the-board offer. Moreover, countermeasures directed against the Community would probably hurt other countries, which in turn also would start withdrawing part of their offers. This could easily set off a chain reaction that would reduce the average cut very significantly. The key to preventing a chain-reaction effect was, in other words, the elimination of most of the third-country problem. Unfortunately, it was impossible in preliminary negotiations to obtain agreement between the EEC and the United States on a general disparities rule. The matter was left for settlement on the basis of detailed negotiations covering individual items.

IV   Other exceptions to the linear rule

Although the disparities issue dominated early Kennedy-Round negotiating sessions, the Ministerial Resolution also outlined three other circumstances in which a general and equal percentage cut was not necessarily appropriate. These were cases where a participating country already possessed "a very low average level of tariffs"; where a participant was a less-developed nation; and where a country, although developed, exported mainly agricultural or other primary products.

The rationale put forth for the first set of special circumstances was the bargaining-power argument, that if low-duty countries reduced tariffs much more, they would have nothing of interest left to offer higher-duty countries in future negotiations. Actually, there is substance to the point that a given percentage cut in a low-duty country's rates is likely to increase exports to that country less than would be the case if the duty level were higher. The reason, as noted before, is simply that the higher the duty on any item, the greater the percentage cut in the product's price that a given percentage tariff reduction produces. Consequently, even if import elasticities are the same for all countries, exporters to low-duty countries will have less to gain from a uniform tariff cut than exporters to high-duty nations.

The answer to the bargaining-power argument is that, if it were valid, the higher-duty countries would be unwilling to undertake across-the-board cuts with the low-duty countries in the present negotiating round. The highs will tend to give more and receive less from the lows not just in the future but in the Kennedy Round as well. This is an important characteristic of the linear approach. Under the traditional item-by-item approach, the bargaining-power notion did influence negotiating policy, and low-duty countries did find that request lists submitted to them usually were much smaller than the requests for cuts that they made of others. This was one of the reasons why the item-by-item technique was proving so limiting in recent negotiations. However, the willingness of the higher-duty nations to cut duties in the Kennedy Round by percentages at least as large as the low-duty countries suggests that the bargaining-power argument loses its strength if a linear approach is followed. It is fortunate, therefore, that no country has claimed special treatment under this provision of the Ministerial Resolution.

The other two conditions for setting aside the linear technique are straightforward. Obviously, the less-developed countries are not willing to make deep tariff cuts at this time. Indeed, in general, they are not prepared to make any meaningful cuts. They consider high duties to be an important means of fostering domestic development. In many instances, high tariffs actually are hindering growth in these countries. However, a new GATT negotiating round, in which discussion of trade matters is isolated from discussion of the general development programs of these countries, is not the appropriate occasion for considering an extensive re-evaluation of their tariff structures. Likewise, this is not the time politically or economically for developed countries to ask for full reciprocity from less-developed participants. The developed nations should concentrate upon using the Kennedy Round as a means of stimulating growth in less-developed countries by opening up their export markets, especially for those manufactured and semimanufactured products in which the less-developed countries do have the ability to compete efficiently.

For a country like Canada, the linear approach does not provide reciprocity. Canada's exports consist largely of primary products on which there are either no duties or only very low duties in foreign markets. On the other hand, Canada imports substantial quantities of manufactured commodities, despite fairly high duties on these items. A general cut, therefore, would increase imports into Canada much more than Canadian exports. For this reason, the ministers recognized that negotiations with countries that have a "special trade structure" would have to proceed in a more traditional manner.

A final novel negotiating approach in the Kennedy Round concerns those items that each linear participant excludes from the general cut. The 1963 Ministerial Resolution states that these exceptions "should be subject to confrontation and justification". Unfortunately, an effective technique for performing this function could not be agreed upon before the start of the actual negotiating process. Each country obviously wanted full sovereignty concerning the determination of its exceptions and did not want any international group set up that might embarrass the country about the size of its exceptions list. However, the Secretariat of GATT, although badly hampered by lack of staff, was aware of the need for a technique of negotiating exceptions on a multilateral basis and was anxious to contribute its services in implementing any such arrangement.

The establishment of a multilateral mechanism for trading off exceptions would represent a major improvement in tariff negotiations under GATT. Previous negotiations have been only partially multilateral in scope. They took place between pairs of countries on items of principal-supplier interest to the two countries, and the resulting cuts were then generalized to all countries. Each country undertook several bilateral negotiations simultaneously, and there was some exchange of information on a multilateral basis, but the balancing of concessions was done essentially on a bilateral basis. As a result, many items were necessarily left out of the negotiations. For example, suppose country A is the principal supplier to B for a list of items on which the likely increase of exports from A to B after a given percentage duty cut is much larger than B's increase in exports to A on the items principally supplied to A by B. To achieve bilateral balance, B will not offer concessions on all its imports for which A is its principal supplier (or else offer only small concessions). This outcome was inevitable in pre-Kennedy-Round negotiations. The bilateral aspects of these negotiations were every bit as restricting as the item-by-item procedure.

In carrying out the 1963 instructions of the ministers concerning confrontation and justification of exceptions, the participating nations had an opportunity to make an important advance in negotiating technique. Instead of trading off exceptions bilaterally and thus insuring a minimum solution to the miltilateral balancing problem, they could have established a formal multilateral arrangement. The GATT Secretariat, for example, could have attempted to find instances where, say, a triangular negotiation on exempted items might prove beneficial to all involved. In other words, the Secretariat could have acted as a broker by determining multilateral trading possibilities and bringing them to the attention of the countries involved.

V   Conclusions

Although the Kennedy Round has not yet been completed, negotiations thus far seem to indicate that the sweeping, uniform cuts in tariff levels expected by supporters of the Trade Expansion Act of 1962 will not be achieved. Instead, right from the outset, the negotiations turned into lengthy, petty haggling similar in many ways to the old item-by-item process. Ostensibly, the reason for this was the objection by the EEC to the linear negotiating approach suggested by the United States. According to the EEC, this technique was not suitable for giving a balance of concessions among the major trading nations. The preceding analysis indicates, however, that the specific reasons presented by the Community in support of their claims are not substantial. It would be most unfortunate for future negotiations if the contentions by the EEC were regarded as anything more than arguments basically put forth to cover up more fundamental reasons for wishing the nature of the negotiations to be different than was originally intended. The reasons for desiring this difference are complex and, in part, obscure, but the goal of the EEC quite clearly was the achievement of a much lower average reduction in duties than the United States wanted. However, since this goal was not popular among most other participants, Community officials found it advantageous to use technical objections to the linear approach as the means of achieving their objective.

SOME ASPECTS OF POLICIES FOR FREER TRADE

Bertil Ohlin

In recent years, several attempts have been made to create institutions for freer trade and for international economic unions. The most general is, of course, the attempt of the General Agreement on Tariffs and Trade to bring about multilateral reductions of tariffs and the elimination of quantitative restrictions on trade, at least for manufactured goods. The European Economic Community is another method of creating freer trade inside a more limited area, its goal in the economic sphere being to create an economic union which will include a customs union. Other customs unions or free trade areas are planned in other parts of the world, particularly in Latin America, Africa, and a part of Asia.

The European Free Trade Association, consisting of Great Britain and six minor states with Finland as an affiliated member, was created when attempts to bring about a large western European territory of free trade had failed. For a time, the generally accepted idea was that sooner or later – and probably after a relatively small number of years – the Economic Community and the Free Trade Association would be in some way combined, or all or most of the members of the latter would enter the Economic Community. In the last few years, it has become clear that there is little chance of this happening in the 1960's, however. Furthermore, the outlook for substantial tariff reductions as a result of the GATT negotiations in Geneva (the Kennedy Round) seems rather gloomy. The elimination of internal duties in the Community and the Free Trade Association by 1967 therefore seems to be the only substantial reduction in the obstacles to trade one can expect in the immediate future, at least as far as Europe is concerned. Moreover, the recent imposition of temporary import taxes in Great Britain (15 per cent) is a serious step backwards.

This is not a satisfactory state of affairs, particularly to countries like the United States, Canada, Australia, and Japan. It is also unsatisfactory from the special point of view of the economically less-developed nations. Under the circumstances, it has been proposed that the Free Trade Association and North America begin cooperating to make trade freer within and between these two territories. This would be accomplished through an agreement to *reduce* duties on commodities traded inside the combined territory; but it would hardly be possible to promise from the outset to eliminate the duties altogether at a fixed date in the future. Consequently, it would be the beginning not of a large free trade association, but of *a preferential tariff association*. This does not conform to the conditions laid down by GATT,[1] being contrary to the rules of the most-favored-nation policy. Since this policy may lose some of its importance anyhow, however, the question of permission to create such preferential tariff associations could possibly be kept open by GATT, and hence the first steps might be taken.

It is not my intention here to discuss the political conditions and the psychology of the political leaders in different countries, which may be decisive for the development of these and other institutions for a new commercial and economic policy. The chances of creating large customs unions, free trade associations, or preferential tariff associations will, perhaps even more than the chances of a general worldwide tariff reduction, depend on how complicated the domestic policy changes that must accompany the new commercial policy will be. In some countries, there is firm belief that it is not possible to eliminate duties on trade among a large number of countries if one does not at the same time bring about a real economic integration, by means of a harmonization of economic and social policy in general. In other words, there is skepticism toward the idea of free trade if it is not combined with the creation of a union involving far-reaching economic integration.

Is a radical integration and harmonization really necessary in order to make free trade function efficiently and advantageously inside an association of a number of states? My intention in this paper is to comment upon this question. If the answer should be in the affirmative, the outlook for some of the above-mentioned attempts to achieve decidedly freer trade would seem to be rather gloomy. It is difficult to see how such an integration

---

[1] In the first German edition of his pathbreaking and well-balanced treatise, *Der Internationale Handel* (Berlin: J. Springer, 1933), Gottfried Haberler had already presented a penetrating analysis of preferential import duties, which remains up to date.

could be brought about in the next decade in most of these new organizations, except perhaps in the European Economic Community.

The chances of arriving at a successful policy for freer trade will be much greater if it is possible to eliminate obstacles to trade without creating a large number of common institutions or requiring a radical harmonization of economic policy in general. It is, therefore, of some importance to know to what extent one can expect that such harmonization will be a useful or necessary precondition of freer trade.

I   Equilibrium analysis

It is generally accepted that the smooth functioning of the international economic system under present conditions of tariffs and quantitative restrictions requires that certain conditions be fulfilled. One of the essential things is that the important industrial nations maintain relatively full employment, but not a state of exaggerated inflationary pressure. Any considerable and more than temporary inflationary or deflationary pressure will, of course, affect foreign trade in an unbalancing way, and thereby bring about changes in the balances of payments not only of the countries directly concerned but of other countries also.

Secondly, it is important that relative cost levels do not develop very differently in the different countries over a prolonged period. In other words, relative variations in wage rates should roughly reflect international differences in rates of productivity increase. If, in some countries, wages per unit of output rise much more quickly than in others, this cannot fail in the long run to affect exports adversely and to stimulate imports. Postwar history is full of examples of this kind which have led to balance-of-payments crises, particularly on several occasions in Great Britain.

On the other hand, it is obvious that extensive structural changes in demand and supply will necessitate a certain adjustment of relative cost levels in order to make the maintenance of balance in international economic relations possible. All this is, I think, conventional theory and accepted by practically every economist, although – alas – not by every government. As the conditions mentioned cannot be fulfilled completely in practice, it is also obvious that sufficient international liquidity and a certain "availability" of international credits are prerequisites of a satisfactory functioning of the international economic system.

It might be argued that a somewhat parallel movement of costs and prices in the different countries – with modifications when the structure of supply and demand has varied – is not essential, as flexible foreign exchange rates can take care of the necessary adaptation. Devaluations and revaluations of currencies may also be used at suitable intervals, when relative costs have fallen out of line. The latter procedure has been practiced by most industrialized countries once – and by some of them twice – since the war. But in my opinion, for which I cannot here give the reasons, both these methods have serious disadvantages and create as many new problems – for example, with regard to irregular international capital movements – as they solve. Anyhow, opinion in ruling financial circles almost everywhere is firmly against them. It is natural, therefore, to choose as the normal case the assumption of fixed foreign exchange rates. By this I mean that only fluctuations of the same size as the margin between the old gold points or fluctuations within otherwise determined very narrow limits are permitted.

As indicated above, many economists and politicians in the EEC countries – of whom some were influential when the Treaty of Rome was worked out and others are still directly or indirectly connected with policy-making in the Community – maintain that a reasonably satisfactory functioning of a customs union presupposes a harmonization of social policy and, in particular, of social payments and contributions by the competing enterprises in the member countries. However, what matters is the total cost per hour of labor – productivity and other things being taken as given – not the share of this cost paid out in contributions to social insurance and to cover the cost of "fringe benefits". Nobody suggests that cash wages per hour for a certain labor quality must be equalized in all member countries to guarantee "fair competition". Why should the other part of labor costs be the same in all the member countries of a free trade union?

Social policy may affect the conditions of competition also by changing the "milieu" in which industry is working, for example, through legislation about hours of work. One country may have a 40-hour week, another will allow a normal working time of 48 hours. In a third country, double shifts may be accepted readily by the workers, while this is not the case in the two countries just mentioned. It is obvious that such legislation and labor practices affect the relative costs of different industries and thereby influence international trade. The same can be said about differences in the peacefulness of the state of the labor market, that is, the frequency and cost of serious labor conflicts. However, let us not forget that climatic conditions and many other things also affect the milieu of production and the relative costs, above all in agriculture. It is not possible to "harmonize" the climate; yet international trade can still run smoothly. Indeed, one of the advantages of trade is that the location of production can be adapted to the climatic conditions. Similarly, production can be adapted to international differences in the milieu that are due to man's actions, that is, to social policies and traditions.

If the responsible authorities do not want to accept the influence on production and trade that is exercised by such milieu conditions, they have, within limits, the opportunity to change the social policy conditions. It is understandable that this may prove difficult and that they may prefer to persuade or compel the other member countries to change *their* policies in a "harmonizing" direction. But there seems to be no justification for the assertion that only if one or both of these two methods are used can trade proceed efficiently and smoothly.

In summary, to avoid a maladjustment of relative cost levels, a certain coordination of wage policies is required in the sense that the sums of all elements that enter into labor costs are kept in a relation that is consistent with international balance. But this should be possible even if social policies diverge. Secondly, cooperation between monetary and financial authorities, which is necessary anyway in the world today, will be even more needed inside a customs union or a free trade area, in order to avoid long-lasting underemployment as well as tendencies to overemployment and inflation.

Let me turn now to another type of policy that exercises an influence on international trade and which has, therefore, been under discussion in connection with the demands for "harmonization". Taxation naturally affects the price system in several ways, since taxes enter as cost items and also change the distribution of income and the character of demand for goods and services. One type of taxes, import duties, has been thoroughly analyzed, but other taxes have received very little attention so far as their influence on international trade is concerned. Yet it is evident, for example, that company taxes proportional to labor costs will have different effects than high double taxation of the profits of business corporations. The former may more easily in the long run be shifted onto the wage earners, whereas the latter will probably be partly paid by the shareholders through lower net profits and dividends. Agriculture and other types of economic activity that are usually not carried on in the corporate form will be favored and expanded in countries where a large part of the tax burden is placed on corporations, and will, conversely, develop less in countries with low corporation taxes.

It is, in my opinion, only by careful study of a number of simplified theoretical models that conclusions can be reached about the effects of different types of taxes on costs, prices, and demand conditions, and, indirectly, on foreign trade. To attempt this is beyond the scope of this paper, which is concerned chiefly with the need for harmonization of policies as a condition for a reasonable functioning of large markets inside customs unions or free trade associations. As long as attention is confined to the influence of domestic taxes, it seems reasonable to draw the same conclusion as has already been reached about differences in social legislation. Trade will adapt itself to differences in the social and financial milieu in the same way it does to differences in climate. If changes in industry and trade can be proved to be the outcome of a difference in tax policy, and if these changes are considered unfavorable to one or several member countries, it will be natural to take up the matter of effecting a change in taxation through action by one or several of them. But, until such an analysis has been made, there is no prima facie case for harmonization of the tax system in general. It should also be kept in mind that identical tax laws may have different effects in countries with different income distributions and varying composition of industries. The way in which the tax receipts are spent is, of course, highly relevant.

So far, I have confined myself to a somewhat static analysis by concentrating attention on the cost aspects and the stability of balances of payments.

II Some aspects of development

The influence that differences in economic and social policies exercise on the economic development of each country is another matter. It may provide a better argument for harmonization of economic and social policies of member countries than considerations of fair competition can do. Let me direct attention first to the movements of the factors of production. Closer contact between countries will tend to stimulate such movements.

Thus, the incentives to migration across borders, which before had been insufficient, may now well bring migration about, at least when the free trade area or union has lasted long enough to affect the psychology of businessmen and of various labor groups.

Such an increase in the mobility of know-how, capital, and labor will strengthen tendencies to locate manufacturing industries in the districts where conditions for those industries are favorable. This will be the case particularly in regions endowed with sources of raw materials that are required for commodities more easily transported than the raw materials themselves, and where transport conditions are generally good. On the other hand, regions far away and destitute of such raw material sources may be depopulated and suffer a loss of capital. If they are concentrated in certain member countries, such a development will naturally be considered unfavorable by these countries. It will mean rapid economic growth in some countries, the opposite in the others. It cannot be denied that such possibilities may be regarded as an argument either for a restriction of factor movements or for special internal policies that provide a better economic climate in the otherwise handicapped countries. Restrictions of the former type are contrary to the spirit of customs unions and would also be regarded as unnatural in free trade associations. Attempts by the "poor country" to create compensating advantages, for example, by especially favorable tax policies, would be more easily accepted, although they might not be in agreement with the goal of achieving the maximum standard of living for the whole population inside the union or the free trade area. Anyway, from the point of view of the individual nation, this is a case for a policy the opposite of harmonization. Such a policy, however, hardly brings about the desired result unless some factor, for example, ordinary labor, is willing to accept lower real wages than in other member countries and yet refrain from large-scale emigration.

There are, of course, many other things than raw material sources and good transport conditions that may attract production and people: a favorable infrastructure with efficient public utilities, good government, legal security, low taxes. The relatively poor countries in the large market areas may have to choose between a permanently inferior infrastructure and a scarcity of good roads and good schools on the one hand, and a relatively high level of taxation on the other. In both cases, entrepreneurs and skilled technical workers may emigrate, unless the burden of taxation is placed chiefly on other taxpayers. It is true that the poorer countries usually have a higher level of interest rates, but this may be less effective in calling forth a movement of risk-taking capital and technically skilled labor to such countries, even though wages of ordinary labor may be at or below subsistence levels.

What I have briefly touched on above seems to me to be enough to justify the statement that the possibility of increased movements of factors of production may under certain circumstances create very serious problems from the point of view of the individual member countries. This may be much more important than the "dislocation" due to changes in the competitive power of some industries which I have pointed out above in the more static analysis.

Protection and the disappearance of protection inside a large market will naturally affect the domestic supply of the factors of production, for example, through the training of skilled labor for new tasks. Protectionist arguments have correctly emphasized this fact, but have often drawn unwarranted conclusions. It may well be that the more lively contacts between the peoples living inside a customs union or free trade area may lead to a spread of knowledge and an increased supply of know-how all around. The growth of large-scale production and further specialization may also favorably affect the supply of certain qualities of labor.

Another aspect of the reaction of domestic factor supply needs to be emphasized. Let us assume that in one country the tax laws contain very generous rules about the right to tax-free depreciation of capital assets (buildings, machinery, ships, etc.). If so, tax-free savings can be accumulated within business firms and used for new investment. This will speed up purchases of new modern machinery and will increase the competitive power of industries in such a country, particularly of industries that use large quantities of capital. The same industries in other countries may suffer through competition from the former. Other things being equal, manufacturing industries will develop more quickly in countries with generous depreciation rules. Similarly, low income taxes on business are advantageous for manufacturing industries that require plenty of capital and need to carry on production on a large scale. Such production is generally handled not in private firms but in corporations. But the decisive factor is not the increased supply of capital alone. Perhaps equally important is the time element – the speedy acquisition of a better technique and new machines that increase competitive power and profits.

The advantages from a tax policy of this kind may be enhanced when tariffs are eliminated. The other side of the story is an increased handicap on competitors in the other countries inside the market area. There is obviously a choice for each member nation between maintaining a very restrictive taxation policy – even though this leads to slower economic development – and changing its policy in order to obtain more rapid economic development. This question already exists under present conditions, but it may be much more important when no tariffs hamper trade inside the area. Of course, one member country can also require other member nations to change *their* taxation policies, that is, to make them more restrictive in order to prevent such favorable conditions for economic development in these countries. Which course of political action can be considered most reasonable is a matter of subjective opinion.

The impression gained from the reasoning above seems to be that there is some risk that the elimination of obstacles to trade inside a customs union or a free trade area will lead to a more unevenly distributed economic development than the member countries with the relatively unfavorable rates of development can be expected to accept. The understandable wish to avoid such an "uneven development" does not, however, lead to a demand for "harmonization" of economic and social policies. On the contrary, there is a case for planned differentiation of policy.

The conditions of economic development may, however, be used as an argument in favor of harmonization of certain elements of policy, such as depreciation rules in the taxation of business profits, if exceptions to such harmonization are accepted when they are necessary to offset unreasonable effects on development in unfavorably situated countries. An unsatisfactory infrastructure may be mentioned as an example of an "unfavorable situation". Such offsetting differences in policy may be considered reasonable when, without their use, a growing difference in real earnings between the member nations would follow the elimination of trade barriers.

The idea behind the demand for harmonization of policy, when development aspects are considered, has usually been that one wants to prevent an advanced social policy – for example, the 40-hour week and extensive social insurance – in an economically advanced country from hampering its ability to compete with countries that are from the point of view of social policy and economic standards less developed. Here again we meet the strange and erroneous idea that equal social legislation is the necessary condition of fair competition between nations. The advanced nation may have many advantages in production and in sales organization which explain both its high living standard and its advanced social legislation. Why should not the less-advanced country be allowed to work longer hours to raise its standards gradually in both ways? If it is not allowed to do so, the influx of capital and initiative and the growth of domestic savings will be restrained, and the cumulative process of economic growth will be hampered. This would in the long run be a social disadvantage of a much more serious kind than the maintenance during a period of transition of a less advanced level of social legislation. When rich nations urge the poorer nations to accept their own social standards even though the economic basis is much weaker, the reason may be either bad economics or hidden self-interest.

To sum up: by far the most important condition for a successful customs union and free trade area seems to be that relative cost levels are kept in such a relation to each other that in each country balance is kept in the payment relations with the rest of the world – including other member nations – in spite of changes in productivity, demand conditions, and so on. But this problem is not greatly different for countries that are members of a large market group than it would be for the same countries – for example, members of EFTA – if no such free trade area existed. The problem is already a dominant one in international economic relations. The same is true for the question of cooperation between the monetary and financial authorities to maintain reasonably good business and employment conditions. The need for such policies will be increased through the formation of the large markets, that is all.

III The preponderance of the relative cost problem

What bearing can the above analysis have on the future chances of the different types of large market organizations that were mentioned at the beginning of this paper? Can one say that only organizations that bring about a radical harmonization and integration between the member countries take all relevant economic and social conditions into account and, therefore, have a chance to succeed? (Strictly political aspects of a noneconomic character are disregarded in this paper.) The answer to this question evidently is in the negative. With the aid of international economic cooperation in the International Monetary Fund and other international institutions, and with reasonable contacts between the monetary and financial authorities in the market group, it ought to be possible to make the adaptations required for growing specialization and trade. The difficulties of obtaining satisfactory international liquidity are much the same for each country, whether it is a member of a market group or not. If the need for liquidity should increase a little, so, it would seem, should the mutual cooperation between the central banks in the area concerned.

The crucial problem with or without large market areas will be how to obtain a balanced development of wage rates, with due regard to changes in productivity and in other conditions that influence costs. Unless it is solved, there will be – off and on – balance-of-payments difficulties and, hence, risks that some country will feel compelled to use restrictions on its foreign trade. To attempt to solve this problem and to go ahead with more and larger free trade areas – the underdeveloped nations not excluded – would seem to be a fruitful and promising policy as long as a general elimination of obstacles to trade is not feasible and only a slow general tariff reduction is to be expected. Economic unions may be excellent where the politically necessary conditions exist. But they are not the only regional method. It is probable that a number of the simpler free trade areas – although like tariff unions they cause some "artificial" distortions of trade – can be an effective instrument to expand international trade, at least if fundamental and long-lasting imbalances in relative cost levels can on the whole be avoided.

PART TWO

Trade, growth, and development

"VENT FOR SURPLUS" MODELS OF TRADE AND GROWTH

Richard E. Caves

In the past decade, the infant industry producing theoretical models of the interaction of international trade and economic growth has enjoyed a take-off into self-sustained expansion. Frequently, the output has originated in studies of the historical pattern of trade and growth in some particular country or class of countries, with the assumptions and analytical objectives of the models closely associated with the institutional traits of the economies which inspired them. This paper contends that several models that have attracted attention for their apparent power to explain historical cases bear a basic structural similarity. While they may require the addition of very different institutional features when transferred from one developing region to another, and while they may give rise to contrasting policy conclusions in different circumstances, it is important to recognize their common foundation. Without seeing that the differences lie in the trimmings and not in the basic logical structure, either we may fail to apply these models to new cases where they may yield enlightenment, or, alternatively, we may apply them mechanically to circumstances for which they require some revision.

One principal model of trade and growth appearing in the literature is the staple theory, developed primarily with reference to the Canadian economy but widely felt to apply to other temperate-zone lands originally settled by European migrant labor and capital.[1] Another is the "vent for surplus" model, proposed by Myint to explain the evolution of trade and production patterns in certain underdeveloped tropical countries

---

[1] For good, brief accounts of this model and citations to the underlying empirical work (primarily that of Harold A. Innis), see Douglass C. North, "Location Theory and Regional Economic Growth", *Journal of Political Economy*, LXII (June, 1955), 243-58; and Melville H. Watkins, "A Staple Theory of Economic Growth", *Canadian Journal of Economics and Political Science*, XXIX (May, 1963), 141-58.

with large indigenous populations.[2] When it is placed in the setting of an international economy, W. Arthur Lewis' model of development with unlimited labor bears a close resemblance to Myint's construction.

These models share an essential common characteristic in that they depict the effects of trade on growth as involving the exploitation of resources lacking, in that place and at that time, any alternative uses of significant economic value. The existence of these "surplus" resources reflects the state of economic organization in general and not a failure of the market mechanism in any narrow sense. The pace of growth and the changes in the pattern of international trade associated with the absorption of such resources gives these models their distinctive stamp, in contrast to models involving resource reallocation and thus lying nearer to the core of traditional trade theory. Therefore, the expression "vent for surplus" provides a good generic name for these theories by touching directly upon their common characteristic. The first distinction to be made among models built upon this central feature concerns what resources are assumed to be in surplus. Expositions of the staple theory focus upon surplus natural resources: the term "staple" designates a raw material or resource-intensive good occupying a central position in a region's exports. Expositions concerned with the underdeveloped countries emphasize surplus labor attached to a self-sufficient economy producing only its own subsistence, although surplus resources combinable with this labor may also play a role.

This paper presents two highly simplified, formalistic versions of the "vent for surplus" theory, assuming in turn that resources and labor are initially in surplus, in order to bring out the basic similarities of their implications and predictions. No attention is given initially to realism or relevance of the results, or to the normative implications, but the concluding section returns to the problem of applying these models and drawing policy conclusions from them.

At the most severe level of abstraction, the "vent for surplus" model still requires the inclusion of a number of commodities, two regions, and labor, capital, and natural resources as factors of production. Multiple commodities are needed because the theory emphasizes both changes in the commodity composition of trade and variations in the growth rate of

---

[2] Hla Myint, "The 'Classical Theory' of International Trade and the Underdeveloped Countries", *Economic Journal*, LXVIII (June, 1958), 317-37.

national income related to the exploitation of new bundles of surplus resources, or to the discovery of new ways to use the surplus at hand. Two regions must be included because the processes of economic change rearrange endowments of mobile factors and commodity trade patterns in both the developing and mature portions of the world economy. Finally, labor, capital, and natural resources must be included as a minimum complement of factors of production, although the "surplus labor" version can make do without the natural resources. Because of the ponderous results of attacking so many variables with the more elaborate and exact of present-day theoretical tools, the following exposition runs in purely literary form.[3]

I   The "staple" version

Let us take up first the staple model of economic growth and international trade, characterized by "surplus" natural resources whose existence or economic usefulness is freshly discovered. Consider a world consisting of very large and mature region I (Europe, if you wish) and undeveloped region II (North America). I is an industrialized economy producing all classes of commodities. Its endowment of capital and labor we suppose for the moment to be fixed in size; its capital is a homogeneous fund capable of unrestricted transfer from any one process to any other. Full employment of these factors is assumed. One group of products, resource-intensive goods $a, ..., i, ..., m$, require for their fabrication capital, labor, and substantial quantities of natural resources. These goods we shall call staples. We suppose that a different specific resource $R_a, ..., R_i, ..., R_m$ is employed in the production of each commodity, with each resource R_i existing in individual deposits of varying quality. Many small deposits of each resource, varying in quality, are worked in region I. The marginal deposit currently in use of the ith resource yields no rent to its owner; a Ricardian rent accrues, however, to the owner of each superior deposit of the ith resource.[4] In best Ricardian fashion, the price of each staple

---

3   The approach owes a good deal to D. M. Bensusan-Butt, "A Model of Trade and Accumulation", *American Economic Review*, XLIV (September, 1954), 511-29; and his *On Economic Growth: An Essay in Pure Theory* (Oxford: Clarendon Press, 1960).

4   The argument implicitly assumes that each deposit can produce a given quantity of raw material up to some maximum per period of time at a constant average (and

under conditions of competitive equilibrium equals the earnings necessary to attract the amount of capital and labor needed to produce a unit of the commodity in collaboration with the poorest resources currently in use. The extraction and refining or processing of natural resource-intensive goods is assumed to be vertically integrated. The process involves diminishing returns to increases in output per unit of time; constant costs would prevail except for the role of diminishing returns in the extraction of resources, *i.e.*, in all processing activities.

Region I also produces manufactured goods $n, ..., r, ..., z$, using inputs of labor and capital. Staples may also enter into the production functions of manufactures as raw-material inputs, but we suppose their importance to be small enough that no variation actually experienced in the price of any ith staple will directly cause any perceptible variation in the equilibrium price of any rth manufacture employing it as an input. All manufactures are produced in region I under conditions of constant cost in the relevant range of outputs, but their production functions show increasing returns of varying importance at smaller outputs. In order to avoid reviewing the thrice-familiar propositions of the factor-proportions hypothesis about international specialization, we shall suppose that all processes (both staples and manufactures) employ capital and labor in the same proportions at any given factor-price ratio. Finally, some outputs in the manufactures group can be construed as services, having the same production-function characteristics and differing only in their inability to enter into international trade.

Region II, at the start of our story, is an empty land, discovered but with its natural-resource endowment as yet unknown and unexplored. Manufacturing could take place there, subject to the same input requirements as in region I, but subject to increasing returns and thus low productivity at small scales. Region II also has the same capital and labor requirements for turning raw materials, once extracted from the land, into staples. Because of the absence of any discovered real-cost advantage for production to take place in II, and thus of any income motive for capital and labor to migrate there, region II's mere existence encourages

---

marginal) cost; the differences among deposits in these constant cost levels permit their ranking in order of quality. The argument would not be changed in essence by permitting each deposit to be worked under conditions of gradually rising marginal costs as output per period of time is increased. The effects of resource depletion are neglected in the following argument.

no factor movements and no trade unless and until its natural resources are discovered. If an economic justification arises for factor movements to take place, they must incur transportation costs, as would commodities moving in trade. These costs would be small enough to allow us to neglect any difference between f.o.b. and c.i.f. prices of commodities, but large enough to make consumers prefer a domestic good to its foreign counterpart when both goods are produced with the same real inputs of capital and labor. By an analogous assumption, we neglect the influence of the costs of factor movements on their equilibrium earnings in the two regions. No tariffs or other trade restrictions are imposed at any time.

Now, suppose that high-quality deposits of resource R_a are discovered in region II. It becomes profitable for capital and labor to move from I to II to exploit the new resources in the production of staple a. Commodity trade commences between I and II, with I importing units of commodity a and exporting $b \ldots z$ in such proportions as to satisfy the consumption patterns of the emigrant laborers (and capitalists, if they have followed their funds), as well as to accomplish the real counterpart of any continuing flows of capital. The process of exploiting deposits of resource R_a in II involves the development of successive deposits of R_a found there. The world price of commodity a falls as its supply increases, with all deposits being opened in II that can be worked profitably at the long-run equilibrium price. The initial bonanza returns to claimants of the first deposits of R_a developed in II are cut back; in I, marginal deposits of the resource become unprofitable to work and are closed down, while the rents yielded by others are reduced. The capital and labor displaced from I's a industry either replace factors migrating to region II or produce whatever goods are now consumed in larger quantities out of world income augmented by the lower real costs of commodity a. The level of trade, after the exploitation of II's deposits of R_a has been pushed to the no-rent margin and long-run equilibrium restored in the world a market, will depend on the relative quality of R_a deposits found in the two regions and the price- and income-elasticities of demand for commodity a. These factors will also determine the portion of a now produced in region II and the relative decline of the price of a.[5] In this equilibrium situation, units

---

[5] We neglect secondary repercussions of the processes described so far, such as changes in the prices of commodities that are close complements to or substitutes for a.

of capital and labor which have migrated to II receive the same rewards as those which have remained at home; all units directly consuming commodity *a* are better off, however. Unimputed real income derived from the production of *a* in II accrues as a rent to the owners of intramarginal deposits of R_a.

The process of exploiting "surplus" resources in II so far is one of eliminating a disequilibrium situation – a wave of growth for the infant economy of region II with a pace constrained by whatever short-run factors restrict the international migration of labor or capital, or the combination of these factors with newly discovered natural-resource deposits.[6] The attainment of equilibrium in the world *a* market will curtail the growth rate of region II – to zero, by our assumptions, since no other sources of growth are included. On the other hand, any discoveries of additional high-quality resources R_b, R_c,... in II will set off the rapid growth process once again. If the constraints on the maximum feasible growth rate of II's over-all regional product and factor endowment are relatively rigid, then any overlapping discoveries of resources in II will simply prolong the duration of surges of growth. Each wave of expansion raises total income in region II, and income per capita in both regions, through the reduction in the real cost of successive resource-intensive goods. The pattern of world trade and production tends to polarize increasingly, with established region I specializing more and more in manufactured goods *n ... z*, importing an increasing proportion of its consumption of staples *a ... m*.

As the scale of region II's economy grows, it becomes increasingly likely that some of goods *n ... z*, without substantial input requirements of natural resources, can be produced more economically at home than through import from region I.[7] Services, facing infinite transportation costs, will be started with the establishment of the first export staple. Manufactures, incurring only infinitesimal transport costs, may also become economical claimants for factors of production in II. Whether or

---

[6] Restrictions may also derive from the maximum rate at which I's *a* industry contracts in the face of falling prices.

[7] Strictly speaking, we refer to the scale of the economy as measured by gross national income (exclusive of factor earnings remitted abroad), as distinguished from gross domestic product. See Jonathan V. Levin, *The Export Economies: Their Pattern of Development in Historical Perspective* (Cambridge, Mass.: Harvard University Press, 1960), pp. 170-77.

not manufacturing industries are established depends on the relative costs of international movement of goods and factors of production, since we have assumed no indigenous growth of II's factor endowment. If the costs (however interpreted) of factor movements are small relative to the discounted present value of the costs of transporting II's exports and imports that can be avoided by their migration, as we shall assume, then at least some manufacturing industries $n \ldots z$ will be established in II. The order of their establishment depends on the scale economies in their production, relative to the level of domestic consumption in II at prices prevailing in I. Important consumption items produced with minor scale economies will be the first manufactures established in II.

At this stage, we may pause to reflect upon the nature of the source of region II's staple-based growth and the permanence of its impact. A more rational process might be substituted for the discovery of natural resources through casual or random search. The quest for and discovery of resource R_i may be correlated with shifts in world demand toward the ith staple, which raise its price and the rent accruing to all R_i deposits in use and also induce the exploitation of poorer-quality known R_i deposits in region I. The production of i begins or expands in region II, and II's factor endowment and gross national product increase. Indeed, if such a motivated search for natural resources in II regularly unearths some superior to those of marginal quality in I, then a transient demand-induced increase in the price of any ith staple is typically followed by a reduction in the long-run equilibrium price below its initial value.

The possibility that demand shifts may play an essential role in pacing the exploitation of natural resources and the export-based growth of II's income inevitably raises the issue of the reversibility of this growth stimulus: if world demand for the ith staple may increase, it may also decline. The model implies that such vulnerability is greater in the early stages of II's development than after the process is well along. Since recessions are assumed absent, demand cannot shift away from all products at once. Suppose that the probability of a given percentage shift of demand away from any one staple is equal to and independent of the probability of the same shift away from any other. Then the central limit theorem predicts a reduction of the expected variance of the value of II's exports as more staples enter into the export lists. If staple growth tends to add one commodity $a \ldots m$ at a time to the national output, the process grows safer from demand shifts as it goes along.

Another defense of the stability of II's national income against external reverses appears as its economy grows large enough to support efficient production of the typical rth manufacture. In the event of a decline of staple exports from II, our assumptions preclude the profitable export of manufactures instead.[8] Labor and capital displaced from II's ith export industry would earn less by producing the rth good in II for export than by returning to mature region I. Thus is because of the assumption made above about the relative transport costs of goods and factors of production. Net reductions in the demand for staple exports must, therefore, result in some net migration from II back to I. How disruptive this proves for any industries established in II to produce goods $n \ldots z$ depends on the number of cases in which the shrinkage of II's domestic market pulls the home demand for the rth manufacture below the level that will sustain domestic production of efficient scale. When production falls below this point, the whole stock of capital and labor employed in II's r industry has no alternative but to join the trek back to region I. The farther II's domestic markets have grown beyond the levels of minimum efficient scale, the less is the chance that a permanent decline of exports will bring the collapse of domestic industries through inability to produce at an efficient scale.

The model so far makes the rate of growth in the aggregate income in region II (and also in world total income and income per capita) depend solely on the timing of resource discoveries and the feasible rate of factor migration and absorption. This process, however, can be visualized as superimposed upon an underlying steady swell of neoclassical growth occurring in I, II, or both. It may take the form, say, of a gradual increase in population, capital stock, and the general level of labor proficiency and technical knowledge as they affect productivity in all production processes. Such neoclassical growth elements are by their nature likely to be stable over time, relative to the variation in growth that may occur in region II due to the discovery of new resources. Thus, export-based growth may explain a large part of the *variation* in the aggregate growth rate of region II, whether or not it explains a large part of the average level of that growth rate.

A neoclassical and an export-based growth process, teamed together,

---

[8] Here, as elsewhere, we exclude from the description all transitional events involved in processes of adjustment to disequilibria in the balance of payments.

would interact in at least one important way. In raising the world's stock of factors other than natural resources, neoclassical growth increases the demand for staples, and thereby their prices relative to manufactures (and services), and also the derived demand for natural resources. If technical progress is neutral among industries, ii's terms of trade tend to improve no matter what the relative rates of neoclassical growth may be in ii and i, and resource owners in both countries benefit as against capitalists and laborers. To the extent that the discovery of new natural resources in ii is an economic process, motivated by the real value of the average earnings of owners of existing resources, greater search efforts are expended. Unless the probability of discovery drops proportionally with such increases in effort, export-based growth in region ii would tend to be positively correlated with the rate of growth from neoclassical sources occurring in both of the two regions.

The most thoroughgoing application of this model has been made to the Canadian economy, in which a development process based upon series of staples has been found in operation over a period of three centuries. They begin with fisheries and run through furs, timber, dairy products, grain, pulp and paper, metals and metallic ores, and petroleum. Random discoveries, shifts in world demand, and specific technological discoveries favoring known Canadian resources have all been identified as important factors unleashing waves of staple growth. The links between staple growth and expansion of other sectors of the economy have been investigated. Significantly, a major competing model of national development, the Rostovian take-off, has been found to possess inferior explanatory power.[9] The staple model, elaborated in some details although shorn of its multiple-region characteristic, has also been applied to the early economic development of the United States.[10] A casual inspection of the evidence suggests that it may be implicit in the economic history of countries such as South Africa, Argentina, Australia, and New

[9]   Gordon W. Bertram, "Economic Growth in Canadian Industry, 1870-1915: The Staple Model and the Take-off Hypothesis", *Canadian Journal of Economics and Political Science*, XXIX (May, 1963), 159-84.

[10]   Douglass C. North, *The Economic Growth of the United States, 1790-1860* (Englewood Cliffs, N.J.: Prentice-Hall, 1961); also see D. A. Farnie, "The Commercial Empire of the Atlantic, 1607-1783", *Economic History Review*, 2nd series, XV (December, 1962), 205-18.

Zealand, and one pioneering application has been made to a tropical country, Thailand.[11]

II   The "unlimited labor" version

The other version of the "vent for surplus" model of trade and growth arises when the surplus to be vented through trade is one of labor and not natural resources. The central hypothesis here is that of "unlimited labor", advanced by W. Arthur Lewis:[12] a region's economic activity includes a large subsistence sector in which the marginal product of labor is zero but, through family income-sharing practices, the going (subsistence) wage is equal to the average product of labor. We shall state these conditions as a theoretical assumption and ignore the issue of their practical appropriateness, except for one remark. The "unlimited labor" assumption leads to about the same theoretical conclusions as if we suppose that the marginal product of labor in subsistence production is positive but low, and the technology in use could be improved with the almost costless dissemination of knowledge. Then substantial amounts of labor might be removed from the subsistence sector, accompanied by a significant increase in its average but not its marginal product in that sector.

Let us embody the assumption of unlimited labor in a model of trade and growth as nearly parallel as possible to that set forth in the preceding section. Again, we assume the existence of a large, economically mature region I producing goods $a \ldots m, n \ldots z$ under the same initial conditions as before. Instead of region II, we have region III, endowed with an indigenous labor force but no significant stock of capital. That labor force, like II's resources, is precluded from migrating to I. Much of region

---

[11]   *E.g.*, I. R. Woods, "Some Aspects of South Africa's Foreign Trade in Relation to Her Aggregate Income, 1910-54", *South African Journal of Economics*, XXVI (June, 1958), 136-51; D. A. Farnie, "The Mineral Revolution in South Africa", *South African Journal of Economics*, XXIV (June, 1956), 125-34; C. G. F. Simkin, *The Instability of a Dependent Economy: Economic Fluctuations in New Zealand, 1840-1914* (London: Oxford University Press, 1951); Eliezer B. Ayal, "A Staple Theory for the Economic Development of Surplus Capacity Underdeveloped Countries", unpublished ms., Center for International Affairs, Harvard University, April, 1964.

[12]   "Economic Development with Unlimited Supplies of Labour", *Manchester School of Economics and Social Studies*, XXII (May, 1954), 139-91; *idem*, "Unlimited Labour: Further Notes", *Manchester School*, XXVI (January, 1958), 1-32.

III's economic activity occurs in the α industry, producing a class of goods that sustain life for their producers. The α sector is characterized by unlimited labor. Its output, we suppose, does not enter into the preference functions of citizens of region I, either directly or as a raw material,[13] and therefore α does not move in international trade. Region III's factor stock may also be used for the domestic production of some services amongst the group $n \dots z$. These cannot enter into international trade, but are exchanged domestically with the producers for subsistence goods. We arbitrarily assume that region III possesses no natural resources R_i except for R_α, specific to the production of nontraded subsistence goods. As a result of these conditions, no trade occurs initially between I and III.

A growth process begins for region III when an entrepreneur perceives that some manufactured good, n, can be produced there at total costs (in terms of region I's price ratios) less than in region I. These costs would include wages equal to the initial average product of labor in the α sector [14] (and below the going wage in region I) plus the capital costs of training III's labor force and supplying the necessary plant and equipment. Capital is exported from I to III. Trade commences, with region III exporting n to region I. III's imports include whatever goods other than n are purchased with additional income accruing to the following agents: persons in III's subsistence sector who receive the increase in that sector's average product, owners of the capital newly invested in III's n industry (if they now reside in III), and entrepreneurs receiving the profits equal to the

---

[13]   If the output of the subsistence sector is traded, then the model takes on some of the proprties of the Manoilesco-Hagen case. See Everett E. Hagen, "An Economic Justification of Protectionism", *Quarterly Journal of Economics*, LXXII (November, 1958), 496-514.

[14]   A problem arises with the "unlimited labor" postulate in that wages assumed equal to subsistence *and* to the average product of labor in the subsistence-goods sector are supposed to stay constant while labor is removed from subsistence production. The average product of labor is increased thereby, and one might ask whether this rent would not increase the supply price of labor to other sectors. See Lewis, "Economic Development ...", pp. 148-50, 172; S. Enke, "Economic Development with Unlimited and Limited Supplies of Labour", *Oxford Economic Papers*, n.s., XIV (June, 1962), 158-72. We shall suppose nonetheless that labor's supply price outside of the subsistence sector remains constant at a subsistence wage, so long as its marginal product in the subsistence sector is less. Adding the classical assumption of an elastic supply of population at this wage would, of course, guarantee the result.

difference between the production cost of n in I (still its market price there) and its production cost in III.

The expansion of n production in III of course corresponds to some contraction of the industry in I, unless all of the increase in world income is spent on n. Labor displaced from I's n industry tends to be absorbed into whatever other industries are now exporting to III or providing goods consumed by the owners of III's imported capital. Displaced capital may be similarly absorbed, insofar as it does not merely offset capital exported from I to III. In any case, a change occurs in region I's domestic endowment of capital relative to labor. Since the n industry eventually operates under conditions of constant costs in both countries, the competing down of I's n industry is not a self-limiting process. It continues until the n industry disappears from region I,[15] at which time the world price of n falls to the level of its cost of production in III, eliminating profits earned there and raising the real incomes of all n-consuming economic units in both I and III. It is frequently suggested that expansion of this output may become habitual and even overshoot the long-run equilibrium level.[16]

The process of establishing the n industry involves the elimination of a disequilibrium situation that has come to light, during which the growth rate for III's national product is constrained only by the speed of the adjustment processes involved. Constraints upon this rate of adjustment may derive from one or more of several sources: the rate at which labor can be drawn from the α sector without a significant rise in the wage rate; the rate at which capital may be transferred from I to III as limited by the adjustment of the balance of payments; the rate at which labor can be trained and factors coordinated in the production of n in III; and the rate at which factors of production remove themselves from the n industry in I. Thus, as in the case of growth based on idle natural resources, the establishment of each individual industry constitutes a constrained process of eliminating a disequilibrium situation.

While the growth process in III can continue with the establishment of other industries of the $n \ldots z$ group, there are several reasons for expecting that they would come into being one at a time. While constant costs

---

[15] This portion of the sequence is stressed by Edward Marcus, "Labor Resources as a Factor in International Competition", *Social Research*, XXVIII (Spring, 1961), 15-22; the article goes on to draw some questionable policy conclusions.

[16] *E.g.*, Charles P. Kindleberger, *Foreign Trade and the National Economy* (New Haven, Conn.: Yale University Press, 1962), chap. vii.

ultimately prevail, scale economies are assumed in each case to be significant in the early stages. To their impact might be added that of economies in the training of labor that are external to the firm but internal to the industry. Such conditions suggest that the establishment of any one industry must proceed with a critical minimum draft upon the available "surplus" labor and inflow of capital. Any industry being successfully established at all must bulk large relative to the constraints upon the total rate of growth. Once the initial push for one industry is past, entrepreneurs may prefer its certain rate of return (protected by the higher, constant costs of the import-competing industry in I) to venturing into the establishment of a new industry, and proceed to push its expansion to long-run equilibrium before tackling a new industry. But the discontinuities involved in starting a new industry and the fall of profits as the expansion of one comes to an end suggest an uneven process of overall growth for region III. As with development based on surplus resources, periods of growth of production and trade at the maximum attainable rate may alternate with periods of doldrums before another industry gets started.

The order in which the formation of manufacturing industries takes place might be explained on several bases, although we have ruled out the popular factor-proportions explanation by assuming that all production functions employ capital and labor in identical proportions in connection with any given factor-price ratio. The relative advantages to producing any manufacture in III might be the same once an investment is made in the training of labor, but that investment per unit of output might vary from industry to industry. After the initial expansion of manufacturing in III, another possible criterion for the selection of new industries arises in potential savings of transportation costs through import replacement, just as in the preceding surplus-resources model.[17] If I's entrepreneurs can perfectly appraise the extent of (transitional) profits attainable through establishing the rth industry in III, then this order of absolute advantage for the use of I's migrant capital would determine the sequence in which industries are established. If, however, a random element of entrepreneurial discovery attends the successful establishment of industries in III, the sequence may be less rational. In any case, the

---

[17] The pattern depends on the disposition of rents accruing to the subsistence sector and any portion of profits and returns to capital consumed in III.

creation of each rth industry is associated with the competing down of the rth industry in I; the mature region's increasing specialization in the production of staples, services, and the remaining manufactures; and the continued decrease in the capital stock per unit of labor in I.

Several different forces may operate, singly or in combination, to bring to an end the development process with surplus labor. One of these is the extraction of labor from III's α sector to the point where the marginal product of labor rises above the subsistence wage. For the first time, the economic growth of region III unambiguously translates itself into an increase in the general wage level of the labor force of that country.[18] When this point is reached, further movement of capital from I to III may remain profitable, along with the development of additional industries. Rising wages will provide something of a brake upon the process, however; and, in any case, the uniqueness of the growth of trade as a vent for surplus labor has disappeared. A different force tending to halt the growth process for region III is the change in relative factor prices in region I. With I's initial factor endowment fixed, the outflow of capital to region III tends to raise the return to capital in all industries of region I, relative to the wage level in I. The margin of advantage (if any) of establishing the rth industry in region III to take advantage of the availability of labor at subsistence wages is reduced, and the ending of the development process made more likely. Finally, the establishment of some portion of industries $n \ldots z$ in region III, by raising world income, increases the demand for staples $a \ldots m$. By the assumptions of the present model, these are produced only in region I. Lower-quality natural resources are drawn into use there, and the prices of these goods rise relative to those of services and manufactures with little natural-resource content. The net barter terms of trade of region III deteriorate, and the real value of the returns to investing I's capital in the rth industry in III is reduced.

Some combination of these forces eventually produces full equilibrium for trade and factor allocation between regions I and III. The returns at the margin to investment of I's capital stock are the same in all industries, at home and abroad, and no new industry can be profitably established

---

18 Any workers consuming goods other than α and locally produced services, as well as the beneficiaries of the increasing average product of labor in the α sector, have already enjoyed such a gain.

in III. Recipients of income from capital and natural resources (in region I) are unambiguously better off than before. Recipients of wage income in I may be better or worse off; more specific assumptions are needed for a determinate result. Recipients of wage income in III are certainly better off if the marginal product of labor in the α sector now exceeds the subsistence wage; and they may be better off if it does not.

The surplus-labor model, like the surplus-resources model, can be grafted onto economic growth occurring as a result of other processes. Perhaps the most obvious extension is to include population growth in region III, either as a steady autonomous rate or a Malthusian elastic supply at the subsistence wage. The familiar effect of this condition is to prevent one factor from halting the creation of new manufacturing industries in III, namely an increase in the wage rate. Such an elastic supply of population (labor) indeed renders the presence or absence of surplus labor irrelevant to the model; *potential* surplus labor has the same consequences for the evolution of production and trade as *actual* surplus labor. Another independent growth element that might be added to the picture is capital accumulation in the mature region. As a reference point, one might imagine a rate of capital accumulation and export from I that would just match the rate of net increase of III's labor force, leaving unchanged the over-all domestic factor endowment of I and the size of the subsistence sector in III.

Finally, the "staple" and "unlimited labor" models might be combined into a single case. Myint gives exactly this interpretation to the "vent for surplus" model of classical economics.[19] In terms of the model developed above, region III may possess some natural resources and have potential access to the production of staples $a \dots m$ as well as to manufactures. With the unlimited-labor assumption maintained, adding this feature makes no substantial changes in the model. It does, however, provide Myint with an adequate explanation of "the characteristically high rates of expansion which can be observed in the export production of many underdeveloped countries" and the failure of expansion to be accompanied by changes in technique or the proportions of factor inputs.

---

[19] Adam Smith's "concept of surplus productive capacity is not merely a matter of surplus land by itself but surplus land combined with surplus labour; and the surplus labour is then linked up with his concept of 'unproductive labour'". Myint, *op. cit.*, p. 323.

Richard E. Caves

III   Using the "vent for surplus" model

Let us consider the extent of the parallel between these two versions of
the "vent for surplus" model and the lessons that may follow for putting
them to empirical use. Considered as models of trade and growth, the
central common features are the use of productive inputs with no alternative uses to produce exportable commodities, and the resulting creation
and development of a pattern of international trade. The associated
growth rates of income and output are not fully constrained by the
normal continuous processes of the growth of factor supplies or the re-
combination of inputs – which is not to say that surplus-venting growth
will necessarily be faster than these other types, but rather that it operates
under qualitatively different determinants and constraints. One is tempted
to suggest that "vent for surplus" growth, with its potential for starts and
stops as the development of particular industries is begun and concluded,
may explain the variation in a growth rate founded upon other, more
continuous forces.[20] On the other hand, in such circumstances it may be
very hard to decide how much of the over-all growth rate may be attri-
buted to the "vent for surplus" mechanism and how much to other
causes; this problem has been central to much of the criticism of appli-
cations of the staple theory.[21]

The two versions of the "vent for surplus" model draw their inspiration
from very different types of national economies – Canada and the other
"areas of recent settlement," on the one hand, the present less-developed
countries, on the other. The authors of various works setting forth and
applying these models have registered differing degrees of approval of the
results. To oversimplify only slightly, they look upon export-based development through surplus resources with delight, and development

---

[20]   Such conditions would call into question the usefulness of the popular distinction
between foreign trade as a leading and as a lagging sector in economic development.
(See, for example, Charles P. Kindleberger, *Economic Development* [New York:
McGraw-Hill Book Company, 1958], chap. xiv.) Foreign trade may be a leading
and lagging sector in alternation, with the whole process explainable within the framework of a single model.

[21]   *E.g.*, Stuart Bruchey, "Douglass C. North on American Economic Growth",
Explorations in Enterpreneurial History, 2nd series, I (Winter, 1964), 145-55; Kenneth
Buckley, "The Role of Staple Industries in Canada's Economic Development", *Journal
of Economic History*, XVIII (December, 1958), 439-50.

through surplus labor with horror. Having stressed the similarities to be found in the models put to these differing uses, one may well ask about the essence of the differences.

These would seem to lie in the different linkages or externalities communicated by the surplus-based export expansion more than in the character of the export development itself.[22] The preceding exposition avoided the mention of these externalities as part of a general statement of the model, for the reason that externalities are by their nature specific to the particular case. They do not automatically assume either importance or unimportance. Any expansion of exports carried out at small opportunity cost provides somebody with a net increase of real income; a model must encompass the use made of that income if it aspires to general-equilibrium status. But the export expansion may or may not communicate any external effects to the output levels of other forms of economic activity or to the supplies of factors of production. That is the difference in generality.

Many attempts have been made to define and classify types of externalities and linkages.[23] Distinctions can be made between technical and pecuniary externalities horizontal and vertical, backward and forward, and the like. The somewhat broader concept of "linkages" may also provide a useful tool of classification and analysis.[24] The substance of these concepts need not detain us here except to note that their application depends on the general setting assumed for the economy; for example, pecuniary externalities in a static environment of competitive markets simply constitute the allocative signals of the pricing system, but where the supply of saving is somewhat related to the volume and charac-

---

[22] "In the economic life of a country and in its economic history, a most important element is the mechanism by which 'one thing leads to another,' and the most important contribution of an industry is not its immediate product ... and not even its effects on other industries and immediate social benefits ... but perhaps even further its effect on the general level of education, skill, way of life, inventiveness, habits, store of technology, creation of new demand, etc." H. W. Singer, "The Distribution of Gains between Investing and Borrowing Countries", *American Economic Review*, XL (May, 1950), 476; see also Levin, *op. cit.*, pp. 179-85.

[23] For a recent inquiry, see Pranab Bardham, "External Economies, Economic Development, and the Theory of Protection", *Oxford Economic Papers*, n.s., XVI (March, 1964), 40-54.

[24] Albert O. Hirschman, *The Strategy of Economic Development* (New Haven, Conn.: Yale University Press, 1958), chap. vi.

ter of apparent investment opportunities, the corresponding notion of backward and forward linkages may become quite apt.[25]

Whatever the mode chosen for analyzing externalities, both theoretical and empirical work has shown the variety of types of externalities that may spread from export-based development and the range of strengths that they may possess – all the way from negligible to vast. On the one hand, studies of national and regional development in North America have found a variety of strong external connections favorable to a rapid and successful pattern of economic development.[26] On the other hand, the literature on "foreign enclaves" and "dual economies" provides cases of the apparent failure of linkages to appear.[27] Theoretical work on circumstances that would make such linkages strong or weak seems to have received less attention than it merits. A notable exception is Robert E. Baldwin's appraisal of the effect of differences in the production functions of staple exports on the character of factors supplies and the potential for a country's general economic growth.[28] The production function's various attributes provide a check-list for many of the possible types of linkages that have been developed. An activity's requirements of intermediate goods convey its backward linkages, while the role of its output as an input to other activities comprises its forward linkage. The input requirements of primary factors carry the export's direct impact upon the evolution of the nation's factor supply, and the resulting income distribution governs the linkages operating through the composition of final demand. Not every force governing the strength and character of

---

[25]   Robert E. Baldwin, "Export Technology and Development from a Subsistence Level", *Economic Journal*, LXXIII (March, 1963), 90-92.

[26]   *E.g.*, North, *The Economic Growth of the United States, 1790-1860*, chaps. x, and xi.

[27]   Singer, *op. cit.*, pp. 473-85. Studies of areas that have failed to enjoy sustained economic growth seem to find linkage effects that are many in number if weak in over-all strength; cf. S. Daniel Neumark, *Foreign Trade and Economic Development in Africa: A Historical Perspective* (Stanford, Calif.: Food Research Institute, Stanford University, 1964).

[28]   "Patterns of Development in Newly Settled Regions", *Manchester School of Economics and Social Studies*, XXIV (May, 1956), 161-79; *idem*, "Export Technology and Development ...", pp. 84-90. For some evidence bearing on Baldwin's hypotheses on the basis of United States experience, see Paul S. Taylor, "Plantation Agriculture in the United States: Seventeenth to Twentieth Centuries", *Land Economics*, XXX (May, 1954), 141-52; and North, *Economic Growth ...*, chaps. x, xi.

externalities can be traced handily through the production function. Some locational and geographic factors certainly lie outside of it, and other economic examples may also be found.[29] And there is, of course, the whole field of possible influences of the pattern of industry upon social and political development.

Knowing what linkages to anticipate from the operation of surplus-venting growth in a particular region requires not only a theoretical shopping list but also some empirical testing. Such analyses of the under-developed countries must probably depend on a qualitative and descriptive approach. For regions with higher per-capita incomes and more diversified production, hypotheses about linkages can be framed on conventional macroeconomic lines. The foreign-trade accelerator is a case in point.[30] Evidence of these types may show what linkages and their progenitors are most important, and thus what specific forms of the "vent for surplus" model are likely to be fruitful empirically. They also provide a much sounder basis for drawing policy conclusions from such models, a particularly important gain since many of the policy options open to the governments of developing regions probably boil down to strengthening the favorable linkages and throttling any unfavorable ones.[31]

If different patterns of linkages can put very different complexions upon the basic "vent for surplus" model, they can cause a wide variety of normative and policy conclusions to be drawn from it. Indeed, the model in its simple form probably yields no normative conclusions. Assuming that one's normative concern centers on some features of the rate or pattern of economic growth for a region, the loosely phrased conclusion that the venting of a surplus through exports may permit "rapid" growth does not automatically support free trade, protection, export promotion, or any other specific policy without a consideration of the alternatives. The difference in the linkages extending from various industries might warrant either artificial restriction or artificial encouragement of the line

---

[29] Watkins, *op. cit.*, pp. 152-53; Kindleberger, *Foreign Trade ...*, pp. 199-202; Maurice Byé, "Internal Structural Changes Required by Growth and Changes in International Trade", *International Trade Theory in a Developing World*, ed. Roy Harrod (New York: St. Martin's Press, 1963), pp. 142-58.

[30] Richard E. Caves and Richard H. Holton, *The Canadian Economy: Prospect and Retrospect* (Cambridge, Mass.: Harvard University Press, 1959), pp. 81-82.

[31] Cf. Levin, *op cit.*, chap. vii. This point was suggested to me by Professor M. H. Watkins.

of export development set by market forces. Even the preference for venting a surplus of productive capacity over promoting outputs that have more substantial opportunity costs becomes only a presumption. The preceding review of the staple and unlimited-labor models has stuck to their positive or analytical side, and one should not underestimate the difficulties of getting any further with them.

Economists indeed have drawn sharply opposed normative conclusions about the merits of surplus-venting growth. One suspects that the staple and unlimited-labor versions have often received their respective laurels and brickbats as a source of guidance for policy on the basis of what the linkages have or have not done in a particular case. Still other differences that, in this context, seem relatively superficial may help to explain this polarity of attitudes.

One is the different behavior of the terms of trade in the two models. While the method of calculating terms-of-trade statistics would substantially influence the results, the net barter terms of region III would tend strongly to deteriorate over time due to two forces: the eventual fall in the price of each manufactured export as I's industry is competed down; diminishing returns to I's staple industries, feeding an element of increasing cost into III's import prices but not III's export prices. In the case of the staple model, the behavior of the terms of trade for region II would be mixed. On the one hand, the prices of new staple exports tend to fall. On the other hand, long-run neoclassical growth favors the improvement of II's terms of trade due to the dominance in her exports of outputs subject to diminishing returns.

These changes are superficial to the extent that they are incidental to the over-all development process described in the two versions of the model. If the terms of trade deteriorate as the growth of surplus-venting production displaces a mature industry abroad, there is hardly merit to carping about the change in the terms of trade apart from the economic growth that caused it. More broadly, in the operation of the "vent for surplus" model the terms of trade give few signals for policy that can be read correctly without a knowledge of the fundamental process controlling the terms.

Another superficial factor that gives development through unlimited labor a bad press is surely its consequences for income distribution. III's labor may not benefit from the inflow of capital (although income per capita in the subsistence sector rises in the absence of offsetting population growth). The foreign capital itself, however, earns excess profits during the transitional process of displacing foreign production. By contrast, the staple version includes no equally likely appearance of a maldistribution of income, especially if the rents accruing to natural resources in II are allotted somewhat randomly among the erstwhile worker and capitalist elements of the population. Thus, in the one case, foreign capitalists may seem to exploit local labor through what could be a very long short run; in the other, a happy partnership of immigrant labor and capital is further cemented by windfall gains to the fortunate finders of natural-resource deposits. Perhaps the unedifying appearance of growth based on unlimited labor must perforce rule it out politically as a path of development, but the economist can hardly derive pride of workmanship for reaching the conclusion by this route.

INTERNATIONAL, NATIONAL, REGIONAL, AND LOCAL INDUSTRIES

Jan Tinbergen

I Nature of concepts

Industries in the widest sense, or activities, may be subdivided into a number of categories enumerated in the title of this essay. By an international industry, we mean an industry whose products can be imported or exported; by national industries, those whose products, for technical reasons, cannot cross the frontier. The technical reasons may be that transportation costs, in a wide sense, are prohibitive. They may also be that cultural reasons prohibit exportation or importation. If we make a subdivision of a nation into smaller units, to be called regions, some of the national industries may be "regional": their products cannot even cross the regional frontiers. Proceeding to even smaller units, to be called localities, we may accordingly introduce the concept of "local" industries.

For the purpose of economic analysis or economic policy, the definition of the areas to be called nations, regions, and localities should not be based on the actual political definitions; there is such divergence in the size of nations as politically defined that they are not comparable among themselves. We do not go into this question in this essay. In fact, there may be a need for new terms and for a larger number of them, adding perhaps continents on the side of the large areas and distinguishing among cities, towns, and villages on the side of the smaller ones. If once we seek to integrate regional science into economic theory, as we should, all this will have to be settled.

II Approximative character of concepts

Clearly, the concepts are of an approximative nature. They replace quantitative distinctions by qualitative ones. In reality, there is an almost continuous series of products with increasing transportation costs – measured best, perhaps, as a percentage of the production costs and assuming a given distance over which to calculate the transportation costs. Yet for practical purposes, we may fairly easily make a concrete sub-division of industries or "sectors" into the categories proposed. Most manufacturing industries, as well as mining and agriculture, may be considered international industries. Well-known examples of national industries are building, the operation of buildings, and a large number of industries producing services, such as personal services, retail trade, a considerable portion of wholesale trade, transportation, government services, and education. In a large number of countries, the production of electricity and water may also be considered national industries. When it comes to separating out regional industries, what remains as "other national industries" are perhaps central government, higher education, portions of wholesale trade, and electricity, whereas the bulk of the national industries will be regional as well. Many of them will even be local.

III   Similarity with assumption on factors in the theory of international trade

The idea of replacing a quantitative characteristic, as a first approximation, by a qualitative one is not new at all. The closest example is the assumption often made with regard to factors of production in the theory of international trade. There, factors are supposed not to move from one country to another, whereas products are assumed to be transportable, often even at no cost. The point to be made in this essay is that it is realistic to apply the assumption of immobility to a portion of the products as well. A superficial inspection of national income breakdowns according to sectors suggests that almost half the national product of many countries may be of this kind. This sometimes even applies to large cities.

IV   Related concepts in use

In fact, the proposed distinction is itself not new. In town and country planning as well as in development planning, concepts are used which are closely related. Thus, in physical planning the activities of a given area are often subdivided into primary and secondary, the latter only serving the area itself, while the former also export their products. This definition of primary activities is not identical with the ones used by Colin Clark, Fourastié, and others to indicate agriculture and mining. In their definitions, secondary activities are those of manufacturing industry, and tertiary ones are services. This is, however, another subdivision than the one used in town and country planning. Primary activities here are indicated in Dutch as "pushing activities", which seems to be – exceptionally – a happier term than the somewhat flat "primary industries".

In development theory and planning, a distinction between infrastructure and superstructure is well known. Although this does not quite coincide with our distinction between national and international activities, many of the national industries as defined in sections I and II are also part of the infrastructure.

Our suggestion that one may even distinguish between a larger number of activities, in order to bring out the necessity of having some activities done within the area considered, takes into account the relevance of the size of the area for such a necessity. Physical planners are usually aware of this, but their terminology does not clearly remind us of it. We should be aware of the fact that the portion of activities which is "pushing" – or dependent on outside demand – is larger, the smaller the area considered. In our terminology, localities have not only the international, but also the "other regional" (*i.e.*, nonlocal) and "other national" (*i.e.*, nonregional) activities as their pushing industries.

V   Balanced growth only for national industries

Professor Nurkse[1] has emphasized the desirability of "balanced growth", consisting essentially in coincidence of the set of proportions between the expansion of production of various sectors with the proportions between the expansion of demand for their products. Professor Hirschman[2] has,

---

[1] Ragnar Nurkse, *Problems of Capital Formation in Underdeveloped Countries* (New York: Oxford University Press, 1953), pp. 11 ff.

[2] Albert O. Hirschman, *The Strategy of Economic Development* (New Haven, Conn.: Yale University Press, 1958).

on the contrary, advocated "unbalanced growth", which I think is an unhappy terminology. He has in mind specific deviations from balance, namely, such deviations as would induce additional activity. The final result must be balanced growth nevertheless, since final unbalance means disruption of equilibria, price shifts, and so on, which nobody wants. We should be aware, however, of another limitation to Professor Nurkse's recommendation: home production is not the only way to satisfy demand, if imports or exports are possible. In our terminology, balanced growth in the Nurksian sense is needed only for national, not for international industries. In small countries, it may be necessary only for about half of the production. The bigger the countries, the more need there is for balanced growth; and for the world at large, Professor Nurkse's re-commendation still stands. The implications for the planning processes of small countries are that there should be planning based on demand forecasts for national industries, and planning based on comparative advantages in international trade for the international industries. In extreme cases, all "nonnational" production (*i.e.*, production in international sectors) may have to be concentrated in one industry – the famous case of complete specialization. It follows at the same time that this complete specialization does not exclude the necessity of having the national industries at home.

VI International division of labor only for international goods, their capital output ratios less dispersed

In other words, the division of labor among the countries of the world only refers to their international industries. Irrespective of their costs, each country must have the national activities at home. This circumstance considerably reduces the possibilities for countries to profit from the international division of labor. Americans cannot profit from the fact that haircuts or postal services are so much cheaper in Europe than in the United States. Neither can Europeans or Asians profit from their lower costs in these activities by exporting their products to the United States. International competition can only operate in a limited range of industries. Unfortunately, especially for the developing countries, the capital-output ratios in this limited range happen to be the middle portion of the range over which all such ratios spread. The extreme values – the highest and the lowest – of these ratios are usually found to apply to national industries. Thus, the highest ratio of some ten or twelve years' purchase applies to the operation of buildings; some quite high ones are those of transportation, communications, and energy – around five years' purchase or so; and many of the lowest refer to building and to several services. A happy exception is the clothing industry, which has a quite low capital-output ratio. These facts mean that developing countries do not have many possibilities of selecting low capital-output ratio industries so as to develop "cheaply": the national industries with low ratios cannot be expanded beyond national demand, the national industries with high capital-output ratios have to be expanded nevertheless, and there only remains a restricted choice in the middle range.

VII   Import-replacing versus export-furthering industries

Within this limited range, it is more attractive, for developing countries, to expand import-replacing than to expand export-furthering industries. Quite apart from the possibilities they have of protecting the former – which may not be such a good thing – there is the fact that capital-output ratios are often lower at the finished-product than at the raw-material end of the chain of production. Thus, the clothing industry is less capital intensive than the weaving industry, and this again less capital intensive than the spinning industry. Again, machine-making and shipbuilding are less capital intensive than steelmaking. Since developing countries are usually exporting raw materials and importing finished products, they can earn more income from an additional unit of capital investment if it is invested in an import-replacing than in an export-furthering industry (assuming that output is limited only by scarcity of capital). Of course, the condition must be added that the market of the country concerned is sufficiently large to establish optimum-size enterprises. Sometimes this can only be done if small countries integrate their economies or at least conclude customs unions for a limited number of products.

VIII   Indirect effects of investment projects: the semi-input-output method

The existence of a considerable number of national industries poses a problem for the development process of any country. For that process to be an equilibrated one, with as little over- or undercapacity as possible, each extension of an international industry must be accompanied by well-defined simultaneous extensions of all national industries. There are good reasons, therefore, for speaking of bunches of investment projects, since the equilibrium between demand and supply in the national sectors will only be maintained if such bunches of projects are carried out jointly. Each bunch, in this train of thought, consists of only one project in an international industry and of a number of projects in the national industries, in fact, as many as there are national industries. This way of grouping projects into bunches also illustrates the fact that there is never a technical necessity to combine one international-industry project with another. It is not even necessary, say, that a capacity extension of the weaving industry entail a capacity extension of the spinning industry, because yarns, if they are needed, can always be imported. The traditional input-output method sometimes suggests that there is such a necessity, but, strictly speaking, it should depend entirely on the attractiveness of the spinning industry to the country concerned whether or not a spinning unit should be added to a new weaving unit. There are examples of countries which have a larger weaving capacity than their spinning capacity, and the other way around.

But the attractiveness of adding to the nation's productive potential a certain weaving capacity should not be judged only from the contributions which this project makes to the aims of national development and from its cost. It should be judged by the attractiveness of the bunch of projects just defined. It may well be, for instance, that the additional need for energy and transportation – both rather capital-intensive activities – makes the bunch less attractive than the single weaving project. The choice of the best extensions of national productive capacity should therefore depend on the characteristics of the bunch. Some recent examples calculated by Dr. Rasul[3] for the Pakistani economy show that these characteristics may in fact differ substantially from those of the single international project involved.

The bunch should not contain only the direct needs for energy, transportation, and so on emanating from the weaving unit (in our example).

---

[3]   Ghulan Rasul, *Input-Output Relationships in Pakistan, 1954* (Rotterdam: N.V. Universitaire Pers, 1964).

An increased production of energy may itself need additional transportation capacity, and so on and so forth. The bunch therefore should contain the cumulated additional capacities needed in all national industries. These cumulated additional needs can easily be estimated with the aid of the "semi-input-output method", described elsewhere. It so happens that the method is considerably simpler than the traditional "full" input-output method, but it seems to fit the problem better.

The idea of considering bunches of projects as described here instead of single projects, international or national, also represents a better approach to the problem once called the problem of the indirect effects of any single project. It has been believed for a long time[4] that projects should not be appraised on the basis of their own merits only, but that account should be taken of some other things which more or less automatically happen concomitantly. This vague feeling was first given precision in Keynes's introduction of "indirect" and, in addition, "secondary" effects of some investment projects undertaken by the government in a period of depression. The setting of his problem, however, was rather different from ours. An ideal development process should not be characterized by the unused capacities assumed for Keynes's problem. On the contrary, we must aim as much as possible at a process without unused capacities. Also, we should not be interested in what will happen "automatically", since we are now considering a planning problem, that is, creating a basis for the most desirable action. Our task, therefore, is to indicate what must be done in order that the development process be an equilibrated one. This requires that the national sectors be expanded "in line with" the international sectors, and this is what the semi-input-output method does.

A final remark should be made on another implication of the idea that bunches are the building blocks of the development process. There is no need to consider separately any projects in the national sectors, such as energy or transportation. They are divided up among the bunches. This represents a major deviation from today's practice. Yet it has another advantage in addition to the arguments already given. The joint consideration of one international project with its complementary national projects avoids, to a considerable extent, the question of what prices to

---

[4] Jan Tinbergen, *The Design of Development* (Baltimore: The Johns Hopkins Press, 1958).

attach to national products such as energy, transportation, and education, since the bulk of these products is consumed by the international sector considered, and positive and negative items cancel in the bunch. This is a happy feature, since these prices are often somewhat arbitrary, and their choice may unduly boost or reduce the apparent attractiveness of the individual international and national projects.

IX   A bunch's contribution to the balance of payments

Among the important aspects of any project's contribution to the aims of development should be considered its contribution to the nation's balance of payments. The problem involved is somewhat trickier than has sometimes been thought. The naive approach is to ask for only the receipts and the expenditures in foreign money to be expected for the project itself, making a distinction between the investment period and the operation period. On the one hand, this is naive in that expenditures made in local currency for, say, automobiles which are assembled in the country from imported parts are not considered expenditures in foreign currency, although they clearly are to some extent. Even the wages paid, however, may entail some additional imports. On the other hand, even if part of the production is sold in the home market, it may nevertheless make a contribution to the balance of payments, since these sales might otherwise have been imports on behalf of the buyers of the product. From all this, it has long been concluded that the real answer to the question of the contribution to the balance of payments is more complicated. The net unspent balance created by the project during its operation phase may all contribute to the balance of payments to the extent that it represents the balance of receipts over expenditures; in fact, this is the well-known macroeconomic formula used to calculate a change in the balance-of-payments surplus by deducting from the change in national income the change in national expenditure. Whether this unspent balance actually represents the project's contribution to the balance of payments depends, however, precisely on the nature of the goods produced and used up – whether they are international or national goods. So again, the concepts discussed in this essay appear to be useful for this purpose. In principle, what should be done in order to arrive at the contribution to the balance of payments is to distinguish an investment period and an operation period of the project; to find for each of them all the changes in production and the changes in expenditure involved; and to pick, from all these items, the ones representing international goods. Again, the semi-input-output method will be the simplest analytical instrument to perform this task, since it specifies the production and uses of all commodities.

If one wonders in what respect the method suggested is an approximation only because the concepts of international and national goods are approximate, the answer is that some commodities may change character depending on their price level: some marginal quantities of an international commodity may not be truly international to the extent that their prices exceed those in the international market.

X The use of our concepts in regional and local planning

The concepts of international, national, regional, and local industries and products are particularly useful for the process of development planning if a subdivision of a national plan into regional and local plans is required. The fundamental requirements for such plans are that local activities must be developed in each locality according to its demand, and regional activities in each region in correspondence with its demand. The precise use which can be made of the concept varies according to the aims of regional and local planning. The simplest and clearest case exists when we make two special assumptions, one concerning the aims and one concerning the input-output structure. Let the aims be formulated for each region and each locality in terms of the income level to be reached. Let the demand for local goods and services depend on local income, the demand for regional goods and services on regional income, and the demand for national goods and services on national income. Then the aims immediately determine the quantities to be produced, in each geographical area, of its local and other regional commodities. These quantities will also determine the incomes to be expected from the local and other regional industries. What remains of the income target values must then be filled up by "other national" and international activities. Here we should choose the ones most attractive from the viewpoint of development aims; if the only aim is to increase income, and the only scarce factor is capital (with the complementary education), then each locality's and each region's income targets should be filled up with the aid of the "other national" and the international sectors showing the lowest capital-output ratio. For the "other national" activities there would still be a total volume determined by national income to be prescribed. The remaining jigsaw puzzle can be solved relatively easily. The advantage of our concepts lies in the structure they give to the determination of the distribution of the joint national production over the geographical parts of the country, and of even larger areas.

THE MULTIPLIER IF IMPORTS ARE
FOR INVESTMENTS

Wolfgang F. Stolper

I

The original foreign trade multiplier models assume constant prices and exchange rates and infinitely elastic supplies of all factors of production, including foreign exchange. When tracing through the interactions of two economies, the balance of payments need not be in equilibrium. The models are essentially demand models in which the only determinant of output is demand. Specifically, there are no restrictions on output due to any scarce factor of production for which there are no substitutes. Investments are exogenously determined, and consumption depends only on income.

When the model is expanded to include the condition that the balance of payments is to be in equilibrium, relative prices or the exchange rate have to be introduced. In the model of Laursen and Metzler,[1] for example, prices in terms of domestic currencies are still assumed to be constant. The balance-of-payments adjustment is made initially through changes in the exchange rate (which is equivalent to changes in the terms of trade) and, of course, through changes in aggregate spending and income. Although there are restraints on foreign spending because of the newly introduced balance-of-payments restriction, there are no complementarities of foreign with domestic factors, and, as long as domestic factors are unemployed, consumers are free to substitute domestic for foreign goods.

When imports are for consumption only, and when consumers are free and able to substitute domestic for foreign goods (or vice versa, depending on how the exchange rate goes), there are no real limitations to a full-

---

[1] Svend Laursen and L. A. Metzler, "Flexible Exchange Rates and the Theory of Employment", *Review of Economics and Statistics*, XXXII (November, 1950), 281-99.

employment policy that cannot be controlled by exchange fluctuations.

A difficulty in defining real income appears when prices in domestic currencies are assumed to be constant, while prices of imported goods in domestic moneys fluctuate with the exchange rate. In discussing the effect of changes in relative prices on real spending, Laursen and Metzler argue that, as relative prices change, the domestic expenditure functions (which are really generalized consumption functions) would shift with the terms of trade in such a manner that a deterioration would lead to increased, and an improvement to decreased, domestic expenditures.[2] They reason that deteriorated terms of trade mean a reduced real income for any given level of money income; that a reduced real income implies a reduced amount of savings for any given money income; that therefore deteriorated terms of trade imply higher domestic spending for any given money income.

This, however, is a reasonable outcome only if foreign and domestic goods are essentially the same. If they are, reducing imports will simply lead consumers to substitute domestic goods, whose prices have not changed in terms of domestic money. But putting it in this manner suggests that the effect of deteriorated terms of trade may not really go via changes in real income at all. Real aggregate spending corresponding to any level of money income will remain the same because the same level of money income really always means the same level of real income, regardless of the terms of trade. The only thing that changes is the distribution between spending at home and abroad.[3]

Elasticity conditions cannot be neglected because of the repercussions on incomes and imports, and they will determine the extent and direction of the change in the terms of trade. The model, however, does not imply any restrictions on domestic policy from the side of the balance of payments. As long as domestic resources are available, a deterioration of the terms of trade is singularly harmless to the welfare of the country. In fact, such deterioration is simply the result of the country embarking on a

---

[2] In my own model, the problem was deliberately and probably illegitimately sidestepped. See W. F. Stolper, "The Multiplier, Flexible Exchanges, and International Equilibrium", *Quarterly Journal of Economics*, LXIV (November, 1950), 559-82.

[3] The discussion of the Laursen-Metzler analysis is summarized in Harry G. Johnson, "The Transfer Problem and Exchange Stability", *International Trade and Economic Growth* (Cambridge, Mass.: Harvard University Press, 1958), chap. vii, particularly pp. 187 ff.

full-employment policy in the knowledge that the deteriorated terms of trade (in the form of fluctuating exchanges) will take care of the balance of payments without in the least interfering with the attainment of domestic policy objectives, and without reducing domestic consumption standards.

However, even when imports are only for consumption, the outcome may be different. When foreign and domestic goods are not close substitutes, the inability to import goods as before may induce consumers not to shift to domestic goods but to spend less. In such a case, the deterioration of the terms of trade may leave the domestic spending function where it was before the deterioration of the terms of trade or shift it only very little upward. If foreign and domestic goods are complementary, the deterioration of the terms of trade may even lead to a decrease in the domestic spending function.

Consider now the case of any area within a large country, and consider that consumption may consist of a great variety of goods. This involves imagining that the expenditure function of a country is broken down into a great many "regional" expenditure functions. If the areas are chosen small enough, the largest component of each area's income will be earned by "exports" to other areas. If now the "terms of trade" of a small area – Detroit, producing and selling cars only – deteriorate, the "domestic" spending function cannot really shift upward very much, since cars are not likely to be substituted for "imported" radios, books, bread, or jam. What will happen to incomes and employment will almost exclusively depend on the elasticity of demand for cars, which in this case is a "foreign" elasticity. If Detroit's terms of trade improve, it seems reasonable to assume that more will be "imported" and that spending will increase with increasing real income. It seems unreasonable to assume that the opposite will occur when the Detroit area is amalgamated with its supplier areas so that previously "foreign" demand becomes domestic. The points of the example are simply that price effects cannot wash out as small areas is aggregated into larger areas, and that the Laursen-Metzler reasoning concerning the probable effect of changes in terms of trade on spending is likely to be the less realistic the less perfect substitutes goods are for each other.

Other examples could be given in which the technologically identical goods may be economically independent of each other, or complementary, or substitutes. Components of the hi-fi system, for example, are such a case: if the radio component becomes cheap enough, the demand for better amplifiers may increase. Therefore, as disaggregation proceeds and consumption becomes a complicated array of goods, it is not only logically difficult to define the meaning of real income, but the possibility that spending functions will shift upward with improved terms of trade becomes a probability.

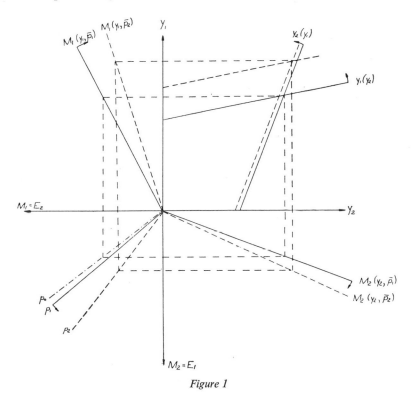

Figure 1

Even when imports (and exports) are all for consumption, the interaction between price and income effects may make it possible for the incomes of both countries to increase, as the terms of trade change. The problem is illustrated by Figure 1, using a technique employed by Romney Robinson.[4] In the northeast quadrant, the incomes of each of two countries are shown as functions of the other country's income (which

---

[4] "A Graphical Analysis of the Foreign Trade Multiplier", *Economic Journal*, LXII (September, 1952), 546-64.

itself is a function of domestic consumption, domestic investment, and exports). On the southeast quadrant, the imports of country II are shown as a function of its income, assuming the terms of trade to be given. On the northwest quadrant, imports of country I are shown as a function of its income, at the same (constant) terms of trade.

The southwest quadrant shows the balance of trade – which is here assumed to be the whole of the balance of payments, except possibly for accommodating gold or short-term capital movements, as assumed in Metzler's *Econometrica* article.[5]

The solid lines indicate the intitial position. Since so far no assumption has been made that the balance of payments must be in equilibrium, no terms of trade have been determined, and nothing is said about whether the balance of payments is or is not in equilibrium. If the terms of trade are p_0, the balance of payments will be in equilibrium.

Suppose, however, that initially the terms of trade are p_1. In this case, the value of country I's imports exceeds that of its exports. Under "normal" conditions, its terms of trade will deteriorate, which means that, graphically, they must move in the direction of the arrow. This, however, will shift the income and the import functions. Under the Laursen-Metzler assumption, the Y_1 (Y_2) function will shift upward, and country I's import function to the right. The Y_2 (Y_1) function will shift inward, and country II's import function downward. This process will continue until the system arrives at the terms of trade at which the balance of payments will be in equilibrium, *e.g.*, at p_2. When that happens, the new intersection of the Y-curves may be to the northeast of the old intersection, in which case the incomes of both countries have increased. If not, only one income will have risen in the process. Under the Laursen-Metzler assumption, it is likely that the country whose terms of trade have deteriorated will have the increased income, if only one country's income may rise.

II

The preceding discussion suggests that for certain purposes, particularly for the analysis of development problems, conclusions drawn from the

---

[5] L. A. Metzler, "Underemployment Equilibrium in International Trade", *Econometrica*, X (April, 1942), 97-112.

"classical" multiplier analysis may be misleading. Writings on under-developed countries stress that the deterioration of their terms of trade has hurt their prospects, and that improvements in their terms of trade are essential if they are to achieve their development objectives with politically endurable sacrifices, within a reasonable time span, and without unrealistically large capital inflows.

The differences in outlook are in part the result of the knowledge that development depends on imports, and that exports are good only to the extent to which they buy imports. They are in part due to the fact that the growth or development problem is a dynamic problem in a different sense from the dynamics of the multiplier analysis needed for the determination of the stability conditions.

The dynamics of the (mathematical) multiplier models can be defined as describing the time path of an adjustment process. There is some initial shock which, with stability, leads to successively smaller adjustments until a final equilibrium is reached. The dynamics dealt with by Schumpeter, for example, deals, however, with the emergence of these shocks themselves. It is also the kind of dynamics that is of interest in connection with the development problem.

In the discussion of the preceding section some of this kind of dynamics is implicit in the examples given. Specifically, consumption is not only a function of real income – provided real income can be defined clearly – and of relative prices, but also of the extent of the assortment of goods available. The upward shifts in the consumption function due to the cheaper availability of more goods which are not close substitutes for each other may look like an instability of the "adjustment" dynamics, but the system may be stable when it is expanded to include more variables. Stability is, after all, the property of a specific system.

In the "classical" multiplier model, investments are exogenously determined. When imports are for consumption only, the level of investment is, by assumption, not affected by the balance of payments, although the balance of payments affects the multiplier effect stemming from any level of investment. In other words, while the multiplier is affected, the multiplicand is not.

If, however, once more the assumption that "investments" are homogeneous is dropped, situations may arise – and they are typical for under-developed countries – in which certain complementary goods are not produced at home. In this case, the level of investments depends also on the availability of imported complementary goods. This is a purely technological relationship. In addition, there is an economic relationship to be discussed presently. In either case, the balance of payments affects both the multiplier and the multiplicand.

Suppose now that we have two countries, or groups of countries. In one, typified by highly advanced countries with sophisticated economic structures and ample and diversified resource endowments, the level of investments depends primarily on the marginal efficiency of capital. The marginal efficiency of capital is influenced by technical progress, governmental policies with respect to taxation and the balance of payments, wage policies, and the like, but there is assumed to be no balance-of-payments constraint.

In the "underdeveloped" group of countries, investments also, of course, depend on the marginal efficiency of capital which, in turn, also depends on governmental policies, as in developed countries, and on the development plans they are likely to have. There is in addition, however, a balance-of-payments constraint on investments because they require certain complementary goods that are imported, and because the economic structure of the countries lacks the necessary sophistication or resource base to produce these complementary goods.

The two aspects of imports for investment will have different effects. The purely technical relationship is simple: cotton goods production must use imported cotton; synthetic fiber production requires imported coal; machinery production requires imported copper, and so forth.

There is, secondly, an economic aspect: changes in the price structure will have an effect on the marginal efficiency of capital. This becomes particularly important when the "imports for investments" consist of raw materials or foodstuffs of mass consumption which cannot be produced domestically at all or only at very high cost.

It is now clear that where there is a technological interdependence, the level of investment can be the higher the more can be imported. When, therefore, the terms of trade of an underdeveloped country improve, and when it is faced with an inelastic demand so that export earnings increase, the level of investments will increase *pari passu*. The multiplicand will therefore increase, not only because exports rise, but also because the rise in exports has allowed an increase in investments via an increase in imports. In such a case, income will rise as a result of the improved terms of trade, even if there is a Laursen-Metzler effect on consumption spending in the opposite direction from the effect on investments. It is not likely, however, that there will be such an effect, partly for the reason that an increasing assortment of goods is likely to have a stimulating effect, partly because the rising income itself is due to increased investments and will affect the expectations of income earners.

If the terms of trade deteriorate and the country is faced with an elastic demand, the results will be the same, as long as the technological aspects are dominant. For what matters to the level of investments is the amount of export earnings, as long as in "underdeveloped" countries the volume of investments depends primarily on the availability of imported complementary factors.

If we deal with a "developed country", the purely technological restraints on investments are less likely to exist, although they were clearly important in Europe in the late 1940's and a major reason for the Marshall Plan. The economic effects on the marginal efficiency of capital are likely to predominate. If the terms of trade improve, and if imports consist mainly of foodstuffs and industrial raw materials, the profitability of production will clearly be improved. Therefore, the level of investments will be stimulated, which in turn will lead to increased imports. The "income" effect of changed prices in this case will be indirect through the increased profitability and hence raised level of investments.

It is therefore likely that improved terms of trade for advanced countries will lead to increased spending via the effect on the marginal efficiency of capital even if there is a Laursen-Metzler effect on consumption spending. And even if there is such an effect, imports for consumption may nevertheless increase also as the result of higher incomes, stimulated by increased investments. The effect on investments and employment may be particularly favorable if the "imports for investments" consist of articles of mass consumption which have an effect on wage levels.

The distinction between imports for consumption and for investments suggests not only that the price effects may be substantially different in the two cases and work through different causal chains; it also suggests that the terms of trade themselves are too aggregative a measure to be useful for theoretical and probably practical analysis.

For an "advanced" country, the ideal situation would be one in which prices of imported raw material and foodstuffs fell, as well as the prices of those industrial goods which could not be produced at home, while the prices of goods competing with domestic goods and the prices of goods competing with the country's exports rose. Such a situation would lead to a substantial effect on investments both for domestic production and exports, and to substantial increases in imports as well.

For an "underdeveloped" country, on the other hand, the ideal situation would be one in which export prices for consumer raw materials rose, when they were likely to meet an inelastic demand; in which the prices of raw materials with close substitutes (which are likely to have an elastic demand) fell; and in which the prices of machinery and industrial materials needed for investments fell, while the prices of such industrial goods as could be produced in the "underdeveloped" country within a reasonable time horizon rose.

It follows that no simple assumption should be made about the effect of changes in terms of trade, but that this effect depends on the structure of trade – itself in part a function of the price structure – on the consumer reaction, and on the precise impact of price changes on the marginal efficiency of capital.

When the two cases are put together it can be seen that, depending on the structure of trade and the domestic policies determining the level of "autonomous" investments, either a deterioration or an improvement in the terms of trade may raise the incomes of both groups of countries. If the terms of trade of "advanced" countries improve, and their imports consist of raw materials and foodstuffs, the value of their imports may increase, even if the demand for raw materials and foodstuffs is inelastic, because the income effects via increased investments may more than offset the price effects via inelastic demands. The "underdeveloped" countries, on the other hand, also can increase their real investments because what matters is total foreign-exchange earnings, which have increased.

It is clear that the effects on investments in both kinds of countries depend on economic policies. In both sets of countries, a favorable effect requires an expansionary policy that avoids price rises if possible. In developed countries, price rises are likely to interfere with the profitability of investments – certainly the experience of the United States since 1960 and the German experience in the fifties suggest that expansionary policies with price stability are beneficial for development. At the same time, increases in the prices of imported goods are not likely to help underdeveloped countries. They would not only reduce the real imports obtainable in exchange for the same amount of export values, but to the extent that they affected development goods that cannot be produced at home, they would also reduce the marginal efficiency of capital in "under-developed" countries. Thus, both the technically feasible and the economically desirable level of investment would be adversely affected.

As far as the case of "developed" countries is concerned, the effects of improved terms of trade were noticed by Folke Hilgerdt in a remarkable

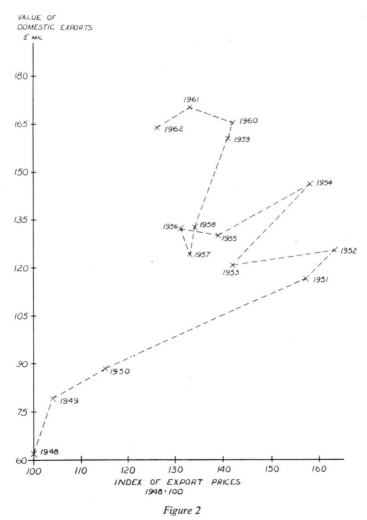

Figure 2

Export prices and value of domestic exports, Nigeria 1948-1962

article that antedates the development of income theory.[6] Hilgerdt observed that industrial production in the short cycle turned down after prices declined. He rejected the hypothesis that this was due to the time

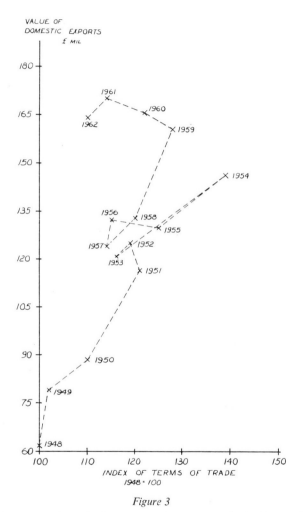

Figure 3

Terms of trade and value of domestic exports, Nigeria 1948-1962

---

[6] "Foreign Trade and the Short Business Cycle: A Study Based on Data for the United States during the Period 1923 to 1929", *Economic Essays in Honour of Gustav Cassel* (London: George Allen & Unwin, 1933), pp. 273-91.

it takes for industrial production to be hit by falling prices. He also rejected the hypothesis that production and prices ought normally to move together. Hilgerdt found that "the curve for industrial buildings... gathered pace very considerably after the downward turn of prices in 1925 and 1928. *The price fall indeed appears to have favored the boom.*"[7] He postulated a logical connection between price movements, the boom, and capital movements, the behavior of which is linked to the terms of trade. "The direct information ... indicates ... that the price fall during the booms differs from that during the depression of 1930-32 insofar as *the producer's margin, in terms of money, between the price of raw materials and manufactured goods rose, and that this increase was distributed over other cost elements (wages, interest, etc. rose) as well as industrial profits.*

Table 1

Import prices, export prices, terms of trade, exports, Nigeria, 1948-62

Year	Import prices (indices)	Export prices (indices)	Terms of trade	Domestic exports (£ mil.)
1948	100	100	100	61.165
1949	102	104	102	79.199
1950	105	115	110	88.488
1951	130	157	121	116.610
1952	137	163	119	125.135
1953	122	142	116	120.889
1954	114	158	139	146.242
1955	112	139	125	129.816
1956	114	131	115	132.261
1957	116	133	114	124.177
1958	113	134	120	132.791
1959	111	141	128	160.597
1960	116	142	122	165.619
1961	116	133	114	170.067
1962p	115	126	110	164.014
1963p				184.800

SOURCES   Federation of Nigeria, *Digest of Statistics* X, No. 2 (1961), 53; XIII, No. 2 (1964), 53. Figures after 1954 rebased to provide continuous series for import and export prices and terms of trade.
p: preliminary.
Federal Republic of Nigeria, *Annual Abstract of Statistics* (1963), p. 62.

---

7   *Ibid* p. 278. Italics in the original.

Even where the profit per unit produced remained unchanged the expansion of production implied an increase in total profits."[8]

A glance at Figures 2 and 3 indicates that there is no obvious positive relation between either export prices or the terms of trade and the value of domestic exports of Nigeria, an underdeveloped country whose exports consist overwhelmingly of raw materials with a supposedly inelastic demand. This is particularly true when the years 1948-50 are neglected. Although year-to-year changes in export prices and the value of exports on the whole suggest an inelastic demand for Nigerian exports, the scatter diagrams suggest the opposite for the period 1951-62. This is also true for the relation of terms of trade to exports. During this period, Nigerian exports consisted overwhelmingly of raw materials for consumption rather than of industrial raw materials.

It is not asserted that the elasticity of demand for cocoa, palm oil, groundnuts, etc., is greater than one – certainly such factual statements need a more sophisticated analysis than is undertaken here. The fact that year-to-year changes suggest an inelastic demand, while the over-all picture indicates the opposite, could, however, be explained in terms of a model in which income and price effects in "developed" countries combine to raise export demand for "underdeveloped" countries.

III

The model of international trade, which rapidly becomes exceedingly complicated mathematically, suggests that by making "autonomous" investments – *i.e.*, investments not determined by previous income changes – part of the system to be analyzed rather than exogenously determined, new restrictions are put into the system, and price effects become very complicated. They suggest that the structures of prices, investments, and production become more important than the final aggregation.

One policy implication remains, of course: the need to assure favorable terms of trade to underdeveloped countries. But as one major object presumably is to assure the underdeveloped countries the means for investments, and as there are repercussions of the terms of trade that are

---

[8]   *Ibid.*, p. 280. Italics in the original.

not summarized by elasticity conditions, it is also clear that one can worry too much about deteriorating terms of trade.

Moreover, if the model were enlarged to include international long-term capital movements as a function of the marginal efficiencies of capital in different countries, a further complication and modification of the policy prescription is introduced. If the demand for the exports of "underdeveloped" countries really is inelastic, an improvement of their terms of trade would, other things being equal, indeed lead to increased export earnings. But under these conditions, traditional export industries would be relatively profitable, and foreign capital and domestic resources would move to build up the existing raw-material production for export. Tariffs, as Metzler[9] has shown, would only emphasize this movement.

If, on the other hand, the indirect repercussions of improved terms of trade for the "advanced" countries lead to increased export earnings of the "underdeveloped" countries, as the Nigerian statistics suggest is the case, this would allow the latter to increase their imports. At the same time, as their terms of trade deteriorated, the domestic or import-competing industries would become relatively more profitable, and the export proceeds would naturally be employed to invest in new industries.

---

[9] L. A. Metzler, "Tariffs, the Terms of Trade, and the Distribution of National Income", *Journal of Political Economy*, LVII (February, 1949), 1-29; and "Tariffs, International Demand, and Domestic Prices", *Journal of Political Economy*, LVII (August, 1949), 345-51.

PART THREE

Money, prices, and the balance of payments

TRADE, SPECULATION, AND THE FORWARD EXCHANGE RATE

Peter B. Kenen

If Great Britain had been paradise for the last two hundred years, economic analysis might still be quite primitive. Our subject advances most rapidly when theorists are challenged by policy problems, and it owes its greatest debt to Britain's afflictions. The history of trade theory illustrates this proposition. So does the theory of forward exchange.

The interest-parity doctrine, constructed by Keynes and christened by Einzig,[1] replied to the dilemma that Britain confronted in the early 1920's – domestic stagnation combined with a payments deficit. Keynes showed that changes in forward exchange rates have the same effect on capital flows as changes in the difference between national interest rates. He urged intervention to support forward sterling in lieu of raising Bank rate higher, thereby to strengthen Britain's reserves without doing damage to the British economy. When Britain faced the same dilemma in the late 1950's, another generation of economists revived Keynes's suggestion,[2] inspiring additional advances in analysis.

The modern theory of forward exchange, as set out by Spraos, Tsiang, and Sohmen,[3] builds upon Keynes's contribution – his treatment of the

---

[1] J. M. Keynes, *A Tract on Monetary Reform* (London: Macmillan and Co., 1923), pp. 122-32; and P. Einzig, *A Dynamic Theory of Forward Exchange* (London: Macmillan and Co., 1961), p. 146.

[2] See, *e.g.*, A. E. DeJasay, "Forward Exchange: The Case for Intervention", *Lloyds Bank Review*, L (October, 1958), 35-45; and J. Spraos, "Speculation, Arbitrage and Sterling", *Economic Journal*, LXIX, No. 1 (March, 1959), 1-21.

[3] J. Spraos, *loc. cit.*; *idem*, "The Theory of Forward Exchange and Recent Practice", *The Manchester School of Economics and Social Studies*, XXI, No. 2 (May, 1953), 87-117; S. C. Tsiang, "The Theory of Forward Exchange and Effects of Government Intervention on the Forward Exchange Market", *International Monetary Fund Staff Papers*, VII, No. 1 (April, 1959), 75-106; and E. Sohmen, *Flexible Exchange Rates: Theory and Controversy* (Chicago: University of Chicago Press, 1961), chap. iv.

forward exchange rate as an ordinary price that must move to equate supply and demand. But the treatment of transactions in forward exchange is much more complete. As the *modus operandi* of Bank rate was usually expounded in respect of bill-market arbitrage – movements of funds between two countries' money markets – Keynes stressed the forward exchange operations arising from this type of capital transfer.[4] Recent writers on forward exchange have studied the many constituents of forward supply and demand, examining separately transactions arising from trade, from the several types of international investment, and from pure speculation on changes in the spot rates. In so doing, they have made important changes in Keynes's chief conclusion. Because the supply and demand for forward exchange reflect commercial "covering" and speculation, as well as interest arbitrage, the equilibrium price for forward exchange can be quite different from interest parity, even when there is just one relevant interest rate in each of the countries concerned.

But this functional classification of forward transactions may also obscure the essential similarity of all such transactions. Purchases and sales of forward exchange are undertaken for one reason, no matter what their form or the principal business activity of buyer and seller. They are used to alter the currency composition of each party's balance sheet – to align his net position in each currency, whether "long" or "short", with his expectations concerning the exchange rates. A merchant, investor, or banker who holds foreign-currency assets or who incurs foreign-currency debts may make profits or take losses in his own currency if the spot exchange rate is subject to change during the life of his assets or debts. To diminish his exposure to exchange risk, he must reduce his net position in foreign exchange, as by incurring foreign-currency debt to offset net

---

[4] Even now, interest parity is usually expressed in terms of the Treasury bill rates: If r_a is the quarterly interest rate on three-month Treasury bills in New York, r_b is the corresponding rate in London, R is the spot price of sterling expressed in dollars, and $R_f = R(1 - \alpha_f)$ is the three-month forward price of sterling, an American investor averse to exchange risk will have no profit incentive to transfer funds between New York and London when:

$$(1 + r_a) = (1 + r_b) \cdot (R_f/R) = (1 + r_b)(1 - \alpha_f).$$

When this condition holds, however:

$$(r_b - r_a)/(1 + r_b) = \alpha_f,$$

describing the bill-rate interest parity for forward sterling.

assets or by acquiring foreign-currency assets to offset net debt.[5] Transactions in forward foreign exchange create these extra debts and claims without imposing interest costs or a loss of interest income. A sale of forward foreign exchange creates a new debt in foreign currency and a new claim in the seller's own currency. A purchase of forward foreign exchange creates a new claim in foreign currency and a new debt in the seller's own currency.

To illustrate the basic similarity of purpose in all forward exchange transactions, I examine the spot and forward operations of an export-import firm. I show that it engages in "covering" (or "hedging"), arbitrage, and speculation in the normal course of business, and I develop the several connections among these activities – connections that cannot appear when the activities are studied separately or assigned to different parties.[6] I also stress the relationship between the firm's balance sheet (a set of stocks) and its transactions in foreign exchange (a set of flows).[7]

I   The trader-speculator

The first version of the model studied here supposes that all foreign trade is invoiced in the exporter's currency and is conducted on a cash basis. Exporters are paid in full on the execution of sales contracts (and employ their cash receipts to purchase or produce the goods they must deliver under the contracts). Importers must borrow to make their cash payments, and can do so readily at foreign or domestic banks. The banks

---

[5]   It is, of course, conventional to define exposure to exchange risk as a long or short position in foreign currency, and I follow this convention here. But a firm whose net worth is always expressed in its home currency also courts exchange risk, for its home currency depreciates whenever any other currency appreciates. No one with financial assets or financial debts can escape exchange risk, properly defined.

[6]   See, *e.g.*, J. E. Stein, *The Nature and Efficiency of the Foreign Exchange Market* ("Essays in International Finance", No. 40 [Princeton, N. J.: International Finance Section, Princeton University, 1962]), pp. 15 ff. Stein regards the banks as the "professional risk bearers" (speculators) who take over exchange risks from merchants and investors.

[7]   In this respect and several others, my treatment of the problem resembles the Fleming-Mundell model (J. M. Fleming and R. A. Mundell, "Official Intervention on the Forward Exchange Market: A Simplified Analysis", *International Monetary Fund Staff Papers*, XI, No. 1 [March, 1964]).

lend freely to all comers, but at rising interest rates; the average rate paid by any one borrower to any one bank is an increasing function of his current borrowing from that particular bank.[8] Finally, I assume that the spot exchange rate is fixed (albeit not immutably), that all bank loans and forward exchange transactions have the same maturity (ninety days), and, at the start, that the volume of trade is given.

To put these assumptions more formally, define:

R, R_e, R_f The spot price of pounds prevailing today (the current spot price), the spot price traders expect to encounter ninety days from now (the expected or deferred spot price), and the ninety-day forward price of pounds prevailing today, all expressed in dollars per pound;

M_a, M_b American and British imports paid for today (current trade), both expressed in dollars;

$_bP, _aP$ Spot purchases of British currency (pounds) and American currency (dollars) resulting from current trade (current spot purchases);

$_bP_e, _aP_e$ Spot purchases of British and American currency ninety days from now resulting from current trade (deferred spot purchases);

$_bP_f, _aP_f$ Ninety-day forward purchases of British and American currency resulting from current trade (current forward purchases);

C_{aa}, C_{ab} New dollar loans to American and British traders furnished by American banks (current American bank loans);

C_{ba}, C_{bb} New sterling loans to American and British traders furnished by British banks (current British bank loans);

r_{aa}, r_{ab} The average rates of interest on C_{aa} and C_{ab}; and

r_{ba}, r_{bb} The average rates of interest on C_{ba} and C_{bb}.

If, then, all imports are financed by bank credit:

$$M_i = C_{ai} + C_{bi} R, \qquad i = a, b. \tag{1}$$

If average interest rates rise with the level of new borrowing, and banks

---

[8] To be more realistic, one should probably assume that the average interest rate is an increasing function of the borrower's total indebtedness, not his new borrowing from a particular bank. But this would greatly complicate the algebra that follows.

do not discriminate by nationality:[9]

$$r_{ai} = \beta_a(C_{ai}), \quad \text{with} \quad r'_{ai} \equiv (d\beta_a/dC_{ai}) > 0, \quad \text{and}$$

$$r_{bi} = \beta_b(C_{bi}R), \quad \text{with} \quad r'_{bi} \equiv (d\beta_b/dC_{bi})/R > 0. \tag{2}$$

Next, define the current dollar value of the change in each importer's balance sheet (his expected net worth) resulting from current trade and from new transactions in forward exchange:[10]

$$V_a = {}_bP_f R_e - {}_bP_f R_f - \left[C_{aa}(1 + r_{aa}) + C_{ba}(1 + r_{ba})R_e \right]$$

$$V_b = \{ {}_aP_f/R_e - {}_aP_f/R_f - \left[C_{ab}(1 + r_{ab})/R_e + C_{bb}(1 + r_{bb}) \right] \} R. \tag{3}$$

A forward purchase of foreign exchange appears twice in each equation – as the expected home-currency equivalent of a foreign-currency asset $({}_bP_f R_e$ and ${}_aP_f/R_e)$ and as an obligation to deliver home currency $({}_bP_f R_f$ and ${}_aP_f/R_f)$. Debts to foreign banks also appear at their expected home-currency value $\left[C_{ba}(1+r_{ba}) R_e$ and $C_{ab}(1+r_{ab})/R_e \right]$. Hence, each balance-sheet change contains two terms weighted by the expected spot rates, R_e and $(1/R_e)$, and these can be collected to define two new terms measuring each trader's exposure to exchange risk:

$$E_a = \left[C_{ba}(1 + r_{ba}) - {}_bP_f \right] R$$

$$E_b = - \left[C_{ab}(1 + r_{ab}) - {}_aP_f \right]. \tag{4}$$

E_a measures the current dollar value of the American's net sterling debt (his "short" position in foreign currency); E_b measures the current dollar value of the British trader's net dollar claim (his "long" position in foreign currency). E_a and E_b are defined asymmetrically so that they will take the same sign when both traders expect the same change in the spot rate.[11]

---

[9]   Note that r_{bi} is defined as a function of $C_{bi} R$, the dollar equivalent of C_{bi}, to facilitate direct comparison between r'_{ai} and r'_{bi}. Note, further, that total dollar interest costs are $C_{ai}r_{ai}$, and that marginal interest costs are $(r_{ai} + C_{ai} r'_{ai})$. If marginal interest costs rise with total borrowing:

$$\frac{d(r_{ai} + C_{ai} r'_{ai})}{dC_{ai}} = 2 r'_{ai} + C_{ai} r''_{ai} > 0,$$

whence $\varepsilon_{ai} \equiv r''_{ai}(C_{ai}/r'_{ai}) > -2$. Similarly, $\varepsilon_{bi} \equiv r''_{bi}(C_{bi} R/r'_{bi}) > -2$. The case for these restrictions appears in the appendix.

[10]   We do not require the corresponding change in each exporter's balance sheet, since the exporter is paid promptly in domestic currency.

[11]   See p. 149, below.

As each trader must pay for his imports in foreign currency, he will exchange the proceeds of home-currency bank borrowing for spot foreign currency. In consequence:

$$_bP = C_{aa}/R, \quad \text{and} \quad _aP = C_{bb} R. \tag{5}$$

He must also buy spot foreign exchange to pay off his net foreign-currency debt, but only when that debt matures. Therefore:

$$_bP_e = C_{ba}(1 + r_{ba}) - {_bP_f} = E_a/R$$
$$_aP_e = C_{ab}(1 + r_{ab}) - {_aP_f} = - E_b. \tag{6}$$

Finally, solve equations (4) for forward purchases:

$$_bP_f = C_{ba}(1 + r_{ba}) - E_a/R$$
$$_aP_f = C_{ab}(1 + r_{ab}) + E_b. \tag{7}$$

If, next, one rewrites R_e as $R(1-\alpha_e)$ and R_f as $R(1-\alpha_f)$, where α_e is the expected percentage discount on spot sterling and α_f is the actual percentage discount on forward sterling, equations (3) give way to:

$$V_a = E_a(\alpha_e - \alpha_f) - [C_{aa}(1 + r_{aa}) + C_{ba} R(1 + r_{ba})(1 - \alpha_f)]$$
$$V_b = E_b[(\alpha_e - \alpha_f)/(1 - \alpha_f)(1 - \alpha_e)]$$
$$- [C_{ab}(1 + r_{ab})/(1 - \alpha_f) + C_{bb} R(1 + r_{bb})]. \tag{8}$$

These equations reproduce Tsiang's important contribution:[12] Although each trader may engage in "spot-market speculation", achieving his desired net position, E_i, by borrowing from foreign banks, his operations can be viewed as comprising "forward-market speculation", combined with covered debt arbitrage that minimizes interest cost. When $(\alpha_e - \alpha_f)$ is positive, a trader can seek speculative profits by selling pounds forward, then buying them spot when he must deliver them. By combining C_{ai} and C_{bi} correctly, moreover, a trader can finance his imports at least interest cost and no net exposure to exchange risk. Note, too, that positive values of $(\alpha_e - \alpha_f)$ invite the American trader to incur net sterling debt $(E_a > 0)$ so as to increase expected net worth, and invite the British trader to incur

---

[12]   Tsiang, *op. cit.*, p. 92; also Spraos, "Speculation, Arbitrage and Sterling", pp. 5-6.

net dollar claims $(E_b > 0)$; similarly, negative values invite the American trader to incur net sterling claims $(E_a < 0)$, and invite the British trader to incur net dollar debt $(E_b < 0)$. In general, any difference between the expected spot discount, α_e, and the actual forward discount, α_f, supplies an incentive for traders to speculate – to take on net positions in foreign currency.

II   The foreign exchange market and interest parity

If the traders represented by these equations can be regarded as "typical", their purchases of spot and forward exchange can be used as proxies for the corresponding aggregates. Hence, current trade and speculation will generate excess supplies of spot and forward dollars when:

$$S \equiv {_b}P R - {_a}P = C_{aa} - C_{bb} R = [M_a - M_b] + [C_{ab} - C_{ba} R] > 0$$

$$S_e \equiv {_b}P_e R - {_a}P_e = E_a + E_b > 0$$

$$S_f \equiv {_b}P_f R_f - {_a}P_f = [C_{ba}(1 + r_{ba}) R (1 - \alpha_f) - C_{ab}(1 + r_{ab})]$$
$$- [E_a(1 - \alpha_f) + E_b] > 0. \qquad (9)$$

When S is positive, of course, current trade and speculation will work to increase British reserves. When S_e is positive, they will work to increase British reserves ninety days hence, provided the exchange rate has not changed in the interim. When S_f is positive, the forward rate must change or must be stabilized by official intervention.[13]

If the forward market is in equilibrium $(S_f = 0)$, the last of these three definitions can be rearranged as follows:

$$\frac{(C_{ab} - C_{ba} R)(1 + r_{ab}) + [E_a(1 - \alpha_f) + E_b]}{C_{ba}(1 + r_{ba}) R} = \left[\frac{r_{ba} - r_{ab}}{1 + r_{ba}}\right] - \alpha_f. \qquad (10)$$

But the first argument on the lefthand side of equation (10) also figures

---

[13] Note, however, that S has no argument denoting the deferred effects of past trade and speculation, while S_e has no argument denoting the then-current effects of future trade and speculation. S_f, by contrast, describes the entire excess supply of forward dollars. Note, too, that S_e is defined at the current spot rate, not the expected spot rate; if an R_e different from R prevails ninety days hence, the definition of S_e will no longer hold.

in the definition of excess spot demand (S), so that equation (10) can be rewritten:

$$\frac{[S + (M_b - M_a)](1 + r_{ab}) + [E_a(1 - \alpha_f) + E_b]}{C_{ba}(1 + r_{ba})R} = \left[\frac{r_{ba} - r_{ab}}{1 + r_{ba}}\right] - \alpha_f. \quad (10a)$$

This equation reproduces another major finding of the recent contributors: Classic interest parity is a very special case. The forward discount on the pound would be at loan-rate parity when the righthand side of equation (10a) vanished completely, when $\alpha_f = (r_{ba} - r_{ab})/(1 + r_{ba})$. In order for this to happen, however, the lefthand side of the equation would have to vanish, too. Loan-rate parity would always emerge if S were zero, trade were balanced, and there were no speculation.[14] But these conditions will rarely prevail, as exchange-rate speculation is not an aberration linked solely to anticipations of devaluation. Whenever α_e differs from α_f, even when α_e is equal to zero, traders have profit incentives to speculate, and will take on net positions; the E_i are not likely to be zero.

III   Maximization and marginal parity

If traders were to maximize expected net worth and were indifferent to risk, they would take on enormous foreign-currency positions whenever α_e was different from α_f. If, instead, the traders were averse to exchange risk, weighing it carefully when reaching for profit, they would not take on net positions in foreign exchange unless prospective gains outweighed prospective risk. To put this second supposition more formally, define the typical trader's utility function as:

$$U_i = \psi_i(V_i, |E_i|), \qquad i = a, b. \quad (11)$$

---

[14]   It would also be maintained in another special case. Spot-market equilibrium requires that $S + S'_e = 0$, where S'_e is the value of S_e generated by past speculation, and can be represented by $E'_a + E'_b$. With spot-market equilibrium and balanced trade, the sign of equation (10a) depends on:

$$[E_a(1 - \alpha_f) + E_b] - [E'_a + E'_b](1 + r_{ab}),$$

reflecting the evolution of speculation, and loan-rate parity will be obtained when $E_a = E'_a(1 + r_{ba})$ and $E_b = E'_b(1 + r_{ab})$. In proof, assume loan-rate parity and substitute for α_f in the argument above.

setting $(\partial U_i/\partial V_i) > 0$ and $(\partial U_i/\partial E_i) < 0$. An increase in prospective net worth raises utility; an increase in exposure to exchange risk reduces utility. Then define $\alpha_a^* \equiv (\alpha_e - \alpha_f)$ and $\alpha_b^* \equiv \alpha_a^*/(1 - \alpha_f)(1 - \alpha_e)$, the prospective profit rates on the net positions E_a and E_b, so as to rewrite equations (8) more compactly:

$$V_i = E_i \alpha_i^* - \frac{[C_{ai}(1 + r_{ai}) + C_{bi} R(1 + r_{bi})(1 - \alpha_f)]}{1 - z_i \alpha_f}, \qquad (8a)$$

where $z_a = 0$ and $z_b = 1$.

The use of the absolute value, $|E_i|$, in equation (11) is meant to imply that traders are equally averse to "long" and "short" positions of identical size – to net debts and net claims in foreign currency. The sign of E_i cannot be inferred from the utility function or its derivatives, but it can be obtained from the sign of the expected profit rate, α_i^*, as $E_i \alpha_i^*$ must augment V_i rather than reduce it. The construction of the utility function also implies that the size of the expected profit rate does not affect the trader's attitude toward risk, save by affecting prospective net worth, V_i. Finally, the utility function is written as though the trader's total foreign-currency position, the series of net debts or net claims acquired in the preceding eighty-nine days, does not affect his current decisions. This supposition is not realistic. But there is little to be gained by writing U_i as a function of past debts and claims as well as current debts and claims, for the former are not altered by the trader's new decisions. It is sufficient to remember that these predetermined debts and claims are quite apt to influence current behavior – that they will alter the indifference curves linking V_i and E_i. If, for example, an American trader has assumed net sterling claims during the most recent eighty-nine days, but has now come to anticipate a positive profit rate on net sterling debt, he is likely to take on larger net debts than he would have incurred if he did not already hold net sterling claims, thereby to offset his net sterling claims.[15]

A trader may be deemed to maximize utility while obeying the trade constraint given by equation (1). To simulate his operations, construct the Lagrangian function:

$$L_i = \psi_i(V_i, |E_i|) + \lambda_i(C_{ai} + C_{bi} R - M_i). \qquad (12)$$

---

[15] For a more elaborate treatment of this problem (with a similar conclusion), see Tsiang, *op. cit.*, pp. 88-90.

Then differentiate this function with respect to E_i, C_{ai}, C_{bi} and λ_i, and set the first partial derivatives equal to zero:[16]

$$\frac{\partial L}{\partial E} = \frac{\partial U}{\partial E} + \frac{\partial U}{\partial V}\left(\frac{dV}{dE}\right) = 0$$

$$\frac{\partial L}{\partial C_a} = \frac{\partial U}{\partial V}\left(\frac{dV}{dC_a}\right) + \lambda = 0$$

$$\frac{\partial L}{\partial C_b} = \frac{\partial U}{\partial V}\left(\frac{dV}{dC_b}\right) + \lambda R = 0$$

$$\frac{\partial L}{\partial \lambda} = C_a + C_b R - M = 0. \tag{13}$$

From the first of these conditions:

$$-\left(\frac{\partial U}{\partial E}\right)\Big/\left(\frac{\partial U}{\partial V}\right) = \left(\frac{dV}{dE}\right) = \alpha_i^*, \tag{14}$$

which asserts that the marginal rate of substitution between net worth, V_i, and exposure to exchange risk, E_i, must equal the marginal profit rate foreseen by the trader. Figure 1 illustrates this condition for the American trader. The curves $_1U$ and $_2U$ are his indifference curves relating E_a and V_a, and $_0V_a$ denotes net worth when E_a is zero. If $\tan \theta$ represents the profit rate α_a^*, the trader will locate at T_1, taking on $_1E_a$ dollars worth of sterling debt and raising net worth to $_1V_a$.[17] By rotating the ray defining angle θ, one can construct an "offer curve" like $_0V_aT_1T_2$, depicting the trader's demand for sterling debt as a function of the expected rate of profit.[18]

From the second and third of the marginal conditions (and the additional assumption that traders borrow in both centers, so that C_{ai} and

---

[16]   I omit the subscript i when it is not needed to avoid ambiguity.

[17]   As the indifference curves are defined in respect of the absolute value of E_a, Figure 1 can be employed to describe the trader's acquisitions of sterling claims when α_a^* is negative. It can also be employed to describe the British trader's acquisitions of dollar claims ($E_b > 0$) and dollar debt ($E_b < 0$).

[18]   Note, in passing, that this curve could perhaps bend backward and that this effect, if sufficiently strong, could cause $_bP_f$ to behave peculiarly. I return to this problem below.

C_{bi} are both positive):

$$\left(\frac{dV}{dC_a}\right)R = \left(\frac{dV}{dC_b}\right). \tag{15}$$

But:

$$\frac{dV}{dC_a} = -\left[\frac{1 + r_{ai} + C_{ai}r'_{ai}}{1 - z_i\alpha_f}\right],$$

$$\frac{dV}{dC_b} = -R\left[\frac{1 + r_{bi} + C_{bi}Rr'_{bi}}{1 - z_i\alpha_f}\right](1 - \alpha_f). \tag{16}$$

Whence:

$$\alpha_f = \frac{(r_{bi} + C_{bi}Rr'_{bi}) - (r_{ai} + C_{ai}r'_{ai})}{(1 + r_{bi} + C_{bi}Rr'_{bi})}. \tag{17}$$

Each trader will arrange his total borrowing so that the discount on forward sterling stands at its marginal loan-rate parity. Unlike the average parity examined earlier, this marginal parity will always prevail (unless the difference in bank lending rates is so large that traders borrow all they need from one country's banks). Marginal loan-rate parity is internal to the cost calculations of the individual trader, and can be maintained by adjustments in the locus of commercial borrowing. Average loan-rate parity, by contrast, depends on a particular constellation of market aggregates.

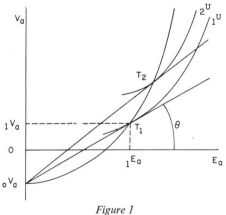

Figure 1

IV Stability, displacement, and adjustment

To study the trader's responses when α_e, α_f and M_i change, take the total derivatives of equations (13), writing:

$$
\begin{bmatrix}
\dfrac{\partial^2 L}{\partial E^2} & \dfrac{\partial^2 L}{\partial C_a\,\partial E} & \dfrac{\partial^2 L}{\partial C_b\,\partial E} & 0 \\[2mm]
\dfrac{\partial^2 L}{\partial C_a\,\partial E} & \dfrac{\partial^2 L}{\partial C_a^2} & \dfrac{\partial^2 L}{\partial C_a\,\partial C_b} & 1 \\[2mm]
\dfrac{\partial^2 L}{\partial C_b\,\partial E} & \dfrac{\partial^2 L}{\partial C_a\,\partial C_b} & \dfrac{\partial^2 L}{\partial C_b^2} & R \\[2mm]
0 & 1 & R & 0
\end{bmatrix}
\begin{bmatrix}
dE_i \\[2mm] dC_{ai} \\[2mm] dC_{bi} \\[2mm] d\lambda_i
\end{bmatrix}
=
\begin{bmatrix}
-\left(\dfrac{\partial U}{\partial V}\right)d\alpha_i^* \\[2mm]
\left(\dfrac{z_i\lambda_i}{1-z_i\alpha_f}\right)d\alpha_f \\[2mm]
-\lambda_i R\left[\dfrac{1}{1-\alpha_f}-\dfrac{z_i}{1-z_i\alpha_f}\right]d\alpha_f \\[2mm]
dM_i
\end{bmatrix}
$$

(18)

Applying Cramer's rule:

$$
\frac{dE_i}{d\alpha_i^*}=-\left(\frac{\partial U}{\partial V}\right)\frac{|H_1|}{|H|}=-\left(\frac{\partial U}{\partial V}\right)\Big/\left(\frac{\partial^2 L}{\partial E^2}\right),
$$

$$
\frac{dC_{ai}}{d\alpha_i^*}=-R\left(\frac{dC_{bi}}{d\alpha_i^*}\right)=-R\left(\frac{\partial U}{\partial V}\right)\left[R\left(\frac{\partial^2 L}{\partial C_a\,\partial E}\right)-\left(\frac{\partial^2 L}{\partial C_b\,\partial E}\right)\right]\frac{1}{|H|},
$$

(19)

where H is the bordered Hessian on the lefthand side of (18), and H_1 is the principal minor of H obtained by deleting the first row and column.[19] As $(\partial^2 L/\partial E^2)$ must be negative when L_i is a maximum, $(dE_i/d\alpha_i^*)$ is always positive.[20] An increase in the profit rate foreseen by the trader will cause him to enlarge his net position. As $R\,(\partial^2 L/\partial C_a\,\partial E)=(\partial^2 L/\partial C_b\,\partial E)$, moreover, $(dC_{ai}/d\alpha_i^*)$ and $(dC_{bi}/d\alpha_i^*)$ are zero. Changes in the profit rate will not directly alter the locus of borrowing. Furthermore:

$$
\frac{dE_i}{d\alpha_f}=\left(\frac{dE_i}{d\alpha_i^*}\right)\left(\frac{d\alpha_i^*}{d\alpha_f}\right)+\frac{R\lambda_i}{1-\alpha_f}\left[R\left(\frac{\partial^2 L}{\partial C_a\,\partial E}\right)-\frac{\partial^2 L}{\partial C_b\,\partial E}\right]\frac{1}{|H|},
$$

$$
\frac{dC_{ai}}{d\alpha_f}=-R\left(\frac{dC_{bi}}{d\alpha_f}\right)=-\left(\frac{\partial^2 L}{\partial E^2}\right)\left[\frac{R^2\lambda_i}{1-\alpha_f}\right]\frac{1}{|H|}=-\left[\frac{R^2\lambda_i}{1-\alpha_f}\right]\frac{1}{|H_1|}
$$

$$
=\frac{-\dfrac{dV}{dC_a}}{(1-\alpha_f)\left[\dfrac{d^2 V}{dC_a^2}+\left(\dfrac{d^2 V}{dC_b^2}\right)\Big/R^2\right]}.
$$

(20)

---

[19] For proof that $|H_1|/|H|=1/(\partial^2 L/\partial E^2)$, see equation (A.6) of the appendix.

[20] See equations (A.4) through (A.6) of the appendix. Note that the sign of $(dE_i/d\alpha_i^*)$ rules out a backward-bending "offer curve" $({}_0V_aT_1T_2)$ in Figure 1.

Hence $(dE_i/d\alpha_f)$ simplifies to $(dE_i/d\alpha_i^*)(d\alpha_i^*/d\alpha_f)$, and this must be negative because $(d\alpha_i^*/d\alpha_f)$ is negative. An increase in the discount on forward sterling causes a reduction in net dollar claims (net sterling debt) because it reduces the profitability of speculation against sterling. In addition, $(dC_{ai}/d\alpha_f)$ is negative and $(dC_{bi}/d\alpha_f)$ is positive, for $|H_1|$ must be positive when L_i is a maximum, while λ_i is equal to $-(\partial U/\partial V)(dV/dC_a)$ and is therefore positive.[21] An increase in the discount on forward sterling causes a shift in the locus of borrowing – more borrowing from Britain and less from America. Finally, one can show that:

$$\frac{dE_i}{dM_i} = -\left(\frac{\partial^2 L}{\partial C_a \partial E}\right)\bigg/\left(\frac{\partial^2 L}{\partial E^2}\right) = -\left[\frac{\partial^2 U}{\partial V \partial E} + \frac{\partial^2 U}{\partial V^2}\left(\frac{dV}{dE}\right)\right]\left(\frac{dV}{dC_a}\right)\bigg/\left(\frac{\partial^2 L}{\partial E^2}\right),$$

$$\frac{dC_{ai}}{dM_i} = \left[1 - R\left(\frac{dC_{bi}}{dM_i}\right)\right] = \left(\frac{d^2 V}{dC_b^2}\right)\bigg/\left[R^2\left(\frac{d^2 V}{dC_a^2}\right) + \left(\frac{d^2 V}{dC_b^2}\right)\right]. \quad (21)$$

Hence, (dE_i/dM_i) takes the sign of $[(\partial^2 U/\partial V \partial E)+(\partial^2 U/\partial V^2)(dV/dE)]$, not yet specified. We do not know how an increase in the level of trade affects the volume of speculation. But $0<(dC_{ai}/dM_i)<1$, and $0<R(dC_{bi}/dM_i)<1$. We can say that an increase in the level of trade will increase traders' borrowing from both financial centers.

We usually suppose that demand curves slope downward, and most recent writers on forward exchange have made the same assumption. Consider, however, the changes in $_bP_f$ and $_aP_f$, the two traders' purchases of forward foreign exchange, attending a decrease in the corresponding prices, R_f and R_f' (where $R_f' = 1/R_f$). Differentiating equations (7) and allowing, in the process, for changes in trade:

$$-\frac{d_b P_f}{dR_f} = \frac{d_b P_f}{d\alpha_f}\left(\frac{1}{R}\right) = \left\{\left[\left(\frac{dC_{ba}}{d\alpha_f}\right)(1 + r_{ba} + C_{ba} R r_{ba}') R + \left(\frac{dE_a}{d\alpha_a^*}\right)\right]\right.$$

$$\left. + \left[\left(\frac{dC_{ba}}{dM_a}\right)(1 + r_{ba} + C_{ba} R r_{ba}') R - \left(\frac{dE_a}{dM_a}\right)\right]\left(\frac{dM_a}{d\alpha_f}\right)\right\}/R^2,$$

$$-\frac{d_a P_f}{dR_f'} = -\frac{d_a P_f}{d\alpha_f}\left(R_f^2/R\right) = \left\{\left[\left(\frac{dC_{bb}}{d\alpha_f}\right)(1 + r_{ab} + C_{ab} r_{ab}') + \left(\frac{dE_b}{d\alpha_b^*}\right)(R/R_f^2)\right]\right.$$

---

[21] For the sign of $|H_1|$ and the final formulation of $(dC_{ai}/d\alpha_f)$, see equation (A.3) of the appendix. As $(dV/dC_a) < 0$, and each of the derivatives in the denominator is also negative, the whole argument will always be negative.

$$-\left[\left(\frac{\mathrm{d}C_{ab}}{\mathrm{d}M_b}\right)(1 + r_{ab} + C_{ab}\,r'_{ab}) + \left(\frac{\mathrm{d}E_b}{\mathrm{d}M_b}\right)\right]\left(\frac{\mathrm{d}M_b}{\mathrm{d}\alpha_f}\right)\left(\frac{1}{R}\right)\right\}/R_f'^2. \quad (22)$$

As $(\mathrm{d}C_{bi}/\mathrm{d}\alpha_f)$ and $(\mathrm{d}E_i/\mathrm{d}\alpha_i^*)$ are always positive, the first argument of each equation will also be positive. Furthermore, C_{ba} and C_{ab} are increasing functions of imports. Yet one cannot attach a sign to the second argument of each equation without first ascertaining the signs of $(\mathrm{d}E_i/\mathrm{d}M_i)$ and $(\mathrm{d}M_i/\mathrm{d}\alpha_f)$.

Some recent writers on forward exchange assume that a decline in the cost of forward cover will stimulate imports – that $(\mathrm{d}M_a/\mathrm{d}\alpha_f)$ is positive and $(\mathrm{d}M_b/\mathrm{d}\alpha_f)$ is negative because α_f is the discount on the forward pound – and some of them lean heavily on this assumption to secure other important results.[22] Traders who "cover" commercial risks, it is argued, will use the forward rate to calculate the home-currency price of imports; they will regard a decline in the cost of forward foreign exchange as equivalent to – and more relevant than – a decrease in the cost of spot exchange. My equations (1) through (8) do not display a separate term that corresponds to "covering". But I can obtain the conventional signs for $(\mathrm{d}M_a/\mathrm{d}\alpha_f)$ and $(\mathrm{d}M_b/\mathrm{d}\alpha_f)$ by supposing that the level of trade depends on a component of expected net worth, and asking how an increase in the forward discount affects that component. One cannot suppose that the level of trade depends on the whole of V_i, for a change in α_f would then give ambiguous results. Holding M_i fixed:[23]

$$\frac{\mathrm{d}V_a}{\mathrm{d}\alpha_f} = \left[E_a + \alpha_a^*\left(\frac{\mathrm{d}E_a}{\mathrm{d}\alpha_a^*}\right)\right]\left(\frac{\mathrm{d}\alpha_a^*}{\mathrm{d}\alpha_f}\right) + C_{ba}\,R\,(1 + r_{ba}),$$

$$\frac{\mathrm{d}V_b}{\mathrm{d}\alpha_f} = \left[E_b + \alpha_b^*\left(\frac{\mathrm{d}E_b}{\mathrm{d}\alpha_b^*}\right)\right]\left(\frac{\mathrm{d}\alpha_b^*}{\mathrm{d}\alpha_f}\right) - C_{ab}(1 + r_{ab})/(1 - \alpha_f)^2. \quad (23)$$

---

[22] See Sohmen, *op. cit.*, pp. 72-76, 137-38; Tsiang, *op. cit.*, pp. 92-94, 105; and Einzig, *op. cit.*, pp. 53-58.

[23] Differentiating V_a with respect to α_f and holding M_a constant:

$$\frac{\mathrm{d}V_a}{\mathrm{d}\alpha_f} = \left[E_a + \alpha_a^*\left(\frac{\mathrm{d}E_a}{\mathrm{d}\alpha_a^*}\right)\right]\left(\frac{\mathrm{d}\alpha_a^*}{\mathrm{d}\alpha_f}\right) - \left[\left(\frac{\mathrm{d}C_{aa}}{\mathrm{d}\alpha_f}\right)(1 + r_{aa} + C_{aa}r'_{aa})\right.$$

$$\left. + \left(\frac{\mathrm{d}C_{ba}}{\mathrm{d}\alpha_f}\right)(1 + r_{ba} + C_{ba}\,Rr'_{ba})(1 - \alpha_f)R\right] + C_{ba}\,R(1 + r_{ba}).$$

But $(\mathrm{d}C_{aa}/\mathrm{d}\alpha_f) = -R(\mathrm{d}C_{ba}/\mathrm{d}\alpha_f)$, while $(1 + r_{aa} + C_{aa}\,r'_{aa}) = (1 + r_{ba} + C_{ba}r'_{ba})$ $(1 - \alpha_f)$, so that the argument in brackets vanishes completely. A similar procedure gives $(\mathrm{d}V_b/\mathrm{d}\alpha_f)$.

As $(d\alpha_i^*/d\alpha_f)$ is always negative, $(dV_a/d\alpha_f)$ might also be negative when E_a is positive, while $(dV_b/d\alpha_f)$ might be positive when E_b is negative. If, however, the level of imports is independent of the speculative argument in V_i, depending only on "nonspeculative" net worth, $(V_i - E_i\alpha_i^*)$, an increase in α_f will increase M_a and decrease M_b because it will cut the cost of American borrowing and raise the cost of British borrowing.

Yet the slopes of the demand curves, given by equations (22), will still be in doubt unless $(dE_a/dM_a) \leq 0$ and $(dE_b/dM_b) \geq 0$. If the demand curves are both to slope downward, one must set $(dE_i/dM_i) = 0$ by setting $[(\partial^2 U/\partial V \partial E) + (\partial^2 U/\partial V^2)(dV/dE)] = 0$ in equation (21). This is tantamount to saying that trade and speculation are *doubly* independent. To obtain $(dM_a/d\alpha_f) > 0$ and $(dM_b/d\alpha_f) < 0$, I had to suppose that a change expected in net worth due to speculation would not alter imports. To obtain $(dE_i/dM_i) = 0$, I have to suppose that a change in "nonspeculative" net worth will not alter the volume of speculation, E_i.

To prove this second statement, denote the marginal rate of substitution between V_i and E_i by ϕ, and differentiate ϕ with respect to V_i, holding E_i constant:

$$\frac{\partial\phi}{\partial V} = -\left[\frac{\partial^2 U}{\partial V \partial E} + \phi\left(\frac{\partial^2 U}{\partial V^2}\right)\right]\bigg/\left(\frac{\partial U}{\partial V}\right) = -\left[\frac{\partial^2 U}{\partial V \partial E} + \frac{\partial^2 U}{\partial V^2}\left(\frac{dV}{dE}\right)\right]\bigg/\left(\frac{\partial U}{\partial V}\right),$$
(24)

as $\phi = (dV/dE)$ when V_i is a maximum. When (dE_i/dM_i) is zero, then, $(\partial\phi/\partial V)$ is also zero, and the trader's indifference curves will be vertically

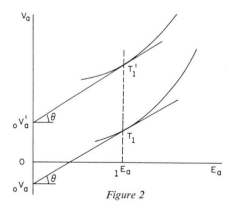

Figure 2

aligned, as in Figure 2. A change in "nonspeculative" net worth, $_0V_a$ in the diagram, due to a change in the level of trade, in interest rates, or in α_f, will not cause a change in the trader's net foreign-currency position, E_i.[24]

Two-way independence between trade and speculation lurks in all the recent models that treat speculation, arbitrage, and commercial "covering" as separate activities. The authors of those models, however, would seem to have chosen this mode of analysis for its expositional convenience, without perceiving its full significance or its role in their results. But two-way independence is an excessively strict supposition, for it rules out several intriguing results, yet does not even guarantee a stable forward market. To be sure of comparative-static stability in the forward market, one must be able to show that a rise in the price of the forward dollar will generate an excess supply of dollars – that (dS_f/dR_f') is positive. This may not be true, even when the two demand curves for forward exchange are negatively sloped. Differentiating equation (9) with respect to the forward price of the dollar, R_f', and using the arguments of equation (22):

$$
\begin{aligned}
\frac{dS_f}{dR_f'} &= -\left[\left(\frac{d_b P_f}{dR_f}\right)R_f^3 + \left(\frac{d_a P_f}{dR_f}\right) + {_b}P_f R_f^2\right] \\
&= R(1-\alpha_f)^2\left\{\left[\sum_i\left(\frac{dC_{bi}}{d\alpha_f}\right)R(1+r_{ai}+C_{ai}r_{ai}')\right]\right. \\
&\quad + \left[\frac{dE_a}{d\alpha_a^*}(1-\alpha_f) + \frac{dE_b}{d\alpha_b^*}(1-\alpha_f)^{-2}\right] \\
&\quad + (1-\alpha_f)\left[\left(\frac{d^2V_a}{dC_{aa}^2}\right)\left(\frac{dC_{aa}}{d\alpha_f}\right)\left(\frac{dM_a}{d\alpha_f}\right) - \left(\frac{d^2V_b}{dC_{bb}^2}\right)\left(\frac{dC_{ab}}{d\alpha_f}\right)\left(\frac{1-\alpha_f}{R^2}\right)\left(\frac{dM_b}{d\alpha_f}\right)\right] \\
&\quad \left. - \left[\frac{dE_a}{dM_a}(1-\alpha_f)\frac{dM_a}{d\alpha_f} + \frac{dE_b}{dM_b}\left(\frac{dM_b}{d\alpha_f}\right)\right] - \left[{_b}P_f R\right]\right\}.
\end{aligned}
\tag{25}
$$

The first three arguments of this equation, representing arbitrage, specu-

---

[24]   One can see the full effects of setting $(dE_i/dM_i) = 0$ by looking at the Hessian H. With $(dE_i/dM_i) = 0$, H can be partitioned into two submatrices: the first contains one element, $(\partial^2 L/\partial E^2) < 0$, supplying a sufficient second-order condition for maximum prospective gains from speculation; the second is H_1 with $|H_1| > 0$, supplying a sufficient second-order condition for minimum borrowing cost. Note, further, that one can obtain $(dE_i/dM_i) = 0$ with $(\partial^2 U/\partial V\,\partial E) \gtreqless 0$. But with $(\partial^2 U/\partial V\,\partial E) > 0$,

lation, and the role of trade, will all be positive, provided $(dM_a/d\alpha_f)$ is positive and $(dM_b/d\alpha_f)$ is negative (*i.e.*, with one-way independence).[25] The fourth argument has an uncertain sign unless one assumes two-way independence, but the fifth will be negative in every circumstance. Hence, one cannot put a sign to equation (25) merely by assuming two-way independence. One must make a separate assumption concerning market

---

the sign of $(\partial^2 L/\partial E^2)$ comes into doubt, as:

$$\frac{\partial^2 L}{\partial E^2} = \left(\frac{\partial^2 U}{\partial E^2}\right) + \phi\left(\frac{\partial^2 U}{\partial V \partial E}\right) + \phi\left[\left(\frac{\partial^2 U}{\partial V \partial E}\right) + \phi\left(\frac{\partial^2 U}{\partial V^2}\right)\right] = \left(\frac{\partial^2 U}{\partial E^2}\right) + \phi\left(\frac{\partial^2 U}{\partial V \partial E}\right),$$

when $(dE_i/dM_i) = 0$, and this may not be negative even if $(\partial^2 U/\partial E^2) < 0$. If further $(\partial^2 U/\partial V \partial E) < 0$, one must have $(\partial^2 U/\partial V^2) > 0$, which is implausible, although not impossible. In short, one can best obtain $(dE_i/dM_i) = 0$ by setting $(\partial^2 U/\partial V \partial E) = (\partial^2 U/\partial V^2) = 0$, which gives strict independence between $(\partial U/\partial E)$ and V_i (between the marginal disutility of exposure to exchange risk and prospective net worth, including gains from speculation), not merely between $(\partial U/\partial E)$ and $(V_i - E_i\alpha_i^*)$ or $_0V_a$ in Figure 2.

[25] The new formulation of the trade term in equation (25) derives from equations (20), (21), and (16). For:

$$\left(\frac{dC_{ba}}{dM_a}\right) R = - \left(\frac{d^2V_a}{dC_{aa}^2}\right)\left(\frac{dC_{aa}}{d\alpha_f}\right)(1 - \alpha_f)\bigg/\left(\frac{dV_a}{dC_{aa}}\right),$$

where

$$\left(\frac{dV_a}{dC_{aa}}\right) = -(1 + r_{aa} + C_{aa}\, r'_{aa});$$

$$\left(\frac{dC_{ab}}{dM_b}\right) = -\left(\frac{d^2V_b}{dC_{bb}^2}\right)\left(\frac{1}{R^2}\right)\left(\frac{dC_{ab}}{d\alpha_f}\right)(1 - \alpha_f)\bigg/\left(\frac{dV_b}{dC_{ab}}\right),$$

where

$$\left(\frac{dV_b}{dC_{ab}}\right) = -(1 + r_{ab} + C_{ab}\, r'_{ab})\,/\,(1 - \alpha_f).$$

It should be remembered that (d^2V_a/dC_{aa}^2) and $(dC_{aa}/d\alpha_f)$ are negative; so, too, are the corresponding arguments for Britain. Note that equation (25) can also be written in the familiar elasticities form:

$$\frac{dS_f}{dR'_f} = [_bP_f\, R_f/R'_f]\left[_b\eta_f + {_a}\eta_f\left(\frac{_aP_f}{_bP_f\, R_f}\right) - 1\right],$$

where $_b\eta_f$ and $_a\eta_f$ are the elasticities of demand for forward exchange. Haberler was among the first to show that the corresponding spot-market condition is, in fact, a statement that the market is stable. (See G. Haberler, "The Market for Foreign Exchange and Stability of the Balance of Payments", *Kyklos*, III [1949], 193-218).

stability. I assume that the market is stable in the sections that follow. I also assume that the level of trade is independent of the expected gains from speculation so as to obtain the conventional signs for $(dM_a/d\alpha_f)$ and $(dM_b/d\alpha_f)$. But I do not impose two-way independence.

V Speculation, intervention, and the reserves

Suppose that the traders come to anticipate a depreciation of spot sterling – that there is an increase in α_e. From equations (9):

$$\frac{dS}{d\alpha_e} = 0$$

$$\frac{dS_e}{d\alpha_e} = \left[\frac{dE_a}{d\alpha_a^*} + \frac{dE_b}{d\alpha_b^*}(1 - \alpha_e)^{-2}\right] > 0$$

$$\frac{dS_f}{d\alpha_e} = -\left[\frac{dE_a}{d\alpha_a^*}(1 - \alpha_f) + \frac{dE_b}{d\alpha_b^*}(1 - \alpha_e)^{-2}\right] < 0. \tag{26}$$

Taken by itself, speculation against sterling will not cause any current change in Britain's reserves, and will cause an increase after ninety days. But the excess demand for forward dollars $(dS_f < 0)$ produced by speculation will lead to a change in α_f, the discount on forward sterling, unless the authorities intervene to stabilize the forward pound. In the absence of such intervention it is necessary that:

$$\left(\frac{dS_f}{d\alpha_e}\right)d\alpha_e + \left(\frac{dS_f}{d\alpha_f}\right)d\alpha_f = 0, \quad \text{or} \quad -\left(\frac{dS_f}{d\alpha_e}\right)\bigg/\left(\frac{dS_f}{d\alpha_f}\right) = \left(\frac{d\alpha_f}{d\alpha_e}\right) > 0. \tag{27}$$

Forward sterling will tend toward a discount $(d\alpha_f > 0)$ when the forward market is assumed to be stable. This change in the forward rate is likely to affect Britain's reserves, though the sign of the change is not at all certain. The current and deferred effects of the increase in α_f take their signs from:

$$\left(\frac{dS}{d\alpha_f}\right) = \left[\left(\frac{dC_{aa}}{dM_a}\right)\left(\frac{dM_a}{d\alpha_f}\right) - R\left(\frac{dC_{bb}}{dM_b}\right)\left(\frac{dM_b}{d\alpha_f}\right)\right] - R\left[\frac{dC_{ba}}{d\alpha_f} + \frac{dC_{bb}}{d\alpha_f}\right] \tag{28}$$

$$\left(\frac{dS_e}{d\alpha_f}\right) = -\left[\frac{dE_a}{d\alpha_a^*} - \frac{dE_b}{d\alpha_b^*}(1 - \alpha_f)^{-2}\right] + \left[\frac{dE_a}{dM_a}\left(\frac{dM_a}{d\alpha_f}\right) + \frac{dE_b}{dM_b}\left(\frac{dM_b}{d\alpha_f}\right)\right]. \tag{29}$$

The first or "trade" term of equation (28) will always be positive, as $(dM_a/d\alpha_f) > 0$ and $(dM_b/d\alpha_f) < 0$ when the level of trade is independent of speculative gains; but the second or "arbitrage" term will always be negative, as $(dC_{bi}/d\alpha_f)$ is always positive. And if the first effect is larger than the second, speculation against sterling can actually add to Britain's reserves, rather than reducing them. Tsiang has also called attention to this possibility, but in a different context. Objecting to official intervention in the forward market, he argues that it may protect a nation's reserves, but "at the cost of worsening, to some extent, the current balance of trade".[26] The "worsening" at issue, however, is the cancellation of the "trade" effect in equation (28), and if there is a case for official intervention, it rests on the supposition that this "trade" effect is too small to offset the "arbitrage" effect, so that $(dS/d\alpha_f)$ is negative. Put differently, official intervention does not worsen the trade balance; it merely forgoes the (insufficient) trade-balance gain concomitant with speculation.

The deferred effects of speculation are also ambiguous, as one cannot attach a sign to (dE_i/dM_i) in equation (29) without assuming two-way independence. Furthermore, $(dM_a/d\alpha_f)$ and $(dM_b/d\alpha_f)$ have opposite signs, so that the second argument of equation (29) might turn either way, no matter what the sign of (dE_i/dM_i). Finally, solve equations (9) for $(S+S_e)$ to obtain the total change in Britain's reserves, current and deferred:

$$(S + S_e) = (M_a - M_b) + (C_{ba} R r_{ba} - C_{ab} r_{ab}) - ({}_b P_f R)\alpha_f - S_f. \qquad (30)$$

Differentiating this equation totally and invoking equation (27) to dispose of its last term:

$$\left(\frac{dS_e}{d\alpha_e}\right) + \left[\frac{dS}{d\alpha_f} + \frac{dS_e}{d\alpha_f}\right]\left(\frac{d\alpha_f}{d\alpha_e}\right) = \left(\frac{dE_a}{d\alpha_a^*}\right)\alpha_f + \left\{\left[\frac{dM_a}{d\alpha_f} - \frac{dM_b}{d\alpha_f}\right]\right.$$

$$+ R\left[\frac{dC_{ba}}{d\alpha_f} + \frac{dC_{ba}}{dM_a}\left(\frac{dM_a}{d\alpha_f}\right)\right](r_{ba} + C_{ba} R r'_{ba})$$

$$+ \left[\frac{dC_{bb}}{d\alpha_f} - \frac{dC_{ab}}{dM_b}\left(\frac{dM_b}{d\alpha_f}\right)\right](r_{ab} + C_{ab} r'_{ab})$$

$$- R\left[\left(\frac{d_b P_f}{d\alpha_f}\right)\alpha_f + {}_b P_f\right]\right\}\left(\frac{d\alpha_f}{d\alpha_e}\right). \qquad (31)$$

All of the arguments of equation (31) are positive, save for the last pair

---

[26] *Op. cit.*, p. 105.

of terms in brackets; the sign of $(d_b P_f/d\alpha_f)$ will always be in doubt unless one assumes two-way independence, and the last term will always be negative.[27] Hence, the total effect of speculation on Britain's reserves – current and deferred, direct and indirect – must remain ambiguous; two-way independence and forward market stability do not suffice to clarify the sign of equation (31).

Yet the case for intervention in the forward market is not weakened by these new results, as the proponents of intervention make no claim at all regarding the total effect described by equation (31). They merely suppose that the (beneficial) "trade" effect of speculation is smaller than the (adverse) "arbitrage" effect – that $(dS/d\alpha_f)$ is negative – so that speculation against sterling will reduce Britain's reserves as soon as it appears. They argue, moreover, that the authorities will be able to "unwind" their forward positions without any later loss of reserves. This modest case for intervention draws strong support from equations (26). If the authorities support forward sterling, meeting the excess demand for forward dollars defined by $(dS_f/d\alpha_e)$, there will be no change in the forward rate (no change in α_f). In this case, $(dS/d\alpha_e)$ and $(dS_e/d\alpha_e)$ in equations (26) will describe the full reserve effects, current and deferred, of speculation against sterling. There will be no current change in British reserves, and the increase in reserves occurring ninety days later will suffice to discharge the commitments incurred by the authorities. They will gain $(dS_e/d\alpha_e)$ dollars ninety days after their intervention and will have to pay out $(dS_f/d\alpha_e)$ dollars. But:

$$\left(\frac{dS_e}{d\alpha_e}\right) = -\left(\frac{dS_f}{d\alpha_e}\right) + \alpha_f\left(\frac{dE_a}{d\alpha_e}\right). \tag{32}$$

The authorities' deferred receipts will exceed their obligations, supplying a profit on counterspeculation if the forward pound stood at a discount when intervention first occurred.[28]

---

[27]   The demand for forward sterling, $_bP_f$, is the difference between $C_{ba}(1 + r_{ba})$ and E_a/R, and it would seem that this could be negative. But if E_a/R is positive (the case that raises doubt), E_b will also be positive, and $_aP_f$ will be positive. As $_bP_f R_f = _aP_f$, then, $_bP_f$ must be positive.

[28]   The comparison between $(dS_e/d\alpha_e)$ and $(dS_f/d\alpha_e)$ deserves special emphasis, as it is the relevant test of the risk incurred by the authorities. Too many people are prone to make an irrelevant comparison between the *level* of reserves and the authorities' forward commitments.

If speculation continued unabated at the end of the ninety-day period, the authorities

VI   Modifications in the model

This entire paper has been constructed on a particular set of assumptions regarding institutional arrangements: Trade was financed in the exporter's currency and was conducted on a cash basis. But similar conclusions can be derived for very different institutional arrangements. I do not examine all permutations, but outline one other case to show how the rest of them can be attacked and that the analysis is very similar to the one presented in the preceding sections.

Suppose that trade is invoiced in the importer's currency and that payments are made when goods are delivered, ninety days after contracts are signed. Let the exporters borrow from foreign and domestic banks to finance their operations while awaiting payment for the goods they have sold. In this case, one can write:

$$(1 - g_i) X_i = C_{ai} + C_{bi} R, \tag{33}$$

where X_i represents export proceeds valued in dollars at the current spot rate, and g_i represents the gap between export proceeds and the dollar total of exporters' costs.[29] Next, write V_i^x, the current dollar value of the change in net worth due to the exporter's current sales and his forward exchange transactions:

$$V_a^x = X_a (R_e/R) + {}_bP_f R_e - {}_bP_f R_f - [C_{aa}(1 + r_{aa}) + C_{ba}(1 + r_{ba}) R_e],$$
$$V_b^x = \{X_b/R_e + {}_aP_f/R_e - {}_aP_f/R_f - [C_{ab}(1 + r_{ab})/R_e + C_{bb}(1 + r_{bb})]\} R. \tag{34}$$

Finally, define the exporter's exposure to exchange risk in the usual way:

$$E_a^x = [C_{ba}(1 + r_{ba}) - X_a/R - {}_bP_f] R,$$
$$E_b^x = - [C_{ab}(1 + r_{ab}) - X_b - {}_aP_f]. \tag{35}$$

---

would have to renew their positions to stabilize the forward rate. But their commitments are not apt to cumulate, as Tsiang suggests (*op. cit.*, pp. 105-6), unless the traders enlarge their net positions, E_i, at the close of the period. Tsiang's error consists in neglecting the fact that the traders must discharge their own obligations after ninety days. One is not likely to make this sort of error if one works with net positions, as in this paper, rather than current flows. (For more extensive comments on "cumulation", see J. H. Auten, "Counter-Speculation and the Forward-Exchange Market", *Journal of Political Economy*, LXIX, No. 1 [February, 1961], 50-51.)

[29]   Hence $0 < g_i < 1$. The use of this device permits me to write equation (33) as an equality, not an inequality.

Whence:

$$V_i^x = E_i^x \alpha_i^* + \frac{X_i(1-\alpha_f)}{(1-z_i\alpha_f)^2} - \left[\frac{C_{ai}(1+r_{ai}) + C_{bi}R(1+r_{bi})(1-\alpha_f)}{1-z_i\alpha_f}\right], \quad (36)$$

which is identical to equation (8a) save for the addition of the trade term, $X_i(1-\alpha_f)/(1-z_i\alpha_f)^2$, which corresponds explicitly to commercial "covering". The addition of this term, however, makes little difference for the analysis if one regards the level of exports as demand-determined. Using the same utility function as in the importer-borrower case, one can form the Lagrangian function:

$$L_i^x = \psi_i^x(V_i^x, |E_i^x|) + \lambda_i^x[C_{ai} + C_{bi}R - (1-g_i)X_i], \quad (37)$$

and can differentiate L_i^x with respect to E_i^x, C_{ai}, C_{bi}, and λ_i^x. The first-order conditions for maximum L_i^x will be the same as equations (13), except that $(1-g_i)X_i$ replaces M_i in the final equation, and the only change in equation (18) describing displacement is the substitution of $dX_i(1-g_i)$ for dM_i. One therefore obtains the same equations (19) and (20) as in the importer-borrower case, while (21) gives way to:

$$\frac{dE_i}{dX_i} = -(1-g_i)\left[\frac{\partial^2 U}{\partial V \partial E} + \frac{\partial^2 U}{\partial V^2}\left(\frac{dV}{dE}\right)\right]\left(\frac{dV}{dC_a}\right)\bigg/\left(\frac{\partial^2 L}{\partial E^2}\right),$$

$$\frac{dC_{ai}}{dX_i} = \left[(1-g_i) - R\left(\frac{dC_{bi}}{dX_i}\right)\right] = \frac{(1-g_i)\left(\dfrac{d^2V}{dC_b^2}\right)}{R^2\left(\dfrac{d^2V}{dC_a^2}\right) + \left(\dfrac{d^2V}{dC_b^2}\right)}, \quad (38)$$

which take the same signs as equations (21).

Finally, define the arguments that correspond to S, S_e, and S_f. As traders must convert foreign-currency borrowing into home currency:

$$S^x = C_{ab} - C_{ba}R. \quad (39)$$

As before, moreover:

$$S_e^x = E_a^x + E_b^x. \quad (40)$$

And equations (35) give:

$$S_f^x = [C_{ba}(1+r_{ba})R(1-\alpha_f) - C_{ab}(1+r_{ab})]$$
$$- [E_a^x(1-\alpha_f) + E_b^x] - [X_a(1-\alpha_f) - X_b], \quad (41)$$

adding a trade-balance term to the argument of S_f in equation (9). When one differentiates these three equations with respect to the expected discount on spot sterling, α_e, one obtains the same arguments as in equation (26) and can make the same case for forward-market intervention in the face of speculation. But these three equations respond rather differently to changes in the forward rate. To isolate this difference directly, examine the response of S^x, the excess supply of dollars on the spot market:

$$\frac{dS^x}{d\alpha_f} = \left[\left(\frac{dC_{ab}}{dX_b}\right)\left(\frac{dX_b}{d\alpha_f}\right) - R\left(\frac{dC_{ba}}{dX_a}\right)\left(\frac{dX_a}{d\alpha_f}\right)\right] - R\left[\frac{dC_{ba}}{d\alpha_f} + \frac{dC_{bb}}{d\alpha_f}\right]. \tag{42}$$

The second or "arbitrage" argument of equation (42) is the same as that of equation (28) defining $(dS/d\alpha_f)$. But the first or "trade" argument is rather different. One could, of course, banish the significant difference between the two "trade" terms by a mechanical substitution of $(dM_a/d\alpha_f)$ for $(dX_b/d\alpha_f)$, and $(dM_b/d\alpha_f)$ for $(dX_a/d\alpha_f)$.[30] The signs of $(dM_i/d\alpha_f)$, however, were obtained by making special assumptions in the importer-borrower case, and these assumptions cannot hold in the present case, as changes in the forward rate can no longer alter the importer's balance sheet.

Yet one can still attach the appropriate signs to $(dX_i/d\alpha_f)$. Equations (34) imply that an exporter can be regarded as "covering" all his commercial receipts and speculating, if at all, on the forward market. If this is true, however, he can be expected to use the forward rate when quoting the foreign-currency prices at which he makes his export sales. One can write:

$$X_a = (p_a q_a)(R/R_f), \quad \text{with} \quad q_a = f_a(p_a/R_f),$$
$$X_b = (p_b q_b) R_f, \quad \text{with} \quad q_b = f_b(p_b R_f), \tag{43}$$

where the q_i are the export quantities, the p_i are the (constant) export prices in the exporters' currencies, and the f_i define the demand for each country's exports as a function of the price paid by the importers. These equations yield:

$$\frac{dX_a}{d\alpha_f} = - X_a(\eta_a - 1)/(1 - \alpha_f),$$

$$\frac{dX_b}{d\alpha_f} = X_b(\eta_b - 1)/(1 - \alpha_f), \tag{44}$$

---

30   There would still be a difference between the two "trade" arguments, since the

where the η_i are the price elasticities of demand for imports defined in the usual way.[31] When, therefore, each country confronts an elastic demand for its exports, $(dX_a/d\alpha_f)$ must be negative and $(dX_b/d\alpha_f)$ positive. The "trade" term of equation (42) is consequently positive, aligning my two models in the most important way.[32]

VII Summary

The model of forward exchange operations with which you have just tangled is quite special and restrictive in several of its features. It assumes a symmetrical aversion to risk – to long and short positions in foreign exchange – and pretends that trader-speculators work with a "point estimate" of the future spot rate. But my model is more general than most of its predecessors, for it does not segregate the several components of the demand for forward exchange. It deals with a single firm involved in foreign trade and shows that such a firm will engage in "covering", "arbitrage", and "speculation" in the normal course of its credit operations.

My model can be made to yield many of the propositions stressed by other recent writers. It shows, for example, that all speculation can be treated as a combination of spot-market arbitrage in assets or debt coupled to open forward positions. It also reproduces the modern formulation of classic interest parity. The forward rate will not stand at "average interest parity" save in special circumstances, but will almost always stand

---

loan weights applied to the trade changes are different. But all the loan weights are positive (see equations [21] and [38]), so that the two "trade" arguments would both be positive.

[31] To be precise: $\eta_a = -f'_a [(p_a/R_f)/q_a]$, and $\eta_b = -f'_b [(p_b R_f) / q_b]$.

[32] Note, further, that a weaker restriction on η_a and η_b suffices to remove any new ambiguity as to $(dS_f^x/d\alpha_f)$: S_f^x differs from S_f by another "trade" term, $- [X_a (1 - \alpha_f) - X_b]$ in equation (41). Differentiating this new term with respect to α_f and using the arguments of equation (44):

$$\left[\left(\frac{dX_b}{d\alpha_f} \right) - \left(\frac{dX_a}{d\alpha_f} \right) (1 - \alpha_f) + X_a \right] = [X_b (\eta_b - 1) + X_a \eta_a (1 - \alpha_f)] / (1 - \alpha_f) ,$$

and the righthand side of this equation cannot be negative unless the elasticities are very low. If, in fact, $X_a = X_b$ to start, the righthand side cannot be negative unless $(1 - \eta_b) / \eta_a > (1 - \alpha_f)$, and this is impossible unless $\eta_b < 1$.

at "marginal parity", because this marginal condition is internal to the profit calculations of the individual borrower or investor. You have also encountered new results. First, this paper has explored the substantive implications of "two-way independence" between trade and speculation. When, as here, trade and speculation are conducted by one enterprise, the demand curve for forward foreign exchange may be backward sloping, and the forward market may be unstable. But my model also shows that "two-way independence" does not guarantee stability; one needs a more restrictive elasticities condition, much like the familiar Lerner-Robinson condition. And when one assumes market stability, one can dispense with "two-way independence", so as to study the several connections between trade and speculation.

Finally, this analysis supplies a strong presumptive case for official intervention to combat speculation. It shows how speculation will affect reserves, allowing for the cross-effects of trade and speculation, and how intervention will dispel these effects, preventing any change in official reserves. Intervention can prevent any "current" loss of reserves; when speculation has died down, moreover, the authorities can unwind their forward positions without any "deferred" loss of reserves. They can "match" their net positions with those of the speculators. The net profit or loss on counterspeculation depends entirely on the forward premium or discount at which the authorities stabilize the forward rate.

APPENDIX

Consider the bordered Hessian $|H|$ appearing in equation (18) of the text. For maximum L_i, it is necessary and sufficient that $(-1)^{(4-m)}|H_m| < 0$, where H_m is the $(4-m)$th order trailing principal minor of the Hessian obtained by deleting the first m rows and columns.[33] In consequence, $|H_1|$ must be positive, being of third order. Furthermore:

$$|H_1| = 2R\left(\frac{\partial^2 L}{\partial C_a \, \partial C_b}\right) - R^2\left(\frac{\partial^2 L}{\partial C_a^2}\right) - \frac{\partial^2 L}{\partial C_b^2}. \tag{A.1}$$

---

[33] See, *e.g.*, J. R. Hicks, *Value and Capital* (2nd edition; London: Oxford University Press, 1946), pp. 304-5.

And:

$$\frac{\partial^2 L}{\partial C_a^2} = \frac{\partial^2 U}{\partial V^2}\left(\frac{\mathrm{d}V}{\mathrm{d}C_a}\right)^2 + \frac{\partial U}{\partial V}\left(\frac{\mathrm{d}^2 V}{\mathrm{d}C_a^2}\right),$$

$$\frac{\partial^2 L}{\partial C_b^2} = \frac{\partial^2 U}{\partial V^2}\left(\frac{\mathrm{d}V}{\mathrm{d}C_b}\right)^2 + \frac{\partial U}{\partial V}\left(\frac{\mathrm{d}^2 V}{\mathrm{d}C_b^2}\right) = \frac{\partial^2 U}{\partial V^2}\left(\frac{\mathrm{d}V}{\mathrm{d}C_a}\right)^2 R^2 + \frac{\partial U}{\partial V}\left(\frac{\mathrm{d}^2 V}{\mathrm{d}C_b^2}\right),$$

$$\frac{\partial^2 L}{\partial C_a \partial C_b} = \frac{\partial^2 U}{\partial V^2}\left(\frac{\mathrm{d}V}{\mathrm{d}C_a}\right)\left(\frac{\mathrm{d}V}{\mathrm{d}C_b}\right) = \frac{\partial^2 U}{\partial V^2}\left(\frac{\mathrm{d}V}{\mathrm{d}C_a}\right)^2 R. \qquad (A.2)$$

So that:

$$|H_1| = -\left(\frac{\partial U}{\partial V}\right)\left[R^2\left(\frac{\mathrm{d}^2 V}{\mathrm{d}C_a^2}\right) + \left(\frac{\mathrm{d}^2 V}{\mathrm{d}C_b^2}\right)\right], \qquad (A.3)$$

where:

$$(\mathrm{d}^2 V/\mathrm{d}C_a^2) = -(2r'_{ai} + C_{ai} r''_{ai})/(1 - z_i\alpha_f) = -r'_{ai}(2 + \varepsilon_{ai})/(1 - z_i\alpha_f),$$

and:

$$(\mathrm{d}^2 V/\mathrm{d}C_b^2) = -\left[(2r'_{bi} + C_{bi} r''_{bi})(1 - \alpha_f)/(1 - z_i\alpha_f)\right] R^2$$
$$= -\left[r'_{bi}(2 + \varepsilon_{bi})(1 - \alpha_f)/(1 - z_i\alpha_f)\right] R^2.$$

For $|H_1| > 0$, $(\mathrm{d}^2 V/\mathrm{d}C_a^2)$ and $(\mathrm{d}^2 V/\mathrm{d}C_b^2)$ must be negative, so that ε_{ai} and ε_{bi} must each exceed -2. In effect, marginal borrowing cost must be an increasing function of current borrowing.

Maximum L_i also requires $|H| < 0$, being of fourth order. But:

$$|H| = \left(\frac{\partial^2 L}{\partial E^2}\right)|H_1| + \left[R\left(\frac{\partial^2 L}{\partial C_a \partial E}\right) - \left(\frac{\partial^2 L}{\partial C_b \partial E}\right)\right]^2, \qquad (A.4)$$

where:

$$\frac{\partial^2 L}{\partial C_a \partial E} = \left[\frac{\partial^2 U}{\partial V \partial E} + \frac{\partial^2 U}{\partial V^2}\left(\frac{\mathrm{d}V}{\mathrm{d}E}\right)\right]\left(\frac{\mathrm{d}V}{\mathrm{d}C_a}\right),$$

$$\frac{\partial^2 L}{\partial C_b \partial E} = \left[\frac{\partial^2 U}{\partial V \partial E} + \frac{\partial^2 U}{\partial V^2}\left(\frac{\mathrm{d}V}{\mathrm{d}E}\right)\right]\left(\frac{\mathrm{d}V}{\mathrm{d}C_b}\right) = \left(\frac{\partial^2 L}{\partial C_a \partial E}\right) R, \qquad (A.5)$$

so that the second argument of (A.4) vanishes completely, and:

$$|H| = \left(\frac{\partial^2 L}{\partial E^2}\right)|H_1|. \qquad (A.6)$$

Hence $(\partial^2 L/\partial E^2)$ must be negative if L_i is a maximum. This result has already been employed in the construction of Figure 1, as the increasing slope of the trader's indifference curves requires that:

$$\left(\frac{\partial^2 U}{\partial E^2}\right) + \phi\left(\frac{\partial^2 U}{\partial V \, \partial E}\right) + \phi\left[\left(\frac{\partial^2 U}{\partial V \, \partial E}\right) + \phi\left(\frac{\partial^2 U}{\partial V^2}\right)\right] < 0, \qquad \text{(A.7)}$$

where ϕ is the marginal rate of substitution between V_i and E_i. In equilibrium, however, $\phi = (dV/dE)$, and the argument of equation (A.7) is the formula for $(\partial^2 L/\partial E^2)$.

MONETARY STABILITY AS A PRECONDITION
FOR ECONOMIC INTEGRATION

Reinhard Kamitz

From the very beginning of history, man's economic life has centered on the problem of scarcity of goods. But an abundant world is no longer a dream: it is fully within the grasp of mankind. We have developed powerful technologies that reduce the amount of human effort necessary to produce the goods required for a prosperous life, while the system of free enterprise has proven its ability to use the tools of production to achieve sustained and rapid growth. And the end of these capabilities for further growth is not yet in sight.

We now stand at the threshold of a new era of economic development. We have completed one period of economic development – the period from the end of World War II to the end of 1962. During that era, the main problem was the reconstruction of those national economies that had been devastated or disorganized during the war. It was also necessary to adopt a policy of full employment in order to avoid unemployment and crises, and to pursue policies of ensuring continuous growth. We are entering a new period of economic growth, a period based on the increase of productivity through the economic integration of national economies. The increase in international trade brought about by the liberalization of trade policies in the postwar period has been remarkable, but integration may have still more spectacular consequences for economic growth and standards of living.

The achievement of these advantages of integration, however, depends on the fulfilment of certain preconditions relating to the policies of national governments. In particular, as I argue in this paper, it requires the pursuit of policies of monetary stability. Such policies have been neglected in the recent past, when governments have allowed inflation and the depreciation of the real value of their currencies to result from their pursuit of full employment and economic growth. I begin with some general remarks on the meaning of economic integration and the policies required to make it effective. I then discuss the two factors which in my judgment have been responsible for the postwar propensity to inflation: the practice of deficit budgeting and the magnitude of the budget in relation to the total of economic activity. Finally, I describe the distortions of prices, wages, and allocation of economic resources that may occur under economic integration as a result of monetary instability, and suggest that monetary stability deserves more attention within the context of integration policies than it has so far received.

I The meaning of economic integration

It is characteristic of our time that the meaning of the term "integration", the importance of which is so obvious to everybody, is rarely understood and arouses little interest. The attempt has been made to trace the meaning of the word in Latin, but that does not provide a satisfactory guide to its economic meaning, which is, after all, what matters. At best, it is regarded as a new kind of economic cooperation between individual countries. It is, however, widely understood to be something resulting in an increase in the volume of foreign trade. Thus, positive results in the form of increased foreign trade are regarded as evidence of integration and of the success of the measures taken to effect it.

The meaning and definition of a term depend essentially on the purpose for which it is required, and it might conceivably be useful to define the concept of integration simply as a rise in foreign trade. I do not believe, however, that such a definition would be useful. What was really the reason for embarking upon economic integration, and what results were expected from it? It goes without saying that the general assumption was that the integration of the free world would bring about an important expansion of its economic potential. That assumption, indeed, anticipates part of what I believe to be a useful definition of the term. In fact, my definition presupposes developments associated with an increase in productivity in the participating countries.

Such an increase in productivity cannot, however, be expected from a mere expansion of the volume of foreign trade. For any national economy, the volume of foreign trade can be expanded either by reducing domestic consumption of a particular exportable product, or by utilizing means of production formerly idle for the manufacture of this product. In either case, productivity remains basically the same, although foreign trade has expanded. The expansion of trade, moreover, must end as soon as all means of production are fully utilized or home consumption cannot be further restricted.

Obviously, economic integration, and the acceptance of the difficulties inherent in achieving it, must have a wider objective than this. *The crux of the problem is to extend the principle of international division of labor;* this principle has been almost completely disregarded since World War I.

The principle of international division of labor, developed and later improved by classical economic theory, demonstrates that it is expedient for all countries to employ their means of production (land, labor, and capital) in the production of those goods and services relatively best suited or least unsuited to local conditions. *Economic integration, as I understand it, is the intensified application of the principle of international division of labor.*

The nature of this process may be illustrated by a specific example. It may happen in the course of the process of integration that one country, where conditions are specially advantageous for the production of paper, will produce far more paper than before, whereas its motor vehicle industry may cease to exist, this line of manufacturing being concentrated in those countries where conditions for it are more appropriate. It is only by such a process of reshaping existing conditions of manufacture that a genuine and significant increase in productivity and total output can be achieved.

It goes without saying that such a process involves many difficulties. It is not merely a question of increasing production or exports above previous levels, as in the case of expanded foreign trade discussed earlier; instead, it may well become necessary to substitute an entirely new type of production for some former line of manufacture – in other words, to make structural changes in the economy. Such structural changes will likely entail a painful process of adjustment to the new circumstances, and they will naturally be opposed by all those who are directly and adversely affected. This fact explains why economic integration, even within an organization such as the Common Market, will not come about as rapidly as some of its proponents expect.

Nevertheless, the conditions for undertaking such a process of structural change have never before been as favorable as they are at present. The reasons are to be found in the fact that governments have assumed responsibility for the maintenance of full employment and economic growth. *An economic policy which has fully accepted the principles of full employment and economic growth, and only such a policy, can and will reduce the transitional losses and difficulties to a minimum.*

In order to give practical effect to the concept of economic integration, it is not sufficient to create conditions that will allow foreign trade to be carried on with as little restriction as possible. If the structural changes required to maximize productivity are to be thoroughly executed in all participating countries, freedom of movement must be assured in other spheres of economic activity as well. I am referring principally to the international movement of capital. Without freedom in this field, there can be no possibility of equalizing the returns to capital on an international level, of accelerating the development of countries that are short of saving, or of advancing the process of division of labor and the exploitation of economies of scale. Similarly, achievement of the full benefits of economic integration requires freedom of movement of labor, and especially the freedom to establish industries abroad, as well as a host of other economic liberties.

I should emphasize that this approach has nothing to do with old-fashioned liberalism. *Appreciation of the benefits of efficient production is not a question of ideology.* The question is simply whether or not we are prepared to acknowledge the fact that conditions for the manufacture of goods differ, and that the best results will be obtained by selecting and exploiting the most favorable conditions.

Understanding of this principle is the motivation, and implementation of it the supreme objective, of the movement toward economic integration. It may be that this ideal cannot be fully realized. National or noneconomic considerations may frustrate its attainment. The more the policy is diluted, the less successful it will be, and the more rigorously it is followed, the greater will be the results.

A new period has commenced and a new course has been embarked upon in order to increase productivity and production; the prospect of a new and mighty growth of economic wealth has been opened up. I call it a new period because it promises new and great development. I do not argue that it calls for a new set of economic policies; on the contrary, I believe that the proved methods of economic policy should be continued and if possible developed further. I would suggest, however, that in this new period, at the threshold of which we now stand, certain policies of the past will have to be reconsidered. Specifically, I argue the necessity of reconsidering policy with respect to monetary stability, and in particular of adopting a less uninhibited attitude toward inflation than has been characteristic of the postwar period. I am not, however, concerned with the question of what system of international monetary organization is most appropriate to an integrated world economy.

II   The sources of inflation: deficit spending

Since the end of World War II, a softening of the currencies of the various countries – a loss of real purchasing power due to inflation – has generally accompanied economic development. There has been no exception to this rule, although there have been national differences of degree in rates of depreciation of money relative to commodities. In view of this indisputable fact, it has been widely asserted that depreciation of the real value of the currency is the inevitable price of a policy of full employment. Personally, I am not of this opinion, but I do not propose to dispute the proposition here.

The boom in the countries of the free world developed during the first years after 1945 under especially favorable conditions with respect to unused capacities and unemployed labor. Sufficient means of production existed which could be put to use with the aid of financial resources created by budgetary deficits or by outside support in the form of gifts. The increase in money in circulation led directly to an increase in the quantity of goods produced. As the supplies of money and of goods rose at approximately the same rate, prices at first changed only marginally; the situation altered radically, however, when the exploitation of existing capacities and means of production came close to its optimum. The application of new methods of production as well as a more intensive use of capital in industry brought a sharp rise in productivity. This rise in productivity also brought about a corresponding rise in wages.

The increase in productivity, however, was not universal; indeed, any such uniformity would have been a quite unnatural process. There are many sectors which still provide opportunities for considerable rises in productivity; on the other hand, there are others where further rises will be very limited indeed. The scale ranges from industry at one end to the service trades at the other. Between these two extremes, we may observe varying degrees of possible development.

Furthermore, a new fact has recently emerged, the importance of which had not hitherto been apparent, a fact which will have to be taken into account in the future: in the modern economy, wage increases are no longer solely determined by increases in marginal productivity of labor in particular employments, but are governed by other influences as well. *The general wage structure presents, indeed, every appearance of rigidity and immobility.* The interrelation between the wage levels of workers in various industries has apparently come to be considered as immutable.

If, in any one branch of industry, wages rise with rising productivity, other groups of labor will demand that the former differential between their wages and the increased wages be restored, even if the rise in productivity, if any, in their particular branch of industry has not been as large. In these sectors of the economy, we will then have wage increases exceeding the increase in the marginal productivity of labor. The costs of the wage increase therefore no longer are covered by the price of the product and will have to be passed on to the consumer in the form of higher prices. The lower the rate of growth of productivity in these industries, the greater will be the effect of wage rises on the prices of the goods concerned. This circumstance is especially obvious in the case of workers in the service trades, for many of whom, as in the case of waiters or hairdressers, an increase in productivity is hard to imagine.

The policy of full employment thus does not in itself produce cost and price increases; these result mainly from the rigidity of wage structures. This development is quite apparent in the United States, where the trend of wages in industry has been very nearly matched by the increase in productivity. Increased costs in the service trades, on the other hand, have led to general increases in prices.

The tendency to maintain the over-all wage structure and the declining influence of the marginal productivity of labor on the wage level have introduced a dynamic factor into economic development. As increases in productivity and rises in wages always occur in some sector or another, adjustments of wages in the other sectors of the economy will constantly occur, thus creating a dynamic upward pressure on costs and prices.

Nevertheless, it would certainly be erroneous to ascribe the resulting depreciation of the purchasing power of the currency to this circumstance alone. It must be borne in mind that in any economy prices and wages can develop only within the limits set by the volume and the velocity of money in circulation. Even the strongest pressure on the wage level could not be effective in securing more than a limited increase in prices – and this at the cost of increased unemployment – if an adequate volume of money did not exist as a basis for wage demands. This aspect of the problem must therefore receive particular consideration when the depreciation of the purchasing power of the currency is discussed.

In my opinion, apart from the influence of credit policy, the causes of the creeping depreciation of currency may be found, above all, in two characteristics of modern economies: the practice of budgetary deficits and the enormous magnitudes of the budgets themselves.

The influence of budget deficits on economic development is uncontested and presents no particular problem. As long as these deficits are incurred in an economy without full employment, there is generally no reason to object to them from the point of view of monetary policy; in such cases, they even may contribute to a fuller employment of the means of production. In an economy with fully employed means of production, however, the extra purchasing power resulting from such deficits will necessarily cause price and wage increases. The extra demand will confront an unchanged supply of goods and services, with the additional demand necessarily resulting in higher prices and wages. In this case, the means of production will be redirected from one sector to another by higher prices, even though no increase in the national product is thereby effected.

Nowadays, the opinion is often voiced that even in an economy with full employment, budgetary deficits may be incurred if they can be met by legitimate financial methods, such as loans. This type of reasoning confuses financial methods with economic effects. From a financial point of view, it is certainly more acceptable to cover a deficit by long-term loans than by immediate recourse to the printing press; yet in principle, the effect on the national economy is the same. In either case, the administration spends more than it earns and appears thus as an additional buyer of goods and services.

The argument that in the case of long-term loans the funds raised by the state cannot be spent by anyone else misses the point. This argument maintains that the state will spend funds which, had they not been borrowed, would have been employed elsewhere in the economy, and that thus no additional purchasing power will be created.

Had they not been borrowed by the state, the funds in question would undoubtedly have been employed for long-term investments in accordance with the structure of the economy, the supply of capital, and the possibilities of employing it. Thus, the funds would have been used for modernizing industries and new profitable investments. Such a way of employing capital is, of course, never inflationary, as long as a noninflationary credit policy is pursued.

However, economic conditions may also be such that available funds are not absorbed for capital investment and thus simply raise the liquidity of the lending agencies. By claiming these funds, the state impedes a noninflationary employment of capital necessary for the long-term strengthening of the economy and uses them to create an immediate demand. Funds which would either not have been used at all, or would have been used to purchase machines or other means of production will, if they are absorbed by the state, be employed instead mainly for the payment of wages, and thereby for the purchase of consumer goods. Thus, an additional demand will be created, the effect of which will inevitably be inflationary.

I certainly do not wish to deny that there may be circumstances under which the situation is somewhat different: this may be the case particularly when a pessimistic view of future prospects has rendered private industry unwilling to use available capital for investments. In this case, utilization of these funds by the state will not cause nonutilization of funds for investment purposes, and the additional demand for public expenditure may possibly serve to compensate for the lack of demand in other sectors of the economy. As mentioned above, the situation may arise when unemployed means of production are available, and thus the use of public funds by way of a deficit may be justified.

On the other hand, the structure of the national economy may be such that the use of funds by the state would produce no greater rise of prices and wages than their employment in other sectors of the national economy: this would be the case where no long-term investment of funds in these other sectors had been intended. Such circumstances will obviously be rare, as economic development normally carries with it a sustained propensity to invest.

Under present conditions (that is, with an economic policy aiming at full employment), this propensity to invest is most certain to prevail strongly in all sectors of national economies; the results of the use of almost any funds by the state will therefore be inflationary.

*III   The sources of inflation: the magnitude of the budget and its influence
on prices and wages*

The effects of deficit spending on the purchasing power of the currency
have been the subject of detailed investigation and have always ranked
prominently in monetary theories and financial policy; on the other hand,
the implications of the magnitude of the budget for the development of
prices and wages have hitherto received hardly any attention at all. Since
the end of World War II, owing to the need to provide for reconstruction
and social exigencies in European countries as well as increasing arma-
ment expenditures, government budgets in the free world have claimed
a growing portion of the national product. This development has not yet
come to an end; to an increasing extent the development of the national
product is directly or indirectly influenced by the state.

This growing claim of the state on the national product influences
prices in two ways: on the one hand, the lack of flexibility of public
expenditure exerts a direct influence; on the other, the reduced possibility
of countering expansive tendencies by using credit policy represents an
indirect influence.

Let us first consider the lack of flexibility. In an economy based on
private ownership which follows the rules of the market and in which the
economic forces are generally permitted to work without interference,
any development away from monetary equilibrium will in itself produce
counterforces which sooner or later restore the economic balance. Even
in the event of an investment boom or the appearance of a so-called
Wicksellian process, the shortage of consumer goods will activate forces
which sooner or later will restore the disturbed balance. This reaction
will take place everywhere in the economy; obviously, though, it will
only develop fully if it is not frustrated, and, above all, if the economy
is flexible enough to adjust to these forces. In any such free economy,
those responsible for the currency will be able to accelerate this development by appropriate measures of budgetary and monetary policy.

However, the part of the economy which is controlled or decisively
influenced by the budget is almost totally devoid of such flexibility. Expenditure decided upon by the administration will be effected, unless
extremely spectacular and dramatic developments render them inadvis-
able. Indeed, it is characteristic of public expenditures that they will most
probably be greater than originally intended. Therefore, they are flexible

in one direction only, *i.e.*, upwards. The part of the economy financed by this type of expenditure can thus not be influenced by the effects of internal economic balancing forces. It is resistant to any restrictions and ensures implementation of the scheduled expenditures, regardless of any opposing force otherwise effective. In fact, the influence of the tendency toward increasing government expenditures is often much stronger than these counteracting forces. The elimination of the counteracting forces which would prevent any excessive expansion means the abolition of an automatic process for the correction of any imbalance in the economy; thus, the creation of new factors favoring continued expansion is facilitated. In the part of the economy influenced by the public sector, one type of development only, *i.e.*, expansion, exists. The larger this sector, the stronger will be the pressure exerted toward uncontrolled expansion.

It goes without saying that the consolidating counterforces effective in other sectors will not be felt in those parts of the economy dependent upon government orders. Thus, the sphere of influence of the stabilizing forces is often too small for these forces to be significant. These forces may be rendered completely ineffective by additional measures of financial and monetary policy introduced because it is considered disturbing to the over-all picture of an expanding economy if some parts are subject to an unfavorable development.

This brings us to the second manner in which excessive participation of the public sector in the national product influences the economy: the reduced capability of those responsible for monetary policy to check an excessive expansion.

Of course, money is put into circulation by the central banks, and it is in their power to restrict the amount in circulation, thereby creating a shortage of money. Similarly, credit policy may be decisively influenced by manipulations of the bank rate and of minimum reserves, and by open market operations. All this is true, but in practice and under the prevailing circumstances, it can no longer be said that the central banks are in a position to exercise a decisive influence on monetary policy.

As mentioned earlier, expenditure in the public sector has risen enormously, and plans once made tend to be implemented regardless of changes in economic circumstances. If the central banks take steps to neutralize a trend of excessive expansion, the result may be that the entire economy will be equally affected, and many provisions of the budget will not be carried out for lack of funds. Or else – and this is much more likely – the public sector will evade any credit restrictions decreed simply by satisfying its requirements by borrowing from the banking system; thus, only the private sector will be affected by the measures of the central bank. However, in my opinion, it is extremely difficult, if not impossible, to restrict one part of an economy sufficiently to compensate for the absence of economic control in another field, in this case in the public sector. But even if this were possible, the private sector would then gradually be choked by the measures of the central bank, whereas the public sector would continue to grow. Any further growth of the public sector would, however, be accompanied by the consequences mentioned above, namely, a dynamic expansion resulting in ever diminishing possibilities for the central banks to stabilize the situation.

Thus, a new phenomenon becomes apparent, that, *under certain conditions,* even a balanced budget cannot prevent a softening of the currency if the volume of the budget is so swollen that the normal economic counterforces become ineffective. This seems to verify the argument of those who maintain that the influence of budgets on monetary stability is a thing of the past, and that the reasons for depreciation of the real value of the currency have to be looked for elsewhere. Apart from political explanations, I have never been able to uncover any actual clue as to where these reasons could really be found.

I hope I have made it clear that the constantly growing participation of the state in the national product presents one of the greatest dangers for economic development in the free world. Similarly, a constantly diminishing capacity to secure monetary stability may finally result in an economic system which is unsuited to the free world. I should think that this aspect deserves increased attention.

This is not the place to discuss the moral effects of inflation. Nevertheless, the economic effects of a general attitude of mind geared to the expectation of constant depreciation of the purchasing power of the currency should not be underestimated.

Quite apart from the fact that a reduction of tax burdens, often excessively heavy in the countries of the free world, would result in a rise in the actual amounts received by the exchequers, a free economic system also requires a certain degree of flexibility. High burdens of taxation nullify flexibility. All those responsible should, therefore, gradually try to reduce the state's participation in the national product. I admit that this is a long-term policy, but it will have to be adopted if we are interested in the continued existence of the free world and an economic system suited to its ideals.

IV Distortions of prices and wages by monetary instability

Hitherto, the increasing share of the state in the national product, the softening of currencies, and occasional enthusiasm for ideas of economic direction by the state have all been tolerated because people have been mesmerized by the manifest success of the economic policy pursued with regard to full employment and economic expansion. It is certainly difficult to achieve everything at once, and it is beyond doubt that the results of the policy will be remembered as a most remarkable achievement in the history of economic development.

However, as we have seen, we are now on the threshold of new developments. Economic integration is to provide a new and powerful stimulus to productivity and production. This is the common goal of all who advocate integration and thereby expect to secure an increase in the wealth of all concerned. In view of these new tasks, will it be possible to assume the same attitude as hitherto with regard to the depreciation of the real values of currencies, or will it be necessary to deal much more rigorously with this problem?

I firmly believe that more rigorous action is necessary, and I shall try to present detailed reasons for this attitude. Indeed, I believe that a successful policy of integration will only be possible if the maximum degree of monetary stability is achieved.

Up to now, the softening of currencies apparently has not interfered with the achievement of the main objectives of economic policy. Many renowned economic scientists and businessmen agree that a decline in the real value of the currency is either the price to be paid for the success of this policy or is essential for the attainment of its goals. Criticisms directed at the long-term detrimental effects on capital formation, the uncertainties created for industrialists, the effect on economic discipline and the confidence of the population in a reliable monetary policy, and many other factors, may have caused misgivings when the problem was discussed over a drink; in practice, however, such criticisms have been ignored.

I do not want to discuss the merits of this attitude; I only want to point out that the disadvantages of depreciation of the currency have been tolerated when balanced against the importance of the objectives and the success of economic policy. What I am asking here is whether, in this new era on whose threshold we now stand, this approach is still acceptable, or whether neglect of the problems of monetary instability may not deprive us of the fruits of integration to which we are looking forward so impatiently. At this point, I should like to refer back to my previous remarks describing the process of integration as an intensified realization of the principle of international division of labor, in which I argued that this process, although it may cause a temporarily painful structural change, will yield the expected results of increased productivity, production, and wealth when it has been successfully completed.

It must be remembered that the international policy of liberalization, affecting the flow of goods as well as that of money and capital, has removed some of the economic barriers between nations that existed before the application of the policy of liberalization. We shall now have to clear the board of everything which, introduced during a hundred years of striving for self-sufficiency, has led to a less efficient use of the means of production. These evils will be eliminated by opening up frontiers and also by gradually removing tariff walls and other obstacles. New, large economic areas will come into being in which a redistribution of the means of production will have to be effected according to their greatest usefulness.

However, this redistribution will not come about in the countries of the free world through the dictates of a planning authority, but will be carried out by private industry, which, competing for capital and labor, will automatically direct the means of production into the most profitable channels. In order to allow such a development to proceed successfully, it is important that currency relations between the countries concerned should correspond to the purchasing-power parities – with all the due limitations that that theory may impose. Only if such relations exist can we assume that the redistribution of the means of production will come about in the right way and be related to the new conditions of profitability.

Let us assume that in one of the countries concerned, a financial policy is pursued which results in considerable economic expansion but carries with it rising prices and wages. According to the present system of agreed rates of exchange, as decided within the framework of the International Monetary Fund, this would result in a gradually increasing deficit in the balance of payments; assistance would possibly be rendered by the International Monetary Fund; and, in the course of time – if the necessary measures had been taken – the result would be a new equilibrium. However, this period of adjustment might extend over several years, due to the conditions already described. During this time, distortions will exist in the relation of costs and profits between this country and other countries. This is mainly the case because an inflationary process does not result in a uniform rise of all prices, but rather in a significantly sharper rise in the prices of the means of production. Such a change in price structure has been analyzed by modern scientific methods, but its principal characteristic is the differentiation of price changes in different sectors. These distortions will prevent the attainment of the economic optimum, because economic decisions will be taken on the basis of wages and prices not corresponding to normal production relations.

Nor will the pursuit of similar inflationary policies by a number of countries prevent the emergence of distortions of the price-wage relationship: the economic development of the free world since 1945 shows considerable variation in the rates of inflation in individual countries, so that in practice we cannot assume a uniform international development of the price-wage relationship.

Those inflationary tendencies which alter the relation between prices and costs should, of course, be clearly distinguished from price fluctuations of the normal kind that occur constantly. I am thinking here of fluctuations in the prices of certain raw materials and supplies dependent on the world market, and also of certain seasonal and cyclical price changes. All these factors are taken into account by the industrialist, apart from his production risks, when he sets out to make his investment plans. It is obvious that he has to run risks. Every industrialist has to be prepared for changes in the market and must always bear in mind that the basis of his calculations may shift. However, these considerations apply more or less to the same extent to similar enterprises in all the countries concerned.

When any given country develops an inflationary boom due to increased activity in the field of capital goods, more advantageous opportunities for investment than would have existed otherwise will apparently present themselves. But for this distortion, investments would probably have been made in other countries and to better advantage. Thus, the distortion of the price structure in a country that shows lack of discipline in its financial policy affects comparative costs and profits. Investments become profitable that would otherwise not have been so.

Undoubtedly, the process of integration which we are now facing will not involve any tremendous differences in the development of costs and profits, and it is likely that these differences will be confined within comparatively narrow limits. If, however, changes in the purchasing powers of currencies cause a constant shifting of the standards on which comparisons of prices and costs are based, the enormous difficulties facing integration – even from a purely mathematical point of view – can be imagined.

I have initially mentioned only purely mathematical considerations. In practice, however, there is still another factor that must be taken into account: the expectations of the industrialists. Industrialists base their expectations on their experience in the past and their evaluation of the future. Should industrialists conclude that, as a result of constant fluctuations in the real values of currencies, redeployment will either become impossible or insufficiently profitable, this attitude could prove to be an even greater handicap to the process of integration than the difficulties of economic calculation by themselves.

The more currency softens, the greater will be the deviation from the basis chosen for the purpose of comparison, the smaller the differences in the results of the calculations of costs and profits, and the weaker the incentive to industrialists to embark upon new developments.

This argument must, of course, be taken with a grain of salt. Within moderate limits, a fluctuation of the basic standard will not form an inordinate obstacle to the process of integration. Besides mere considerations of profitability, there are, moreover, from the viewpoint of business, other factors involved in the process of integration which may cause a change in the production concerned. Life is much too varied to be pressed into a simple mold, and it is surely impossible to present a particular set of related factors as the only valid ones, however clearcut the relation may be. *But it seems important to me to show that monetary stability, with its great importance for any economic development, deserves more attention within the context of integration policies.* As I have argued, the greater the currency discipline, the greater also the likely success of integration. Monetary policy has gained a new significance in connection with integration. Its task will be to pursue the goal of monetary stability and thus establish those conditions most favorable for the achievement of the goals of economic integration.

ADJUSTMENT, COMPENSATORY CORRECTION, AND FINANCING OF IMBALANCES IN INTERNATIONAL PAYMENTS

Fritz Machlup

The theory of the adjustment of the balance of payments is nearly 250 years old, if we consider Isaac Gervaise (1720) as its first successful expositor; and well over 200 years, if we credit David Hume (1752) with this feat. Improved by Smith (1776), Thornton (1802), Ricardo (1812), and John Stuart Mill (1849), to mention only the major architects of the classical design, and renovated by Taussig (1927), Haberler (1933), Viner (1937), and Meade (1951), to cite some of the chief builders of the neoclassical style, the theory is still being remodeled.

Continual remodeling is unavoidable, partly because of changes in general economic theory, which require the replacement of obsolete concepts by others consistent with the currently adopted analytical system, and partly because of changes in economic institutions, which call for adaptations taking account of relevant facts of modern life. In the last few years, so many refinements of analysis have been incorporated into international-adjustment theory that the accounts of Viner and Haberler, the standard expositions until very recently, now seem old-fashioned. This can be appreciated by comparing them with the most up-to-date exposition, contained in the "Report of the Group of 32" – which, incidentally, had the benefit of the active participation of Haberler as one of the thirty-two members.[1]

Yet, we have not achieved a truly satisfactory exposition. We have not even reached a common understanding of the two fundamental concepts of the theory: "adjustment" and "financing" of an imbalance of international payments. In an attempt to clarify the essential relationships

---

[1] *International Monetary Arrangements: The Problem of Choice. Report on the Deliberations of an International Study Group of 32 Economists* (Princeton: International Finance Section, Princeton University, 1964), pp. 25-28, 43-53.

between these two concepts, I have found that a third concept is needed
for the analysis of certain developments and policies which may *correct* an
imbalance of payments but cannot be regarded as *adjustment* in the
classical sense nor as *financing* in any sense. The third concept, for which
I propose the designation "compensatory corrections", is introduced only
at a later part of this essay. At first, I discuss various policy issues and
theoretical considerations concerning the "proper" roles of adjustment
and financing, using these two terms only. I do not commit myself on
whether the policy issues are selected to illuminate the conceptual
problems or whether the conceptual dissection is designed to assist in the
understanding of the policy issues.

I   Misunderstandings, confusions, obscurities

Is the conceptual clarification and delineation really necessary? Granted
that some writers claim that certain occurrences – say, movements of
private short-term capital, induced by international interest-rate differentials – are part of adjustment, whereas others regard them as financing,
is it worth while adjudicating such a conflict in the use of words? Does it
really matter?

In economic analysis, it often makes no difference which things are
called what, especially if the analysis is internally consistent and if one
knows what the speaker or writer is talking about. There are instances,
however, where more is involved than differences in the use of language,
calling for simultaneous or subsequent translation. Theoretical analysis
may be seriously hampered where semantic inconsistencies reflect conceptual confusion. Differences in policy recommendations may remain
hidden behind unnoticed equivocations; or, conversely, mutually compatible or even identical positions may appear contradictory because of
different connotations being attached to the same terms.

Rarely have people bothered to ask, for example, whether "adjustment"
is meant to refer to a *process* or to a *state* of affairs. Those who insist on
operational definitions, and must therefore look for statistical indi-
cations, are constrained to focus on empirical observations of "states" –
say, the state of foreign reserves or of certain accounts in the balance of
international transactions – rather than on processes, which are essentially
theoretical abstractions. The confusion between a state of adjustment and

a process of adjustment frequently leads to misunderstandings in discussions of policy, as, for example, on the question whether "prompt" adjustment ought to be sought. Many *oppose* prompt adjustment, thinking that it refers to an *achieved state* of adjustment; others *favor* prompt adjustment, thinking of the *initiation of the process,* a process which may be quite gradual and slow. There is, of course, no contradiction between a demand to *begin* the process promptly and a warning against trying to rush it toward a prompt *conclusion.*

There is, on the other hand, a genuine contradiction between two groups of persons who think that they are in full agreement when they all insist on the need for "adjustment"; yet, for one group, adjustment has a definite connotation of changing cost-price relations between surplus and deficit countries, associated with reallocations of productive resources in all countries concerned; while, for the other group, adjustment comprises many alternatives to changes in relative costs and prices, including certain adaptations in movements of capital, short-term as well as long. The former meaning is expressed, for example, in the report of the thirty-two economists, which stresses "a fall in money incomes, wage rates, costs, and prices in the deficit countries relative to those in the surplus countries", brought about by changes either in exchange rates or "in the absolute levels of money incomes, wage rates, costs, and prices".[2] The second meaning is expressed in the official report of the Group of Ten (Annex Prepared by the Deputies), which presents in the section on "The Importance of International Balance and the Process of Adjustment", a list of "instruments" including "measures relating to international capital transactions", "commercial policies", and "selective policies directed to particular sectors of the economy", but omits exchange-rate adjustments.[3]

Some writers – including the present one – attempt to make fine analytical distinctions by resorting to a discriminating use of terms. They let "balance" and "imbalance" stand for *concrete,* observable situations (regarding the foreign-exchange market, the foreign reserves held by the monetary authorities, and the statistics of international transactions); and they reserve "equilibrium" and "disequilibrium" for purely analytical

---

[2] *Ibid.,* p. 25. The report proceeds, however, to list "alternatives" which are also regarded as "adjustment policies". See p. 28.

[3] *Ministerial Statement of the Group of Ten and Annex Prepared by Deputies* (August 10, 1964). The ten nations in question are those participating in the General Arrangements to Borrow of the International Monetary Fund.

purposes, with the terms relating to purely *abstract* models containing a specified set of variables, some of unknown magnitude. Other writers, innocently or maliciously, spoil this ritual by using the two pairs of terms interchangeably. The meaning of the term "adjustment" is then quite uncertain: it may mean either restoring "balance" or restoring "equilibrium". But if the sophisticated (or are they merely pedantic?) complain about the disregard of the difference which they want to be recognized, they themselves have not made it clear what they want "adjustment" to denote: full *equilibration* (of all variables relevant in their theoretical system) or just getting back into *balance* (concerning a few observable items)? If they are consistent, they ought to insist that adjustment involves full equilibration – but this has no definite meaning as long as the set of variables that must become mutually consistent remains unspecified.

II   An awkward definition of adjustment

Not to define a term is bad enough, but to define it badly may be worse. A definition is "bad" if it deviates too drastically from the meaning that most experts on the subject have been attaching to the term in question, or if it does not express the meaning in which the definer himself uses the term in his discourse. The latter evidently happened when several economists defined adjustment as "the process by which surpluses and deficits in international payments are eliminated".

The definers were probably thinking of the classical process or mechanism, which comprises for surplus (deficit) countries the following steps: inflow (outflow) of foreign reserves; increase (decrease) in domestic availability of credit; increase (decrease) in effective demand; increase (reduction) of prices and costs relative to those abroad; reduced (increased) allocation of resources to the production of goods for export and goods competing with imports; decrease (increase) in proceeds of foreign exchange from exports, and increase (decrease) in demand for foreign exchange to pay for imports; as a result, the movement of foreign reserves is stopped or reversed. This sequence is completely covered by the proposed definition of adjustment.

Many economists, however, like to think also of an alternative and equally long sequence of events, which starts with a variation of foreign-exchange rates and to which they also refer as "adjustment process". Yet, in the absence of induced movements of private short-term capital, no deficits or surpluses can ever develop in a system of perfectly flexible exchange rates. The exchange rates would at any moment of time make the amounts of foreign exchange demanded equal to the amounts supplied. The sequence comprises the following steps: reduction (increase) in the prices of foreign currencies; reduction (increase) in the domestic prices of imports and in the domestic proceeds from exports; reduced (increased) allocation of resources to the production of goods for export and goods competing with imports; decrease (increase) in proceeds of foreign exchange from exports, and increase (decrease) in demand for foreign exchange to pay for imports; as a result, the movement of foreign-exchange rates is stopped or reversed. Now, this sequence of events is not covered by a definition of adjustment in which the criterion is the "elimination of surpluses or deficits". In this sequence, there are only *potential* surpluses or deficits; they never become a reality.

It stands to reason that many economists want the term "adjustment" to apply to both sequences. To be sure, the two sequences need not end up with exactly the same allocation of resources and the same composition of foreign trade; for, in the sequence that starts with foreign-reserve movements, there are likely to be changes in interest rates which have no part in the sequence that starts with foreign-exchange-rate movements. With this exception, the outcome of both sequences – the commodity terms of trade, the volume of trade, and all the rest – may be quite similar. Is it then not a bit thoughtless to choose a definition of adjustment that embraces the whole of one sequence but excludes the other? Incidentally, if exchange rates are not perfectly flexible but are "adjusted" by deliberate measures, then most economists explicitly refer to this as a method of adjusting an imbalance. Yet, if at the adjusted rate the imbalance is completely corrected, a number of the subsequent steps in the sequence described would again, under the proposed definition, be left outside the adjustment process. I conclude that the definition ought to be amended.

III A political bill of fare

Let us forget the unintended exclusions under the half-baked definition, and attempt instead an enumeration of the measures, policies, or mechanisms that have been recommended under the heading of "adjustment".

Fritz Machlup

Table 1

Comparative monetary expansion in the United States, France, and Western Germany, 1957-63

A. In billions of domestic currency units, end of year.

	Money			Money plus quasi-money			Domestic assets of central bank		
	U.S.	France	Germany	U.S.	France	Germany	U.S.	France	Germany
1957	138.0	71.4	35.1	194.3	75.4	72.1	29.2	36.1	8.6
1958	143.9	75.7	39.7	207.2	80.2	83.4	31.1	38.6	7.5
1959	144.0	83.9	44.4	210.0	90.2	97.0	32.5	30.3	9.3
1960	143.4	95.8	47.4	215.0	104.8	107.8	33.7	31.7	7.6
1961	149.3	110.6	54.4	229.5	122.3	121.7	36.0	31.4	11.3
1962	150.6	130.7	58.0	247.5	144.6	134.6	39.2	34.1	14.2
1963	155.3	149.8	62.2	266.2	164.3	150.8	42.3	36.6	14.2

B. Index numbers (1958 = 100) for average of year[a].

	Wages			Wholesale prices			Cost of living		
	U.S.	France	Germany	U.S.	France[b]	Germany[c]	U.S.	France	Germany
1957	97	90	94	99	90	100	97	87	98
1958	100	100	100	100	100	100	100	100	100
1959	104	107	105	100	105	99	101	106	101
1960	107	115	115	100	107	100	102	110	102
1961	110	126	127	100	110	102	103	114	105
1962	113	137	142	100	113	103	105	119	109
1963	117	149	152	100	116	104	106	125	112

SOURCE   International Monetary Fund, *International Financial Statistics, Supplement to 1964-65 Issues.*

a   For the purpose of international comparisons, index numbers of domestic wage rates and prices should be adjusted whenever the exchange rates of the currencies in question are changed. The French franc was devalued in 1958; perhaps we may simply disregard the French index figures for 1957. The German mark was upvalued in 1961; to correct for this, 5 per cent could be added to the German index figures for 1961 and the later years.

b   Home and import goods.

c   Industrial prices only.

These recommendations have been directed both at countries in deficit and at countries in surplus. But there has been an increasing tendency to place more of the responsibility for adjustment upon the surplus countries. It used to be the standard prescription for deficit countries that they contract the volume of bank credit and allow money incomes, earning rates, and prices to decline. This is no longer so, since "deficit countries cannot be expected to create unemployment and deflate their price levels".[4] But the call for a fairer "sharing of the burden of adjustment" need not imply that the surplus countries are called upon to create over-employment and inflate their price levels. For there are some other things they can do to facilitate the restoration of balance: for example, they may reduce their import barriers and increase their long-term capital exports. In any case, the demand, voiced chiefly by public and private authorities of deficit countries, is to the effect that "the surplus countries must play a larger role in the adjustment process".[5]

These exhortations are of course the reverse side of complaints that "the surplus countries are not adequately meeting their responsibilities in the adjustment process".[6] If one were thinking of monetary expansion and contraction, or inflation and deflation, as the essential mechanism of adjustment, the complaints would be untenable. For there has been no absolute reduction in the supply of money, in the central-bank holdings of domestic assets, in wage rates, or in the price level of the largest deficit country, the United States. On the other hand, in the largest surplus countries, France and Western Germany, most of these indices of expansion have shown conspicuous increases. Table 1 presents the relevant data supporting these statements. Since the statistical facts were known to all those who complained about the failure of the surplus countries to do their share in the adjustment process, the complainants evidently must have meant other things than the essentials of the "classical mechanism".

Our list of "policies and measures prescribed for correcting the balance of payments of deficit countries and of surplus countries" (Table 2) is for the most part authentic in the sense that recent publications could be cited

[4] Arthur Smithies, "The Balance of Payments and Classical Medicine", *Review of Economics and Statistics*, XLVI (May, 1964), 113.

[5] Joint Economic Committee, Congress of the United States, 88th Cong., 2nd Sess., *The United States Balance of Payments* (Washington, D.C.: Government Printing Office, 1964), p. 10.

[6] *Ibid.*

as sources. A few items, however, chiefly the "old-fashioned" remedies of the deflationary type, have had little support in recent years. As a rule, each prescription for deficit countries is the exact opposite of one for surplus countries; but there are exceptions, especially in the group of price and income policies, largely because of the asymmetrical side-effects of, and consequent attitudes toward, expansion and contraction. A few items in the list may call for explanation and elaboration, but considerations of space suggest that this not be undertaken here. (By the way, readers who do not share the author's fondness for tabulations are invited to skip the list.)

Table 2

Policies and measures prescribed for correcting the balance of payments

	Deficit countries (D)	Surplus countries (S)
Domestic monetary policy	1. Stop increasing domestic bank assets (*i.e.*, stop "offsetting" of loss of foreign reserves)	Stop reducing domestic bank assets (*i.e.*, stop "offsetting" of gain of foreign reserves)
	2. Reduce domestic bank assets (*i.e.*, "reinforce" loss of foreign reserves)	Increase domestic bank assets (*i.e.*, "reinforce" gain of foreign reserves)
	3. Retard increase in domestic bank assets (*e.g.*, below the normal rate of growth)	Accelerate increase in domestic bank assets (*e.g.*, above the normal rate of growth)
	4. Raise short-term interest rates	Lower short-term interest rates
	5. Raise long-term interest rates	Lower long-term interest rates
Price and income policy	6. Allow prices to decline	Allow prices to rise (*i.e.*, stop resisting inflation)
	7. Keep price level stable	Promote rise in price level
	8. Allow wage rates to decline	Allow wage rates to rise
	9. Keep wage rates stable	Promote rise in wage rates
Commercial policy	10. Raise tariffs and other import barriers	Reduce tariffs and other import barriers
	11. Introduce or raise export subsidies	Abolish or reduce export subsidies
	12. Tie foreign loans to exports	Untie foreign loans from exports
Fiscal policy	13. Increase personal income taxes	Reduce personal income taxes
	14. Reduce business taxes (to attract foreign and domestic exportable capital)	Increase business taxes (to discourage foreign capital imports)
	15. Reduce government spending at home	Increase government spending at home

Table 2 (continued)

Policies and measures prescribed for correcting the balance of payments

	Deficit countries (D)	Surplus countries (S)
Foreign spend-	16. Reduce government spending abroad	Increase government spending abroad
ing, lending,		
and investing	17. Reduce government grants abroad	Increase government grants abroad
	18. Reduce government lending abroad	Increase government lending abroad
	19. Discourage private long-term capital exports	Promote private long-term capital exports
	20. Control private long-term capital exports	Decontrol private long-term capital exports
	21. Encourage private long-term capital imports	Discourage private long-term capital imports
	22. Discourage private short-term capital exports	Promote private short-term capital exports
	23. Control private short-term capital exports	Decontrol private short-term capital exports
	24. Encourage private short-term capital imports	Discourage private short-term capital imports
Exchange-	25. Control foreign-exchange market (*i.e.*, ration foreign exchange or prohibit certain payments)	Abolish or liberalize foreign-exchange controls
rate policy		
	26. Allow exchange rate to depreciate slightly to a stipulated lower limit	Allow exchange rate to appreciate slightly to a stipulated upper limit
	27. Devalue the currency against foreign exchange (and gold)	Upvalue the currency against foreign exchange (and gold)
	28. Allow exchange rate to seek level at which supply and demand balance	Allow exchange rate to seek level at which supply and demand balance

IV   Protests and disqualifications

While every one of the 28 items (or rather 56 items, if recommendations to surplus countries (S.1-S.28) and to deficit countries (D.1-D.28) are counted separately) has been proposed as a policy or measure aiding the "adjustment process", several of them have been denied this characterization by critics using stricter criteria of what constitutes adjustment. Since a variety of criteria have been used, we must not be surprised to find that several inconsistent conclusions have been reached. The critical assessments of the various types of prescriptions, and the grounds on which many of the prescribed measures or policies have been disqualified as genuine methods of adjustment, are examined below. I do not attempt to reproduce the reasoning of particular authors, nor to disentangle the strains of thought spun on the basis of diverse criteria. If the result looks messy, this should make the reader more receptive to the conceptual and terminological innovation to be proposed later on in this essay.

Use of direct controls   Policies D.20, D.23, and D.25 (and possibly some quantitative import controls under D.10) are contested as "adjustment", to the extent that the controls are of a discretionary kind. It is claimed that discretionary restrictions do not really "correct" or "remove" a deficit, but only "suppress" it. Rationing a scarce supply of foreign exchange under direct controls does not reduce the demand, but merely leaves part of it unsatisfied. The excess demand persists. The imbalance may no longer be visible in balance sheets and payments statistics, but its existence is very noticeable to the control authorities, who have to cope with it in daily battles.

In contrast to the imposition of controls, the relaxation or removal of direct controls by surplus countries (S.20 and S.25) is widely accepted as a proper measure in a program of adjustment. This is not very logical; the direction of change in varying the strictness of control measures in deficit and surplus countries should not be made the criterion for a categorical difference. (In any case, if relaxing the direct controls in the surplus country actually results in an improvement of the payments imbalance, we shall find it preferable to speak not of adjustment but rather of a compensatory correction reducing the need for adjustment.)

Use of trade barriers   What was said about the imposition of direct controls need not apply to the recommendations of higher import tariffs, export subsidies, and the tying of loans (policies D.10, D.11, and D.12). That these interferences with foreign trade may impair efficiency in the use of productive resources is no valid argument against their recognition as means of correcting a payments deficit. One must point, however, to the probable emergence of repercussions which can in the long run counteract the first impact of the commercial policies upon supply and demand in the market for foreign exchange. Yet, to the extent that the interferences with foreign trade succeed in reducing or removing the payments imbalance, they may be regarded as corrective measures, whether we approve of them or not.

The reverse policy, the liberalization of trade restrictions in the surplus countries (S.10, S.11, and S.12), is widely and urgently recommended as a "contribution to adjustment", but the last remark made in connection with direct controls applies also to the use of trade barriers: raising barriers in deficit countries and lowering barriers in surplus countries should not be regarded as different categories, even if the effects on trade volume are different. As to the trade balance, the effects may be the same, although they are far less certain than most of the advocates of these policies seem to think.

Measures producing unemployment It has been claimed that measures that improve the payments position of a deficit country at the expense of employment do not deserve recognition as "adjustment". All the recommendations in the areas of domestic monetary policy and of price and income policy (D.1-D.9), and some of fiscal policy (D.13 and D.15), may lead to an increase in unemployment. Writers who adopted the condition of full employment as a criterion of equilibrium and used the term "adjustment" as an equivalent of "equilibration" resolved to deny the designation "adjustment" to a process which in removing a payments deficit creates or increases an employment deficit. I submit that it is not helpful to mix policy objectives with terminological decisions for theoretical analysis.[7] Under these critics' terminology, a loss of foreign reserves and subsequent decline in effective demand which effectively removes a deficit would have to be called adjustment if wage rates were reduced, but not called adjustment if employment was reduced in the process.

Government spending abroad The main item under this heading that proponents of remedial action have in mind is the military expenditure of the United States Government. Some proponents bracket this item with another of a different sort, namely, grants to foreign governments in the name of military or economic assistance. The idea is that the major

---

[7] See my "Equilibrium and Disequilibrium: Misplaced Concreteness and Disguised Politics", *Economic Journal*, LXVIII (March, 1958), 1-24 (reprinted in my books *Essays on Economic Semantics* [Englewood Cliffs, N.J.: Prentice-Hall, 1963], pp. 43-72; and *International Payments, Debts, and Gold* [New York: Charles Scribner's Sons, 1964], pp. 110-35).

deficit country ought to reduce government expenditures abroad, and surplus countries ought to increase them (recommendations D.16 and S.16). Such changes in foreign spending would probably be partly offset by changes in merchandise trade, but some net improvement of the payments imbalance could perhaps be achieved.[8] Some writers, nevertheless, refuse to recognize such measures as "adjustment" and prefer to treat these government responses to the payments imbalance as a sort of "compensatory official finance".

No matter what label is used for policy decisions of this sort, it should be recognized that the call upon surplus countries to increase their contributions to the free world's burden of defense and economic assistance cannot reasonably be supported on grounds of the favorable payments position of these countries. Not the surplus balance of payments but only the "real wealth" of these nations is the appropriate criterion for assessing the adequacy of their "contributions to common international tasks".[9]

If *private* persons in a deficit country reduce their foreignspending, this is usually recognized as part of the "adjustment" process. It may then seem pedantic to deny this designation to a curtailment of *government* expenditures abroad. There is a difference, however. The reduction of private foreign spending is probably the result of a general decline in incomes in the course of the monetary contraction associated with a payments deficit when the central bank abstains from a policy of offsetting. The reduction of government spending abroad, on the other hand, may be undertaken without any previous or subsequent contraction of effective demand. Hence, the effects would not be the same, and a terminological distinction may be helpful in analyzing the outcome.

Private long-term capital movements   Some critics object to the recent habit of treating all policies that seek to reduce capital exports from deficit countries and to increase capital exports from surplus countries as

---

[8]   The effect upon merchandise trade would depend partly on whether the reduction in foreign spending by the government of the deficit country would or would not be accompanied by an increase in domestic spending. If total government expenditures remain unchanged and are merely switched from abroad to at home, the trade balance is likely to react adversely. A somewhat more detailed discussion is found later in connection with private long-term capital movements.

[9]   Joint Economic Committee, *op. cit.,* p. 9. The Committee is to be commended for this insight, so often not in evidence in pronouncements from official sources. More on this issue is found in the last section of this essay.

"adjustment policies", regardless of the methods used and the probable effects achieved. The effects may be different indeed.

Raising long-term interest rates (D.5), for example, may mean that portfolio investment in the deficit country becomes more attractive to both foreign and domestic investors, which would either invite additional finance to meet the existing deficit or reduce the deficit for which finance is needed. However, it may also mean that capital becomes too expensive for some domestic investment opportunities to be taken up for the time being, and this would reduce domestic business spending – and subsequently also consumer spending – so that, as a result, the demand for merchandise imports would be reduced. Some analysts would like to call attention to these differences by reserving the term "adjustment" for the latter effect.

Business tax incentives (D.14) may increase the attractiveness of both portfolio and direct investment, and thus may have a positive effect on the balance of payments (through reducing capital exports and increasing capital imports), but they may also have a negative effect (through the increase in business spending and associated imports). If the net effect is in doubt, some would object to prejudging the policy either as "adjustment" or as "correction".

What kind of effects can be expected from the nonspecified incentives for capital exports from surplus countries (S.19) and from the nonspecified disincentives introduced in deficit countries (D.19) is impossible to say. With respect to one such disincentive, the United States tax on foreign long-term securities sold in American markets, the so-called Interest Equalization Tax, one may tentatively conclude that its effects are likely to reduce the payments deficit of the United States – though not by promoting adjustment but by reducing the need for adjustment.[10]

There is one recommendation in this area on which no dissent is heard in deficit countries: that surplus countries remove the barriers by which

---

[10]   Two comments may be permitted regarding the reaction of the financial community to this legislative action. Some of the same critics who objected to the proposal that foreign long-term borrowers be discouraged by a federal tax had openly favored higher long-term interest rates. Did they believe that the effects on the balance of payments would be any different if the Treasury rather than the investment bankers imposed a surcharge upon foreign borrowing? Some opponents of the tax urged instead the institution of direct controls on issues of foreign securities in United States markets (D. 20). How can one explain the fact that spokesmen of groups representing "free enterprise" prefer discretionary controls over indirect taxation?

they restrict exports of private long-term capital (S.20). Some proponents explicitly include the removal of these impediments among "adjustment measures".[11]

If all policies that influence private long-term capital to flow into, rather than out of, deficit countries, and out of, rather than into, surplus countries, are called adjustment policies, it appears that the effects of these changes in capital movements are prejudged. The effects, in fact, are far from certain. Let us first take an "extreme" case which would bear out the hopes of the adjustment optimists. Assume that capitalists residing in the deficit country are dissuaded from continuing to invest, and capitalists residing in a surplus country are persuaded to invest, in some industrial ventures in a third country. If the capitalists in the deficit country are not using their funds for anything else – that is, if they leave them inactive – and if the capitalists in the surplus country are not omitting any outlays that they would have made had they not decided to invest in the third country – that is, if they are activating otherwise inactive funds – and if the third country uses the funds of the capitalists of the surplus country in exactly the same way in which it has used the funds of the capitalists of the deficit country, then foreign trade need not be affected, and the new flow of capital will imply a net improvement or correction of the previous imbalance.

Assume now that the capitalists in the deficit country are not "hoarding", and the capitalists in the surplus country are not "dishoarding". In this case, total domestic spending will be increased in the deficit country and decreased in the surplus country. These changes in effective demand will tend to raise the imports of the deficit country and the exports of the surplus country, and to reduce the exports of the deficit country and the imports of the surplus country. These effects on the balance of goods and services need not, and are not likely to, offset completely the changes in the balance of capital movements. In certain circumstances, however – for example, if the third country shifts many of its purchases from the deficit country to the new source of its finance, the surplus country – the effects on the trade balance may even more than offset the changes in the capital balance. Those who insist that an adjustment process is one that actually achieves or promotes adjustment naturally refuse in this case to recognize that the measures which induce the changes in the flow of private long-term capital are "part of an adjustment process". And even if the changes

---

[11] Smithies, *op. cit.,* p. 113; Joint Economic Committee, *op. cit.,* pp. 12, 15.

of capital balance did achieve a correction of the imbalance, a term other than "adjustment" would help to keep apart things which ought not to be confounded.

Government long-term funds   Much of what has been said about "government spending abroad" and about "private long-term capital movements" holds also for attempts to correct imbalances of payments through changing the movements of government long-term funds. Indeed, we have already referred to recommendations to the deficit country that it curtail its military and economic assistance to foreign countries, and to recommendations to surplus countries that they assume a larger share of this burden. Perhaps we should restate the reasons why critics have resisted recognizing such measures (D.17 and D.18, S.17 and S.18) as adjustment. (a) To an undetermined extent, the curtailment by the deficit country of its government remittances to foreign countries will affect the ability of these (and some third) countries to purchase its goods and services, with the result that its exports, and probably the supply of foreign exchange, will be reduced. (b) The reduction of demand for foreign exchange is the direct result of a government decision motivated specifically by balance-of-payments considerations, and is in the nature of "compensatory official finance" rather than "adjustment". The weight of this objection can be seen only after the meaning of "financing" an imbalance of international payments has been examined.

Private short-term capital movements   The recommendations to influence the flow of private short-term capital range from interest-rate policies (D.4, S.4) to other incentives and disincentives (D.22 and D.24, S.22 and S.24) and to the removal of controls (S.23 and S.25) and the imposition of controls (D.23 and D.25). Critics of the indiscriminate use of the concept of adjustment for all these policies point to a variety of needed distinctions. With respect to the short-term interest rate, they wish to separate the effects upon domestic activity from the effects upon the international flow of funds, and prefer to designate only the former as part of the adjustment process, the latter as a financing process. Disincentives to hot-money movements (S.24), such as service charges or taxes on balances that foreign depositors hold in surplus countries, should probably not be regarded as adjustment measures, although they may be viewed as reductions of the need for adjustment.

The imposition of direct controls has been peremptorily rejected as an adjustment, not only because of the reasonable distinctions between adjustment and suppression and between adjustment and reduced need for adjustment, but also because their negative effects may well offset (or more than offset) their positive effects in that they discourage inflows as much as (or more than) outflows. At times, a country could expect more help for its payments position from private short-term money returning from abroad than it could from stopping additional funds going abroad. Finally, there is again the question of the relationship between adjustment and financing, a question which many have answered to the effect that flows of short-term capital can at best compensate, but not adjust, an imbalance of payments. To this point we shall return.

Variations of foreign-exchange rates   In spite of the awkward definition of "adjustment", which may have inadvertently read some of the effects of exchange-rate adjustments out of the adjustment process, most economists do agree on the semantic, analytical, and political verdict that variations in exchange rates may be in the nature of adjustments of payments imbalances. To be sure, many hold that it would be unwise, perhaps disastrous, to resort to this "adjustment route" (D.27) in the case of a deficit country whose currency is used as an official reserve asset of many other countries. There is less opposition to adjustment by appreciation of the nonreserve currencies of countries in persistent surplus.[12]

There is, moreover, widespread agreement that a greater role in the adjustment process might be assigned to moderate exchange-rate variations (D.26, S.26) by broadening the limits of permissible variations around the fixed parity.[13] Some of the proponents of such narrowly limited variations, however, think less of their effects on the balance on current account than of their effects on private short-term capital movements.[14] And this raises again the question whether these induced flows of liquid balances function as means of adjusting or as means of financing an international imbalance.

---

[12]   "If international imbalance consists of deficits by the reserve-currency countries and surpluses by others, so that the former must not devalue, appreciation of the surplus countries' currencies might then be in order". Joint Economic Committee, *op. cit.*, p. 12.

[13]   "It would permit exchange-rate variations to play a somewhat larger role in the adjustment process than is now possible". *Ibid.*, p. 18. On "limited flexibility", see *International Monetary Arrangements:...*, pp. 98-99.

[14]   "... the authorities would have greater scope for short-term intervention in the forward exchange market to offset interest-rate differentials". Joint Economic Committee, *op. cit.*, p. 18.

V   The meaning and scope of financing

We shall not make the mistake of trying to compose a definition of financing before we have found out what purposes the concept is to serve. By defining it too narrowly or too broadly, we run the risk of encumbering analysis and judgment. But in order to circumscribe the notion tentatively, we may say that by financing a payments deficit (surplus) most people mean a reduction (increase) in a country's holdings of current foreign assets (especially gold, foreign currencies, and other short-term claims) and/or an increase (reduction) in the country's current foreign liabilities.[15]

When a "country" is said to increase or decrease its holdings of current foreign assets and its current foreign liabilities, the parties involved may be public authorities or private persons and firms residing in the country. The question arises whether both private and official financing or only official financing should be included in the concept of "financing" an imbalance in international payments.[16]

Financing a payments deficit (surplus) in any other way than through the export (import) of monetary gold is now often referred to as engaging in "accommodating" capital imports (exports). When I coined and defined this term,[17] I included both private and official transactions. But I now recognize that a strong case can be made for confining "accommodating" foreign lending and borrowing to *official* transactions. For only official financing of a deficit (surplus) is clearly motivated by a desire to avoid external depreciation (appreciation) of the currency by pegging the foreign-exchange rates. *Private* financing is usually profit-

---

[15]   There are at least three other meanings in which "financing" or "foreign financing" is used in international parlance. One is the foreign financing of the long-term capital requirements of a developing economy. Another is "financing" international trade by "trade credits" to nations which lack working capital. A third uses "financing international transactions" in the sense in which in a domestic economy the total money supply finances all money transactions. None of these meanings should be confused with financing payments deficits and surpluses.

[16]   The question is even more complicated when the deficit and the surplus countries are considered at the same time, for it may well be that one of the parties to a financing transaction is public while the other is private. It is customary in such instances to characterize the financing as private or official according to the status of the asset-holder or debtor in the country for which the particular statement is made.

[17]   *International Trade and the National Income Multiplier* (Philadelphia: The Blakiston Co., 1943 [reprinted, New York: Augustus M. Kelley, 1961]), pp. 134-35.

motivated, induced either by differentials in interest rates or by expectations of slight movements in exchange rates, or both. Its inclusion among accommodating capital movements seems justified insofar as the profitable interest-rate differentials and exchange-rate spreads result directly from a payments deficit or surplus. But margins in interest or exchange rates are often generated by other causes. Hence, private short-term movements can properly be characterized as "accommodating" only on the diagnosis that they are the consequences of a deficit (surplus); and such a diagnosis is merely an analyst's hunch. One may, therefore, prefer to discard the use of causation, and take motivation instead, as the criterion of accommodating transactions. On grounds of motivation, private foreign lending and borrowing could not be designated as accommodating. In defense of my earlier inclusion of private transactions, I may submit, however, that the latent supply and demand by private exchange dealers may still be presented as "accommodating" out of *stocks* the demand and supply not satisfied out of *flows*.

Treating *both* private and official accumulations of "currencies in excess supply" and decumulations of "currencies in excess demand" as financing of a payments imbalance is most effectively justified on two grounds. (a) For the real consequences which the transactions are likely to have for the economies concerned, that is, for the volume and composition of output, income, employment, consumption, etc., the only differences between private and public institutions engaging in the transactions lie in the effects of variations in interest rates. Where monetary authorities influence interest rates so that they are virtually the same as the rates that would have induced private flows of capital, the *real* differences may be minute. (b) Although profit-induced, private financial transactions may for good reasons be regarded as parts of an adjustment mechanism of sorts, they do not (certainly no more than official financing) constitute a *long-run* adjustment; they are only "holding actions", tiding things over until the disturbances that caused the imbalance have disappeared or until "real" adjustment has been achieved. Since they do not constitute real adjustment,[18] they have to be included, along with "compensatory official finance", among "financing" – unless there is a third category. (As a

---

[18] Note, however, that the change in interest rates which induces the flow of private short-term capital may at the same time affect domestic spending. This effect, we may repeat, is an unquestioned part of real adjustment.

matter of fact, private short-term capital movements may, in certain circumstances, be most appropriately regarded as "compensatory corrections" of an imbalance, reducing the need for adjustment.)

VI Financing as an alternative to adjustment

Financing as a holding action, permitting a payments deficit to endure, is sometimes regarded as an alternative to adjustment. It may well be an alternative, inasmuch as it is possible to defer the initiation of the adjustment process as long as foreign finance is available. The practice of surplus countries of accumulating the currency of the deficit country and thus, in effect, lending back to that country every day the funds it has paid the day before – leaving its holdings of gold and foreign assets undiminished – does, in fact, enable the "overspending" nation to continue its overspending and to put off correcting its imbalance.

It would be mistaken, however, to assume that foreign financing of the deficit *per se* implies avoidance or postponement of the adjustment process. The sale of foreign exchange to domestic buyers (importers of goods, services, or securities) siphons domestic money from actively circulating balances, and it does so no matter whether the foreign exchange sold has been held in the owned foreign reserves or has been freshly borrowed abroad or will be borrowed back tomorrow. The act of satisfying the excess demand for foreign exchange through sales by the accommodating agencies involves a contraction of domestic spending power, which is part and parcel of the classical adjustment process. This process is neither prevented nor delayed by foreign financing of the deficit; it can be prevented or delayed only by domestic offsetting policy, that is, by a policy of returning, by means of domestic expansion of credit, to domestic spenders the domestic money collected for the foreign exchange sold.

In order to avoid confusion, we should strictly distinguish this *domestic* financing of the excess demand for foreign exchange from the *foreign* (or external) financing of the payments deficit. Domestic financing restores domestic money to domestic spenders and enables them to spend tomorrow as much as today and to demand tomorrow as much foreign exchange as today. External financing restores foreign reserves to domestic reserve holders and enables them to sell tomorrow as much foreign exchange as today. It is *domestic* financing which delays adjustment. To be sure, foreign financing may encourage the monetary authorities to continue domestic financing, but one cannot reasonably regard it as a true alternative of, or in any sense a contradiction to, adjustment.

VII   A third category

As we have seen, analysts have sometimes found it difficult to decide whether certain measures, transactions, movements, or changes had better be treated as foreign financing or as adjustment of an imbalance in international payments. They used different criteria, which led them to different findings. Some focused on the motivation behind the transactions in question; others on the accounts in the balance of international transactions on which the balancing transactions were entered or the corrective changes appeared; and still others asked whether the measures were likely to succeed in removing or reducing the imbalance and for how long one could expect the achieved balance, or reduction of imbalance, to last in the absence of new, independent disturbances. Some adhered to preconceived definitions and found that the change in question fitted both "adjustment" and "foreign financing", or that it fitted neither. To some, the concept of adjustment was so wide that it covered virtually everything that reduced current variations in official foreign reserves, to others, it was so narrow that many things failed to gain recognition as adjustment although they did not qualify as financing either.

This state of analytical affairs can be greatly improved by recognizing a third category between the two customary ones. The concept of adjustment may then be confined to the working of the classical mechanism, involving changes in relative costs and prices and in the allocation of productive resources, induced by specific effects of the imbalance of payments and leading to its correction through changes in the international movement of goods and services. The concept of foreign financing, in turn, may be confined broadly (with exceptions) to private and official short-term funds made available to meet an excess supply of, or excess demand for, foreign currencies. Between these two lies the concept of "compensatory corrections" of the imbalance of international payments, corrections which are neither in the nature of temporary financing nor in the nature of adjustments of the balance on current account induced by variations of relative prices and incomes.

This concept of compensatory corrections was anticipated several times in my discussion of the various recommendations for remedial policies. There I referred to it as a "reduction of the need for adjustment," and this is in fact its most significant feature. It ought to be clear – and it is amazing that it has not been so to all analysts – that *adjustment* is one thing and reduction or removal of the *need* for adjustment is another. In medicine, no one would doubt for a moment that there is a difference between a surgical operation (or some painful treatment) and a disappearance or removal of the need for it. That the condition in need of remedial action improves or disappears – either by itself or by therapeutic actions other than those first indicated – is, of course, the hope of anybody suffering from an affliction, and the distinction is surely essential. This holds for balance-of-payments troubles: it may be necessary to go through the operations called "adjustment", or, with luck, the troubles may "go away" without these operations, as a result of either independent developments or deliberate policies. These developments and policies we put under the heading of "compensatory corrections". That temporary financing is required in both cases – during the process of adjustment or until the imbalance is removed through compensatory corrections – is understood.

VIII   Types of compensatory corrections

Compensatory corrections may occur on current account, on donations and long-term capital accounts, and on short-term capital account. They may, I repeat, be the result of independent and spontaneous developments that have nothing to do with the imbalance, or they may be the result of government measures designed to reduce or correct the imbalance. Such government measures may be restrictive (usually on the part of deficit countries) or liberalizing (on the part of surplus countries).

Like most distinctions, ours may be protested as too arbitrary. Regarding the proposed criteria of real[19] adjustment, it may be argued that the line drawn between the current account and other accounts is artificial,

---

[19]   The adjective "real" is not meant as the opposite of unreal, imaginary, or illusory, but rather as referring to the allocation of productive resources and the production of goods and services.

and that the differences between the "four legitimate changes" labeled "real adjustment" and all other changes labeled "compensatory corrections" are even more fictitious. What the distinction amounts to is that it separates the processes described by the classical theorists from all other events or policies. The four legitimate adjustment forces are (a) price and income deflation in deficit countries, (b) price and income inflation in surplus countries, (c) external depreciation of the currencies of deficit countries, and (d) external appreciation of the currencies of surplus countries. Everything else gets another label.

There are no reliable operational criteria by which changes on current account may be readily diagnosed as parts of the real adjustment process or rather as compensatory corrections. Such diagnoses call for largely speculative judgments by the analyst. Assume, for example, that a deficit country experiences a brisk increase in exports of particular goods. Was it due to an increase in foreign demand, induced by an increase in money incomes abroad which resulted from the financing of the payments imbalance? Or was it due to an independent and spontaneous shift of foreign demand in favor of the export articles of the deficit country? Or, again, was it due to a tariff reduction by surplus countries? Only the first case would be "adjustment", the other two compensatory corrections. Alternatively, the increase in exports may have been due to a reduction in export prices by the deficit country, perhaps as a consequence of a loss in domestic markets that goes back to a credit contraction associated with the financing of the imbalance. Or, the export increase may be attributable to independent developments in the exporting industries, by which their production costs were lowered or product qualities improved. Or, again, it may have been the result of open or concealed subsidies, or of the tying of foreign loans, by the deficit country. Only the first of these three causes of the increase in exports would be adjustment, the other two would be compensatory corrections of two different kinds. To ascertain which of these six or many other causes have been responsible would be a difficult task indeed. (In reply to such skepticism, one might submit that an ex post examination of a record of observed changes, however important for purposes of verification, is rather different from the formulation of ex ante propositions on alternative courses of action.)

That, under the proposed classification, commercial policy is treated differently from exchange-rate policy will possibly be condemned as capricious. Theorists have often shown that a depreciation of the currency is analogous to a universal tariff surcharge on all imports and to a uniform subsidy for all exports. Consistent with this analogy, every single tariff increase and every single export subsidy could be regarded as a partial depreciation of the currency, similar to the introduction of a system of multiple exchange rates. Since we recognize exchange depreciation as one of the adjustment forces, but trade interventions as compensatory corrections, the proposed distinction focuses on the question whether a change in exchange rates is uniform or, instead, selective and discriminatory. Whether this speaks for or against the distinction may be partly a matter of taste. But one may point to important differences, particularly to the probability that discriminatory exchange-rate differentials, like discriminatory duties and subsidies, will result in retaliations which may jeopardize any remedial effects on the balance of payments, and also in allocative distortions which may have disconcerting welfare implications.

In the case of remedial changes on long-term capital account, the analytical and operational difficulties are much less serious. For one may expediently classify them as compensatory corrections no matter what brought them about, as long as they reduce the need of adjustment in the long run. Having decided to confine the concept of adjustment to changes on current account (induced by certain changes in relative prices, incomes, and resource allocations), we can assign all corrective changes in long-term capital movements to the category of compensatory corrections. The advantage of the decision is clear: viewing adjustment as the "classical medicine", which acts through the market mechanism and allocative adaptations, any long-term capital movements which reduce or remove the payments imbalance are in fact reducing or removing the *need* for adjustment. The only judgment required may concern the question whether the correction is likely to be temporary or lasting; for if it is patently temporary, one ought to reassign the particular capital movements from "compensatory corrections" to "compensatory finance". Some analysts, however, may prefer an operational convention of treating only the short-term capital account as the visual locus of compensatory finance.

This same convention, if adopted, would militate against assigning any corrective changes on short-term capital account to the category of compensatory corrections. Yet, a strong argument can be made for doing so in certain circumstances. Compensatory financing "meets" or "accommodates" an excess supply or excess demand in the foreign-exchange market by a compensating (accommodating) demand or supply. But there are short-term capital movements of an entirely different nature. Assume, for example, that there has been a persistent outflow of private short-term capital, either because of interest differentials or because of a latent fear of devaluation. If these causes are removed, or offset by various disincentives, and the outflow is thereby checked or a reverse flow induced,[20] it would be misleading to regard the resulting change on short-term capital account as compensatory finance. It is a compensatory correction, obviating the need for adjustment as well as the need for compensatory finance.

IX   A taxonomic summary

I am aware of the disdain some of my fellow economists have for my propensity to engage in taxonomic exercises. Yet, my passion for pedagogy overcomes my desire to please my antitaxonomist brethren, and I tabulate below the types of actions, policies, events, or developments that may restore balance (enduring or temporary) of (autonomous and accommodating) supply and demand in the foreign-exchange market.

Table 3

Adjustments, corrections, and financing of imbalances of payments

Description of changes in the balance of payments	Examples and commentaries
A. *Real adjustments*	
reducing or removing the imbalance through changes in relative incomes, prices, and resource allocations,	
1. induced by reductions of money incomes and prices in deficit countries	*Current account* The relative reduction in money incomes and/or prices in deficit countries raises exports and lowers imports
2. induced by increases of money incomes and prices in surplus countries	
3. induced by devaluation or depreciation of currencies of deficit countries	*Capital accounts* No long-run effects, since "adjustment," by definition, operates only on the current balance
4. induced by upvaluation or appreciation of currencies of surplus countries	

---

[20]   It is quite likely that a large part of the payments deficit of the United States

Table 3 (continued)

Description of changes in the balance of payments	Examples and commentaries
B. *Compensatory corrections* reducing or removing the need for adjustment in the long run, through changes on current account, not induced by the forces of adjustment, and/or through changes on donations and capital accounts, induced or independent,	
1. resulting from independent, spontaneous developments in deficit countries	*Current account* Cost reductions due to increased productivity may increase exports and reduce imports; shifts of demand from imported to domestic products may reduce imports *Long-term capital account* Improved profit expectations may increase capital imports *Short-term capital account* Increased interest rates may check outflow and attract inflow
2. resulting from independent, spontaneous developments in surplus countries	*Current account* Cost increases may reduce exports from and increase imports into surplus countries; shifts of demand from domestic to imported goods may increase imports *Capital accounts* Worsened profit expectations or reduced interest rates induce capital outflows
3. induced by restrictive government measures in deficit countries	*Current account* Import restrictions (higher tariffs, smaller quotas) reduce imports; subsidies and tying of loans increase exports *Capital accounts* Restrictions reduce private capital exports; stinting on official foreign aid
4. induced by liberalizing government measures in surplus countries	*Current account* Relaxation or removal of restrictions (lower tariffs, larger quotas) increases imports;

---

in the last few years has been caused by an outflow of private short-term capital. If this flow were stopped or reversed, much of the imbalance would be corrected without the need for "real adjustment".

Table 3 (continued)

Descriptions of changes in the balance of payments	Examples and commentaries
	removal of subsidies and untying of loans reduce exports *Capital accounts* Relaxation or removal of restrictions increases private capital exports; more liberal foreign aid
C. *Temporary financing* accommodating the excess demand or excess supply in the foreign-exchange market (until adjustment is accomplished by A or made unnecessary by B),	
1. through sales of gold or foreign exchange by monetary authorities of deficit countries	*Compensatory official finance* Reduction in foreign reserve of deficit country
2. through purchases of gold or foreign exchange by monetary authorities of surplus countries	*Compensatory official finance* Increase in foreign reserve of surplus country
3. through direct loans of foreign currencies to the monetary authorities of deficit countries by private or official, foreign or inter-national institutions or authorities	*Compensatory official finance* Increase in current official foreign liabilities of deficit countries
4. through accommodating timing of scheduled official long-term capital transactions	*Special transactions on government capital account* Premature payments of long-term debts by surplus countries and to deficit countries; deferment of payments by deficit countries and to surplus countries
5. through stabilizing movements of private short-term capital, induced by interest-rate differentials or expectations of strengthened exchange rates of deficit currencies	*Short-term capital account* Flow of private funds from surplus countries and into deficit countries *Errors and omissions* Unrecorded flows of private funds as above
6. through leads and lags in payments for goods and services	*Errors and omissions* Prepayments or earlier payments for imports into surplus countries; deferred payments for imports into deficit countries
7. through variations in inventories of imported materials	*Current account* Accumulations of stocks of imported materials in surplus countries, depletion of stocks of imported materials in deficit countries

X A theoretical summary with policy implications

The proposed distinctions – particularly those between real adjustment, compensatory corrections, and temporary financing – are not ornamental but functional taxonomy: they serve analytical purposes and have policy implications as well.

Real adjustment – improvement of the trade balances of deficit countries through resource reallocations induced by deflation or depreciation in deficit countries and/or by inflation or appreciation in surplus countries – is often painful and troublesome; temporary financing is a stopgap, often embarrassing and, of course, of limited duration. Hence, to secure compensatory corrections of the imbalance is the fervent hope and sanguine expectation of the authorities in the countries concerned. Sometimes they hope that independent spontaneous developments, lucky accidents, will correct the imbalance and spare their country the pain of real adjustment. More often they hope that their policy measures, designed to remove the imbalance, will be effective. And quite frequently they hope that the governments of the other countries will take the corrective measures.

It is a sad fact, however, that policies designed to bring forth the desired compensatory corrections will, more often than not, have repercussions that frustrate the attempts. Restrictive measures by deficit countries often remain ineffective, or an initially corrective impact will fizzle out in short order or will be offset by unintended side-effects, reactions, repercussions. Liberalizing measures by surplus countries, even if beneficial in other respects, may likewise fail to be lastingly effective in remedying the payments imbalance.

The theory of international trade has furnished ample explanations of why policies designed to produce compensatory corrections are so undependable. It is known that import restrictions are likely to lead to retaliations and, even if they do not, may divert purchasing power to the domestic use of exportable goods and of goods using means of production that are withdrawn from the production of exportables. The result is that the intended reduction of imports may be offset, partially or fully, by an unintended reduction of exports. It is known, furthermore, that cutbacks in unilateral payments such as foreign aid may reduce exports; that restrictions on capital outflows may raise the domestic demand for imports and lower the foreign demand for exports. It is known, finally, that an increase in long-term capital exports by surplus countries may be largely offset, as regards its effect on the balance of payments, by induced changes in the movement of goods and services. (The reasoning underlying the last statement was briefly outlined when we discussed "private long-term capital movements" as one of the proposed corrections of an imbalance.)

Apart from the likelihood of failure, one ought to consider the consequences which policies to induce compensatory corrections may have upon allocative efficiency. To be sure, for liberalizing measures, for the removal of restrictions, the presumption is that efficiency in the use of resources will be furthered in the process; but the danger is that, whenever the balance turns from surplus to deficit, the restrictions will be "turned on" again. If restrictions on the international division of labor are recognized as harmful, it is unwise to demand their abolition or relaxation just in order to remove a surplus in the balance of payments; for then one will hardly be able to resist their reinstitution when a payments deficit arises. It would be naive to expect that countries in deficit will never impose and strengthen restrictive measures, whereas countries in surplus will always relax and abolish existing restrictions. Even if countries were so disposed, the sequence of liberalizing measures would eventually reach its natural end, when all restrictions are gone and nothing remains to be liberalized. Then the reimposition of restrictive measures would be the only possible policy with which governments could induce compensatory corrections of the current account. In actual fact, the pressures of special interests would always favor restrictive measures in deficit countries and oppose liberalizing measures in surplus countries. With the presumption that restrictions are injurious to efficiency in the allocation of productive resources, the whole emphasis on commercial policies designed to secure compensatory corrections of imbalances is suspect.

This verdict holds true for the proposal to have countries in surplus try to correct imbalances through increasing their long-term capital exports. Some of the top experts in international finance have called for some "assurance that the more developed countries match their export surpluses with an outflow of real capital," and for ways of "incorporating into the adjustment process a place for methods of influencing movements of long-term capital".[21] That such a policy may be largely ineffective has

---

[21]   Robert Roosa, "Movements of Long-Term Capital and the Adjustment Process", *Review of Economics and Statistics*, XLVI (May, 1964), 164.

been pointed out but, even when it succeeds, "the principle underlying this remedy is a false one".[22] The efficient flow of long-term capital is determined by relative wealth, real incomes, thrift, and the productivity of capital – not at all by the state of the balances of trade or payments, which are largely determined by relative costs and prices. Thus, to look to induced movements of long-term capital as desirable compensatory corrections of surpluses in the balance of payments is to disregard some well-established findings of economic theory.

The policy implications of the distinctions proposed in this essay seem to be clear. Although real adjustment seems to be the hard road, and compensatory corrections the easy way out, the easy way does not lead to external balance consistent with the economic principle. Our task, therefore, remains to find how our political idiosyncrasies can be made compatible with the unpleasant necessities of real adjustment.

---

[22] Friedrich A. Lutz, *The Problem of International Economic Equilibrium* ("De Vries Lectures" [Amsterdam: North-Holland Publishing Co., 1962]), p. 56.

INTEREST RATES AND
THE BALANCE OF PAYMENTS: AN ANALYSIS
OF THE SWISS EXPERIENCE

Jürg Niehans

I The problem

Interest rates and the balance of payments on current account can be regarded as two of the endogenous variables in a (unspecified) model of the economy. For any given change in one of the exogenous variables, e.g., in the foreign demand for exports, the consequent change in interest rates will be accompanied by a certain change in the balance of payments. Once the model is specified, the exact nature of these reactions will depend on the exogenous variable that sets it in motion. If there has been an increase in export demand, theoretical reasoning would lead to the expectation of a surplus in the current account, probably accompanied by a fall in the rate of interest. If, on the other hand, there has been an influx of hot money, one would rather expect a fall in interest rates, accompanied by a growing deficit (or diminishing surplus) on the current account.

This paper presents the results of some empirical investigations into the working of these mechanisms in the Swiss economy. In some respects, the case of Switzerland is almost ideal for a study of this kind, for during recent decades the fluctuations both in interest rates and in the balance of payments have been large and frequent, the interrelations between the domestic credit market and the balance of payments are very close, and both the credit market and the balance of payments have been largely – though certainly not absolutely – free from interference by the government and the central bank. In other respects, however, the Swiss case is far from ideal: the investigator is often driven to near despair by the paucity of statistical data about some of the most important aspects of the problem. While there are fairly good monthly statistics on merchandise exports and imports, invisibles are available only on an annual basis, and the results leave much to be desired. On capital movements, there are almost no data at all, except the record of foreign bond issues in the Swiss market. As a consequence, such an investigation assumes something of the character of a detective story in which some links in the chain of evidence consist of rather tenuous clues. This study is mainly based on quarterly data for the seventeen years from the fourth quarter of 1946 to the third quarter of 1963. In addition, it has been possible to apply some of the main findings to the period from the third quarter of 1930 to the second quarter of 1939.[1]

II   *Some statistical observations*

Sometime in 1954, it occurred to me that Swiss interest rates as measured by the yields on government bonds were closely related statistically to the excess of merchandise imports over exports. This was not true, to be sure, for monthly fluctuations, which, in fact, appeared to be quite erratic. For medium and long-term movements, however, the correlation was striking. If a three-quarter moving average of quarterly data is used, a simple regression of interest rates on the import surplus for the 28 quarters from 1946 IV to 1953 III yields a correlation coefficient of $R=0.83$, and the regression coefficient is about three times the 99 per cent confidence interval.

An explanation of this observation did not seem difficult to find. The import surplus dominates the fluctuations of the current account as a whole, the invisibles being relatively stable.[2] The balance on current account is, in turn, an important determinant of monetary reserves which, again, influence the supply of money. On the other hand, an increase in imports is often a consequence of an increase in national income, which

---

[1]   The computations on which the argument is based are the work of Reinhard Salzmann.

[2]   In the absence of quarterly estimates for the invisibles, this statement can be tested only on an annual basis. A correlation of the annual surplus on the current account with the annual export surplus (which is usually negative) for the period 1947-63 yields a correlation coefficient of 0.96. The regression coefficient is 0.77. This means that the invisibles tend to dampen the fluctuations in the merchandise accounts. The positive sign of the constant term reflects the fact that the invisibles usually show a surplus.

at the same time induces a rise in the demand for money. An increase in imports relative to exports, being accompanied by a contraction of money supply relative to money demand, should thus be followed by a rise in interest rates. Theoretical reasoning thus seems to tie in quite nicely with statistical observation. From this point of view, the Swiss monetary system promises to offer a striking illustration of the liquidity preference theory of interest rates.

While this reasoning may be quite plausible, it obviously requires closer examination. Graphical analysis of monthly data shows at once that interest rates lag behind foreign trade by about four or five months. If quarterly data are used, but with a lag of one quarter, the correlation coefficient in fact increases to 0.90, and even with a two-quarter lag it is still 0.86. In a sense, this lag is welcome, because it permits the forecasting of interest rates. From 1954 to 1959, the development of the trade balance could, in fact, be used to predict successfully the movements of interest rates (and in two cases also the timing of some private bond purchases). In retrospect, this success is not surprising, the lagged correlation coefficient for the period 1953 IV to 1959 III being no less than 0.96. The hypothesis formulated in 1954 was thus nicely confirmed. On the other hand, there is the question of the reasons behind this lag. Repeated inquiries and experiments produced no specific explanation, and I was thus forced to fall back on some unspecified inertia of the Swiss monetary and credit system. This was clearly not satisfactory, since in other respects the system did not give the impression of being particularly inert. The problem of the lag thus remained a troubling one.

There was, in addition, the problem of capital movements. If the current accounts affected the rate of interest via their effect on the money supply, why was it possible to explain interest rates without reference to capital movements, which presumably affect the money supply in roughly the same way? This question could not be answered simply by referring to the smallness of capital movements or of their fluctuations, because during the period of observation capital movements were quite considerable and irregular. It seemed, however, that during this period Swiss international capital flows behaved approximately as if they had been largely motivated by the fluctuations of Swiss interest rates, capital exports being encouraged by low rates and discouraged by high rates. Inflows and outflows of destabilizing hot money, on the other hand, seemed to be small relative to those that occurred in the 1930's and again in the early 1960's. This would mean that fluctuations in capital movements from 1946 to 1959 have to be regarded as an effect rather than as a cause of interest-rate changes. They probably dampened the fluctuations in interest rates that would otherwise have occurred under the influence of the current account, but they were not an exogenous force acting on the rate of interest.

This reasoning receives support from the further observation that, for the 1930's, when "exogenous" hot-money flows dominated the picture, no correlation between interest rates and import surplus could be detected, the correlation coefficient never exceeding 0.02, no matter what lag was used. When in 1959-60, after the restoration of convertibility, speculative capital movements again assumed large proportions, I thus anticipated that the import surplus would lose its predictive power. This was indeed the case: for the period 1959 IV to 1963 III the correlation coefficients promptly dropped below 0.30. This gave additional support to the impression that there must have been significant changes in the nature of capital movements. However, direct observations bearing on this point were still lacking.[3]

The correlation between the import surplus and interest rates poses still another and more subtle problem. Inasmuch as imports move parallel to the demand for money, the stock demand for money may be presumed to be related to the flow of imports. On the other hand, inasmuch as the import surplus affects the supply of money, the stock supply of money must be assumed to depend on the stock of monetary reserves and thus much more on the cumulative sum of past trade balances than on the current balance. In light of this consideration, the theoretical reasoning presented above seemed to require more detailed inspection.[4] These were the main questions the statistical observations seemed to raise. They are the subject of the following sections. Section III presents certain preliminary conjectures which are examined in more detail later in this essay.

---

[3] On the argument as presented so far, see Jürg Niehans and Rudolf Bitterli, "Der schweizerische Kreditmarkt und das Gesetz von Angebot und Nachfrage", *Schweizerische Zeitschrift für Volkswirtschaft und Statistik*, XCVI (March, 1960), pp. 12 f.; and my "Das schweizerische Geldsystem und die Zinstheorie", *Zeitschrift für die gesamte Staatswissenschaft*, CXVI, No. 4 (1960), pp. 577 f.

[4] It was Karl Brunner who first suggested that I look into the time dimensions of the underlying monetary theory.

III Some conjectures

If the demand for money moves parallel to national income, which, on the other hand, determines imports, the level of interest rates will be statistically related to the level of imports. If, at the same time, exports are relatively stable, the level of interest rates will also appear to be closely related to the excess of imports over exports. On the supply side, however, the case is different. If the rate of interest depends (among other things) on the supply of money, which in turn depends (among other things) on monetary reserves, then the level of interest rates should reflect the cumulative sum of past surpluses and deficits in the balance of payments. If, for some reason, capital movements and invisibles do not matter greatly, interest rates will thus appear to be related to the cumulative sum of past import surpluses. Now imagine for a moment that the fluctuations of the import surplus display the form of a sine curve. In this case, the cumulative total of past import surpluses would move in a similar sine curve lagged by one-quarter of the cycle. If interest rates were linearly related to both the current import surplus and the cumulative sum of past surpluses, they would thus lag behind current surpluses by, say, about one-eighth of the cycle, the exact lag depending on the relative weights. Now, during the period 1946-59, the Swiss import surplus seems to have moved in cycles of roughly four years' duration (1946-49, 1950-53, 1954-58). On the basis of the foregoing conjectures, one would thus expect a lag of interest rates behind the import surplus of, say, half a year. This is not far from what is actually observed. The fact that interest rates are related to both the import surplus and its cumulative sum thus seems to promise an explanation of the curious lag of four or five months.

Nobody would pretend, of course, that Swiss foreign trade and interest rates move in sine curves. Still, if the above conjectures are along the right track, one would expect a close multiple correlation of interest rates with the import surplus and the cumulative sum of past surpluses, both unlagged. Alternatively, one could use first differences and thus relate the first difference of interest rates to both the unlagged import surplus and its first difference. The standard of comparison would then be the simple correlation between the first difference of interest rates and the lagged first difference of the import surplus. The resulting correlation coefficients are as follows (i=interest rate, I=imports, E=exports):

	1946 IV– 1953 III	1953 IV– 1959 III	1959 IV– 1963 III	
$di/d(I-E)_{-1}$	0.80	0.80	0.28	(1)
$di/d(I-E), (I-E)$	0.80	0.67	0.67	(2)

For the first period, the correlation coefficients are almost identical. For the second period, the simple lagged correlation is somewhat better, but in the last period, on the other hand, the combination of the first difference of the import surplus with the import surplus itself produces a remarkable improvement. On the whole, these results seem to warrant a more detailed analysis.[5]

IV   The primary model

It is the general line of this argument that the balance of payments provides a more or less reliable shorthand or summary expression of those underlying forces which "really" determine the course of Swiss interest rates. A detailed analysis must thus begin with the specification of the "true" or "complete" theory. For this purpose, there is now available a quarterly two-market model of the Swiss money and credit market for the period 1947-63, developed jointly by Heidi Schelbert and myself.[6] It is based on the idea that interest rates (i), prices (p), and the quantities of money (L, M) and credit (A, B) are jointly determined by demand and supply functions for money and credit. Its elements include a money demand function,

$$L = l_0 + l_1 i + l_2 p + l_3 W + l_4 X, \qquad (I)$$

where W and X signify real wealth and income, respectively; a money supply function,

---

[5]   If both $d(I - E)$ and $(I - E)$ are lagged one quarter, the correlation coefficients are somewhat higher still. The additional improvement is small, however, compared to the great importance of the lag if the change in interest rates is expressed in terms of $d(I - E)$ only.

[6]   Jürg Niehans and Heidi Schelbert-Syfrig, "Interactions of Demand and Supply of Money and Credit in Switzerland", unpublished paper presented at the meeting of the Econometric Society, Zurich, 1964.

$$M = m_0 + m_1 i + m_2 \bar{G}, \tag{II}$$

where G is the symbol for the monetary base; a function for the demand for credit,

$$A = a_0 + a_1 i + a_2 p + a_3 \bar{W} + a_4 \bar{X}; \tag{III}$$

and, finally, a supply function for credit,

$$B = b_0 + b_1 i + b_2 p + b_3 \bar{W} + b_4 \bar{B}_{gb}, \tag{IV}$$

where B_{gb} is the volume of outstanding government bonds minus the bond portfolios of banks. The model is completed by the equilibrium conditions $L = M$ and $A = B$. It permits the determination of each of the endogenous variables, including the rate of interest, in terms of the (barred) exogenous variables. The model is actually expressed in terms of the logarithms of the variables. It was applied both to the levels of the variables and to their changes. For further explanations, the reader is referred to the original paper.

For the purposes of the present analysis, this model must be modified in several respects. First, since the balance of payments analysis is most conveniently put in terms of first differences, I use the simultaneous model only in its differential form. Wealth thus becomes investment (J). Second, it is not possible in the present context to work with logarithms, because in the course of the argument several variables have to be split up into additive components. This is an obvious source of error, particularly for longer periods with a strong growth element. As a consequence, one's expectations with respect to correlation coefficients, the constancy of regression coefficients, and the significance of coefficients should not be too high. Third, investment, national income, imports, and exports are uniformly expressed in terms of current prices. Fourth, in equation (II) the monetary base (G) is replaced by monetary reserves (R); in view of the smallness of central bank credit this is a change of little importance.

The resulting "theory" of interest may be written:

$$\mathrm{d}i = c_0 + c_1 J + c_2 \,\mathrm{d}\bar{Y} + c_3 \,\mathrm{d}\bar{R} + c_4 \,\mathrm{d}\bar{B}_{gb}. \tag{V}$$

For the purpose of this paper, this expression is called the "primary" theory of interest rates. Despite its limitations, it is here taken to represent the "true" theory.

Before the "primary" theory can be applied to empirical data, it is necessary to relate the variables to certain statistical series. Interest rates are assumed to be represented by the average yield of twelve government bonds published by the Swiss National Bank. Unfortunately, there are no quarterly data on investment and national income. I was thus compelled to use annual figures interpolated on the basis of the quarterly series of employment. For investment, the separate employment indices for the machinery and metals industries and for construction were used with equal weights. For national income, employment in all manufacturing was combined with construction in the ratio of 12:1. R includes gold and foreign exchange reserves of the central bank and also the net position of Switzerland with the European Payments Union. The net changes in the volumes of government bonds and of bank bond holdings are derived from series published by the Swiss National Bank. All figures are quarterly. For interest rates, investment, and national income I used a three-quarter moving average in order to smooth "erratic" fluctuations without at the same time completely eliminating the seasonal. In the case of monetary reserves, however, I was forced to use a four-quarter moving average, because for purely technical reasons there used to be wide swings at the turns of the year which did not affect the general state of the credit market. The series of B_{gb}, finally, consists of the end-of-quarter figures from a six-month moving average of monthly data.[7] Interest is measured in per cent per annum, whereas the exogenous variables are expressed in billions of Swiss francs per quarter.

Applying these data to equation (V) by least squares for the period 1946 IV to 1963 III, one obtains the following estimating equation:

$$\mathrm{d}i = 0.013 + 0.001 \ J + 0.407 \ \mathrm{d}Y - 0.197 \ \mathrm{d}R + 0.546 \ \mathrm{d}B_{gb} \qquad (3)$$
$$\underset{(\pm 0.04)}{} \quad \underset{(\pm 0.26)}{} \quad \underset{(\pm 0.13)}{} \quad \underset{(\pm 0.22)}{}$$
$$R = 0.67$$

The 95 per cent confidence intervals are given in parentheses. Considering that this equation relates to first differences and that the underlying simultaneous model is in terms of logarithms, the correlation coefficient is reasonably high. The coefficients all have a plausible sign. While the investment coefficient is far from being significant, the other coefficients

---

[7] For further details about these specifications, see *ibid.*

are significant at the 99 per cent level. For different subperiods the correlation coefficients are

	1946 IV- 1953 III	1953 IV- 1959 III	1959 IV- 1963 III
di/J, dY, dR, dB_{gb}	0.79	0.84	0.76 (4)

That the correlation coefficients for the subperiods are considerably higher than for the period as a whole is probably due, at least in part, to the fact that the errors from not using logarithms are less important for short periods. The regression coefficients for the subperiods are affected by a considerable degree of collinearity between certain variables. For this reason, they are not given here.[8] Since these cases of collinearity are different for different periods, the coefficients for the entire period inspire more confidence than those for individual subperiods. It should be added that for the subperiods 1946 IV-1959 III and 1959 IV-1963 III, the coefficient of investment is significant at the 80 per cent level. For this reason, I retain investment as one of the factors affecting the rate of interest, the lack of significance for the entire period and for some subperiods notwithstanding.

On the whole, it seems permissible to conclude that the primary theory is able to explain the course of interest rates with a relatively high degree of approximation. The question now is to what extent the factors appearing in this theory are reflected in certain components of the balance of payments. To what extent can the balance of payments be used as a proxy for the "real" forces determining the course of interest rates?

V   The balance of payments as a proxy

To answer this question one may begin with investment. From a causal point of view, one would expect Swiss imports to be strongly influenced by investment activity. From a purely statistical point of view, investment would then appear to be closely related to imports. Actually, in a simple regression of investment on imports, based on four-quarter moving averages, the correlation coefficient for the entire period 1946 IV-1963 III is no

---

[8]   It may be added, though, that they nevertheless have the same signs as the coefficients for the entire period.

less than 0.98. The regression coefficient of 0.834 means that, on the average, investment was just five-sixths of imports, the regression coefficient being about 25 times the confidence interval at the 95 per cent level. For no subperiod is the correlation coefficient lower than 0.84. This means that imports can be used as a proxy for investment to a high degree of approximation. It is, in fact, conceivable that the proxy works even better than the magnitude it represents, for the statistical data on imports are presumably much more reliable than my rough quarterly estimates of investment.

The second factor is national income. It is also highly correlated with imports, the correlation coefficient amounting to 0.97 for the whole period. However, what we are interested in is not the level of national income but its change. In general, one would expect rising imports to be accompanied statistically by rising national income. This is exactly what is observed, although with a value of 0.63, the correlation coefficient is, not unnaturally, lower than the one observed for the relation of the level of investment to imports. I conclude that to a large extent changes of national income are statistically reflected in the changes of imports.

Postponing consideration of monetary reserves to a subsequent paragraph, I turn to the changes in the volume of government bonds and bank bond portfolios. There is little prima facie reason why there should be any particular relation between these exogenous components of bond supply and the balance of trade. The respective correlation coefficients are, in fact, generally low, and the regression coefficients are not significant. There is, however, an exception. During the first subperiod, 1946 IV–1953 III, the correlation coefficient between dB_{gb} and imports amounts to 0.55 and is significant at the 99 per cent level. This happens to be the same subperiod for which dB_{gb} is of particularly high significance in the explanation of interest rates. In the very period in which dB_{gb} is of particular importance, a considerable part of it is thus reflected in import figures. This may be nothing more than a coincidence, but from the point of view of this analysis it is an important point.

If it is true that the level and change of imports are, at least for certain subperiods, reasonably good proxies for investment, changes in national income, and changes in the volume of government bonds and bank portfolios, one would expect a rather close multiple correlation between interest rates on one side and imports, changes in imports, and changes in monetary reserves on the other. Again using four-quarter moving averages for monetary reserves and three-quarter moving averages for the other variables, the respective correlation coefficients are, in fact, as follows:

	1946 IV– 1963 III	1946 IV– 1953 III	1953 IV– 1959 III	1959 IV– 1963 III	
$di/I, dI, dR$	0.69	0.85	0.81	0.84	(5)

These correlation coefficients are, on the whole, just about as high and mostly even a trifle higher than those for the primary theory, equations (3) and (4). The proxies seem to do very well indeed. Although one step removed from the "true" causal forces, they may work even somewhat better statistically than their masters.

There is, finally, the change in monetary reserves, dR. It is identically equal to the net capital inflow (C) plus the surplus on the invisibles (U) minus the import surplus $(I-E)$:

$$dR = C + U - (I - E).$$

Imports have already been used as one of the arguments in the previous regression. The introduction of E poses no particular problem. Unfortunately, there are no direct estimates of capital movements and also no monthly or quarterly data for the invisibles. As a consequence, figures for $(C+U)$ can only be obtained indirectly by adding the import surplus $(I-E)$ to the change in monetary reserves (dR). By making these substitutions, one arrives at a regression of the changes in interest rates on imports, exports, changes in imports, and capital imports plus invisibles. Considering the way in which $(C+U)$ was derived, it is not surprising that the correlation coefficients are again quite high:

	1946 IV– 1963 III	1946 IV– 1953 III	1953 IV– 1959 III	1959 IV– 1963 III	
$di/I, E, dI, (C+U)$	0.70	0.89	0.86	0.82	(6)

While the closeness of these results to the ones obtained earlier is not, in itself, particularly enlightening, it is at least a check against statistical mishaps. Also it brings us still closer to the balance of trade.

At this stage, it becomes necessary to pay attention to the different types of capital movements. A detailed analysis is, unfortunately, impossible because of the lack of data. Some progress can nevertheless be made if one separates from the total $(C+U)$ the volume of foreign bond issues in the Swiss market which, for the present purposes, may be called long-term capital movements (C_L). One may then hypothesize that the remainder (C_S), taken as a whole, will behave just about as speculative short-term capital movements are assumed to behave. Positive signs of C_L and C_S will signify net inflows, while net outflows will have negative signs. For nonspeculative long-term capital flows (which are usually negative), one would expect a positive correlation with Swiss interest rates, more capital moving in (or less moving out) when interest rates are high than when they are low. One can hardly hope for very high correlation coefficients, though, for besides Swiss interest rates there are obviously some other important determinants of foreign bond issues in the Swiss market. Using for C_L a three-quarter moving average of foreign bond issues, I actually obtained the following correlation coefficients:

	1946 IV–1963 III	1946 IV–1953 III	1953 IV–1959 III	1959 IV–1963 III	
C_L/i	0.21	0.69	0.76	0.68	(7)

The regression coefficients for the subperiods, all of which are significant at the 99 per cent level, gradually increase from 48.2 in the first subperiod to 305.7 in recent years, thus reflecting the growth of the economy and the growing scale of international capital movements. The rather high correlation coefficients for the subperiods are, therefore, much more relevant than the low correlation for the entire period.[9] They leave no doubt that foreign bond issues in the Swiss market are strongly influenced by Swiss interest rates.

If these considerations are valid, it should be possible to express C_L as a function of the other factors that have been found to influence interest rates, *i.e.*, as a function of imports, exports, changes in imports, and short-term capital imports. The respective correlation coefficients are

	1946 IV–1963 III	1946 IV–1953 III	1953 IV–1959 III	1959 IV–1963 III	
$C_L/I, E, dI, C_S$	0.82	0.70	0.84	0.91	(8)

---

[9] A regression coefficient of 100 would mean that an increase in interest rates by 1 per cent per annum induced an increase in long-term capital inflows or – what is much more likely – a decrease in capital outflows by 100 million Swiss francs per quarter.

I conclude that it is illegitimate to consider foreign bond issues as an exogenous determinant of interest rates. Rather, they may be compared with a safety valve which, controlled by the rate of interest, automatically dampens excessive fluctuations of the credit market.[10]

If long-term capital movements are excluded, the rate of interest becomes a function of imports, exports, changes in imports, and short-term capital movements. This is at last the proxy theory alluded to in the title of this section. It is interesting to note that the correlation coefficients obtained in this way are just about the same as those obtained in equation (6), where long-term capital movements were included:

	1946 IV– 1963 III	1946 IV– 1953 III	1953 IV– 1959 III	1959 IV– 1963 III	
$di/I, E, dI, C_S$	0.70	0.89	0.85	0.81	(9)

For the period as a whole, all regression coefficients are significant at the 99 per cent level, while for the subperiods the level of significance is sometimes lower.

At this point, it is desirable to look back for a moment. In section III it was said that a large part of interest movements could be statistically explained in terms of the import surplus and of its first difference, *i.e.*, in terms of imports, exports, and their respective change. The proxy theory, while including some of the same variables, also includes short-term capital movements, whereas the changes in exports are now omitted. This means that on the basis of the theoretical and statistical analysis there is no reason why the changes in exports, dE, should appear in an explanation of interest rates. Actually, it can be shown that the conjectural theory, equations (2) of section III, would have been somewhat improved if dE had been omitted from the start:

	1946 IV– 1953 III	1953 IV– 1959 III	1959 IV– 1963 III	
$di/(I-E), d(I-E)$	0.80	0.67	0.67	(2)
$di/(I-E), dI$	0.89	0.68	0.71	(10)

In the light of this result, it seems that the relatively good result for the

---

[10] It is very likely that this is not due solely to the spontaneous working of the market, but also partly to the influence of the Swiss National Bank.

conjectural theory was partly due to the fact that changes in exports were relatively small, at least much smaller than the changes in some other variables. As a consequence, their inclusion, faulty as it was in principle, did not affect the results very much.

There remains the problem of short-term capital movements (which, it should be remembered, automatically include the invisibles). In section II it was observed that, for the period 1959-63, the simple correlation of interest rates with the import surplus, which for 1946-59 had been surprisingly high, dropped to a very low level. My tentative explanation was that in about 1959-60 there must have been significant changes in the behavior of capital movements. Now, in long-term capital movements (as measured by foreign bond issues) there are no traces of such changes. One would thus expect a marked change in the behavior of short-term capital movements as measured by the residual item. This is just what is actually found. From 1946 to 1959, the graph of C_S moves nicely up and down with the rate of interest, capital inflows being high when rates were high and vice versa. In 1959-60, however, there was a clear break in this pattern, characterized by a huge inflow of capital accompanied by relatively low interest rates. A simple regression of short-term capital inflows on interest rates confirms this picture. For the three subperiods it yields the following correlation coefficients:

	1946 IV- 1953 III	1953 IV- 1959 III	1959 IV- 1963 III	
C_S/i	0.85	0.76	− 0.44	(11)

For the first two subperiods, short-term capital imports seem to have paralleled interest rates even more closely than long-term capital imports. For the most recent subperiod, however, the relation is reversed, short-term capital inflows being high just when interest rates were low. While up to about 1959 interest rates behaved as if international capital movements did not matter very much, short-term capital flows have since become one of the important exogenous factors acting on the Swiss credit market.

VI Applying the proxy theory to the 1930's

The proxy theory developed in the previous section has so far been applied to postwar data only. The reason is that the underlying primary theory partly relied on data that are not available for the 1930's. This is not true, however, for the proxy theory itself, for which all the data are readily available back to 1930. It is thus possible to apply the proxy theory to the 1930's, *i.e.*, to explain the course of interest rates during that period in terms of imports, exports, changes in imports, and short-term capital movements. It was noted above that for the 1930's a simple correlation between changes in interest rates and changes in the import surplus fails completely. The results are not much better if the changes in interest rates are correlated with both the import surplus and its changes, the correlation coefficient being 0.26. If the reasoning leading up to the proxy theory was valid, the proxy theory should bring a marked improvement. Actually, the correlation coefficient now rises to 0.61. While it is still lower than for the postwar period, it is very much higher than before. One of the reasons for this improvement is again the behavior of capital flows. While net long-term inflows (or negative outflows) as measured by foreign bond issues were positively correlated with interest rates in this period, too, short-term capital, although the relevant correlation coefficient was low, tended to move in when rates were low, and vice versa. Another reason is that the inclusion of export changes, for which I have found no theoretical or statistical justification, was much more disturbing in the 1930's than in the postwar period. Although for the 1930's the proxy theory works less well than for the postwar period, the reasoning on which it was based thus seems to be largely confirmed. I therefore feel entitled to conclude that the proxy theory is, on the whole, a reasonably good substitute for a "true" explanation of the course of Swiss interest rates.

VII Concluding remark

The Swiss economy is characterized, among other things, by the dominating influence of the balance of payments on the monetary base and, on the other hand, by a close relation between domestic output and imports. This paper has tried to show that under these conditions certain components of the balance of payments can be used as indicators or proxies of those forces which actually determine the rate of interest. In conclusion, I should like, for a moment, to change the perspective and to ask whether the resulting proxy theory in turn offers certain suggestions for the possible improvement of what I have called the primary theory. This does indeed seem to be the case. If imports reflect domestic investment, changes in the monetary base, contrary to the specifications of the primary model, are not really independent of investment. If, on the other hand, long-term international capital flows are significantly influenced by Swiss interest rates, it is not entirely legitimate to consider the monetary base as exogenous. These considerations lead to an enlarged version of the primary model, in which changes in the monetary base appear as an endogenous variable to be explained in terms of the rate of interest, domestic investment (and possibly output), exports, and short-term capital flows. At the same time, international capital flows may also have a role to play in the demand and supply functions for money and credit. For the time being, important elements of the data required for such a model are still lacking. As a consequence, the simultaneous explanation of interest rates and the balance of payments as envisaged in the opening paragraph of this paper remains a task for the future.

GERMANY'S PERSISTENT
BALANCE-OF-PAYMENTS DISEQUILIBRIUM [1]

Charles P. Kindleberger

Once bitten, twice shy. Having explained the persistent balance-of-payments surplus of the United States, I have for years been expecting the German surplus to go away, as my colleague, Paul Samuelson, continuously reminds me. Perhaps an attempt to "explain" this surplus would exorcise it, too, in medieval fashion. This paper, however, is more a catalogue of explanations than a positive statement. It may have value as a review of balance-of-payments adjustment analysis, if that subject can be said to need further attention after the Brookings report and its exegesis. We start with a list of explanations, by no means mutually exclusive; a table of the principal items in the German balance is presented at the end of this article (Table 2).

    I Inflation abroad

    II Beggar-thy-neighbor policies by Germany

    III The structure of German trade

    IV The German propensity to export

    V The docility of German labor

    VI Competition in German markets

    VII The German propensities to save, or not to absorb

    VIII Deficiencies of the German capital market

    IX German innovation and technical progress

[1] This paper is written in the course of research undertaken with the support – gratefully acknowledged – of the Center of International Affairs, Harvard University. Thanks are due to a considerable number of economists with whom I have discussed the topic. The list is too long to set out in full, but I cannot forbear mentioning Professors Herbert Giersch and Hans Möller, of the Universities of the Saar and Munich, respectively.

I   Inflation abroad

Gottfried Haberler thought that the persistent balance-of-payments surplus of the United States after the war was in important respects a result of inflation "pure and simple."[2] More would agree that the German surplus of 1963 and 1964 follows from inflations in Italy, France, and the Netherlands. DM 2.4 billion out of the DM 3.0 billion increase in the merchandise surplus in 1963 over 1962, for example, were with the European Economic Community countries, and much of the 1963 private capital inflow was Italian. If the surplus of the 1950's is taken as having been corrected by the appreciation of 1961 (see the loss of Bundesbank reserves in 1961 and 1962), the case can be made that 1963 and 1964 present us with a new and different surplus, entirely the consequence of foreign inflation.

But the problem is to explain the 1950's; why adjustment took so long then, and why inflation should have occurred in Italy, France, and the Netherlands, rather than in Germany, with its strained use of resources. The new surplus may be a pure accident, although Nature and social science abhor such explanation. It is likely that there is an asymmetry in the system somewhere, which makes Germany come out with surpluses each time, rather than now a surplus, now a deficit.[3] The asymmetry may lie in the skills of the authorities, in their sensitivity to price changes, in the way the economic system responds to surpluses and deficits – in the German case, slowly to the former and rapidly to the latter. Inflation is part of the explanation, to be sure, but it is not an explanation in itself, and it fails to cover the 1950's.

II   Beggar-thy-neighbor policies by Germany

The German balance-of-payments surpluses are characterized by Thomas Balogh as "beggar-thy-neighbor," but as he has not yet developed his thought on the subject, it is not clear why.[4] The economy was not de-

---

[2]   See "Dollar Shortage", in *Foreign Economic Policy for the United States,* ed. S. E. Harris (Cambridge, Mass.: Harvard University Press, 1948), p. 434.

[3]   C. P. Kindleberger, "L'Asymetrie de la balance des paiements et le problème du dollar", *Revue économique,* No. 2 (March, 1954), 166-89.

[4]   *Unequal Partners* (Oxford: Basil Blackwell, 1963), II, 25, n. 3.

pressed during the 1950's. Apart from the 1951-53 period, there was a continuous inflationary gap. Efforts were made to get rid of the surplus, in unilateral tariff reductions in 1956, which had no effect on the net surplus, and in the 5 per cent revaluation of 1961, where the effect is more debatable. The export drive begun during the Korean-boom deficit of 1950 was virtually abandoned in 1955. Wells states that "no substantial part of the German export effort can be explained in terms of specific government fiscal aid."[5]

We shall have occasion to discuss monetary, fiscal, exchange, and trade policies below, but it seems clear that the Germans worked hard to rid themselves of the surplus, consistent with policies addressed to other objectives. Without these efforts, the surplus might have been larger.

Something more sophisticated than merely foreign stupidity or German guile, then, is required by way of explanation.

III   The structure of German exports

Economists from less developed countries argue that it is the export structure that counts. It counts, they say, against them in primary products. As a manufacturer of capital equipment and consumers' durables, Germany was lucky. In a world of reconstruction from war and self-conscious development, the demand curve for capital equipment moves rapidly to the right. In Europe, where automobiles are the symbol of the rising level of living, high growth abroad produces higher growth in automobile exports. Germany's short-run comparative advantage lay along the same lines as its long-run advantage, in contrast with Belgium, say, where a short-run comparative advantage in capital-intensive, semi-finished, industrial materials – steel, glass, soda ash, nitrogenous fertilizers – was continuously being eroded in the long run by higher foreign demands for, and higher gains of, productivity in other lines of activity.[6] But a couple of points are worth making.

In the first place, international-trade theorists of the Heckscher-Ohlin persuasion, as most of us are, would have been wrong in thinking that

---

[5] S. J. Wells, *British Export Performance: A Comparative Study* (Cambridge, Eng.: The University Press, 1964), p. 81.

[6] See A. Lamfalussy, *Investment and Growth in Mature Economies: The Case of Belgium* (London: Macmillan and Co., 1961).

Germany with its large capital losses and gains of population after the war should have changed to more labor-intensive lines of export activity.[7] It is easy to underestimate the hysteresis effect which virtually requires cities to be built on the same sites after destruction, block by block, and economies to specialize in the same directions. Capital as a whole may be suddenly scarce and labor abundant, but the marginal product of new investment is highest in the familiar lines, where it combines with surviving equipment and trained labor and management. Second, as has been widely remarked, Germany not only did not lose economically by having the agricultural portions of East Germany lopped off at Potsdam; it improved its terms of trade with the world by buying its food more cheaply, and increased its degree of specialization in the heavy industry of the Ruhr and the mechanical and chemical industries of Frankfurt and Stuttgart. Third, however, and this perhaps is the main point, Germany responded to its market opportunities by increasing its specialization still further. Seventy-four per cent of 1950's exports were manufactures; 89 per cent of 1960's. Whereas total exports of manufactures expanded sevenfold over the decade, machinery and transport-equipment exports rose tenfold.

Finally, it must be stated here, in the next several sections, and in homilies to the less developed countries, that structure is not necessarily related to equilibrium. The absorption approach is addressed in section VII below, but note should be taken of it now and in the interim.

IV The German propensity to export

If Germany was favored by its export structure, the individual entrepreneur pushed hard in selling abroad. The high status of exporting goes back to the "Export or Die" period at the end of the nineteenth century, and has often been remarked.[8] But specific reasons are advanced for the

---

[7] See, among others, K. W. Roskamp, "Factor Proportions and Foreign Trade: The Case of West Germany", *Weltwirtschaftliches Archiv*, XCI, No. 2 (1963), 319-26.

[8] See W. N. Parker, "Entrepreneurial Opportunities and Response in the German Economy", *Explorations in Entrepreneurial History*, VII, No. 1 (October, 1954), 16; Henry C. Wallich, *Mainsprings of the German Revival* (New Haven, Conn.: Yale University Press, 1955), pp. 244 ff. For a contrary statement about French incapacity for exporting, see my *Foreign Trade and the National Economy* (New Haven, Conn.: Yale

German interest in exports today. For almost twenty years, from 1931 to 1950, the German businessman's attention was perforce turned inward. Moreover, starting from scratch in 1950, he found it difficult to enter new foreign markets, with the necessity of incurring costs to build dealer organizations, to gear production to foreign requirements, and so on. (Incidentally, he may have been aided by the demise over the twenty years of the old merchanting houses that used to stand between the producer and his customer, which demise now makes direct selling mandatory.) Export markets, so hard to enter or re-enter, once entered were the last to be abandoned.

Whatever the explanation, there seems to be little doubt about the facts. German businessmen reacted to the slight recession of 1961-62 with a strong drive to sell exports. One aspect of this drive was dumping, more politely referred to as price differentiation or price concessions for foreign customers.

An important and interesting puzzle is presented by the disparate behavior of export unit values and the general price level in the United States, on the one hand, and in European countries and Japan, on the other. Prices have been rising more outside the United States than in that country since 1958, but the development of export unit values has not been parallel. A striking diagram is set out in *Lloyd's Bank Review* for April, 1964, showing export prices of manufactures above consumer prices and unit wage costs in manufacturing in the United States, but below them in the United Kingdom, Germany, Italy, France, and Japan. The *Review* states: "The recent upsurge in costs and prices on the Continent has found little reflection in export prices".[9]

Impressions are cheap; facts, elusive. The disparate behavior of external and internal prices may be due to differences in productivity, or in competition, between the export sector and the domestic market. If the export sector is subject to decreasing costs, and domestic output, including services, to increasing, the general picture for all but the United States could be explained. United States experience in turn may be ex-

University Press, 1962), p. 230. The success of the French in exporting after 1958, despite a "built-in aversion for exports", throws doubt on the validity of such a generalization.

   [9] P. 54. The effect is most marked for the 1950's, and a similar diagram based on 1961, rather than 1953 as in the *Review,* shows United States unit values also below consumer prices and (in this comparison) industrial wholesale prices. See *Monthly Report of the Deutsche Bundesbank*, XVI, No. 1 (January, 1964), 31. But the gap in the United States series is narrower than that for the other countries.

plained by the nature of competition in steel, discussed in section VI below. But price differentiation between the export and the home market does occur. An outstanding example is furnished by the automobile industry. In April, 1962, Volkswagen raised its domestic prices by from $60 to $97, but kept its export prices unchanged. It was followed by the rest of the industry in May, despite the strong adverse reaction of (then) Economics Minister Erhard.[10] The *Monthly Report of the Deutsche Bundesbank* for January, 1964, states explicitly: "In some measure the increase of foreign demand continued to be due to the fact that, under pressure of insufficiently employed capacities, some industries tried to expand their foreign sales even at the cost of price concessions".[11]

The German export drive of 1950-55 has been mentioned. Present means of stimulating exports – guaranteed medium-term credits, remission of turnover taxes on exports, and the application of a cascaded tax to imports – may be no greater than those of European countries in general, but the export interests have forced Chancellor Erhard to state categorically that he will not again revalue the mark. Exchange policy in Germany can be regarded as a contest between the savings banks, which favor flexible exchange rates as a means of stabilizing the internal price level, on the one hand, and export interests, which want the rate kept stable, on the other.[12] As of the summer of 1964, the export interests were winning.

V   The docility of German labor

An early explanation for the German economic miracle was love of work.[13] Today, it is denied by a German sociologist that his countrymen

---

[10]   *New York Times,* May 31, 1962.

[11]   *Loc. cit.* See also the statement of Ifo-Institut für Wirtschaftsforschung in its Ifo-Schnelldienst *Berichte zur Wirtschaftslage* for April 10, 1964, under the heading "Anhaltend starkes Exportwachstum" ("Continued Strong Growth of Exports"), p. 1: "For the first time in a long while it was anticipated in many industrial circles that export prices would rise more than inland prices."

[12]   See "Savers Prefer Revaluation", *The Economist,* CCXII, No. 6314 (August 29, 1964), 840. For a detailed statement of the export point of view from a German source, see "No Fear of Export Surpluses", *Die Welt* (Hamburg), February 1, 1964, translated in *The German Tribune,* February 22, 1964.

[13]   See, *e.g.,* Wallich, *op. cit.,* chap. xii, esp. pp. 332-34, 340, 341.

are particularly industrious,[14] and one can even hear echoes in Germany of dislike of Italians because they work too hard at piece-rate jobs. But it remains true that German labor is unaggressive in pushing for higher pay. An early postwar labor leader, Hans Boechler, is regarded in the German press as "unforgettable" because he sold German labor on moderation in wage demands. German industrialists and public opinion find Rosenberg, the top leader – and even Otto Brenner of the metal workers, who cultivates an image of militancy – fundamentally ready to hold back where exports are threatened by domestic price increases. It was feared that the 1962 settlement of the metal workers, which was regarded as eminently reasonable (a two-year contract with 6 per cent increases annually instead of the 10 and 12 per cent of the earlier years), would be followed in 1964 by an enormous wage push, especially in view of high profits and a statement by the Economics Minister that the productivity increase in 1964 had reached a new record. Instead, the metal workers surprised even German public opinion by their moderation[15] – a fifteen-month contract of great complexity, which came to a 7.3 per cent increase a year, and an agreement to postpone for another year the reduction in the working week.

It is difficult for an economist to enter into the discussion as to whether German labor is unusually submissive; takes a long-run rather than a short-run view of its economic advantage, and is really maximizing with low time-preference; is deeply disturbed that present rapidly improving conditions will not last, so that nothing must be done to upset the applecart; or whether the lag of German wages behind profits is merely longer than in most countries. Informed opinion in Germany, however, is persuaded that labor organizations, like businessmen, are sensitive to competitive conditions on export markets and rising prices on the home front, in a way which is true of few other countries. This is income policy from below.[16]

One view is that it is not self-restraint that limits the grasp of labor unions, but competition. This may have applied to the 1950's, with their

---

[14] Ralf Dahrendorf, "The New Germanies", *Encounter*, XII (April, 1964), 56.

[15] *Frankfurter Allgemeine Zeitung,* July 8, 1964.

[16] But note that Chancellor Erhard held a meeting of business and labor leaders, along with the economic and financial leaders of the government, to discuss wage policy *(Frankfurter Allgemeine Zeitung,* July 10, 1964). This was after the metal workers' settlement in which government intervention, if any occurred, was not overt.

initially large number of unemployed, of movements off the farm and of refugees from the East before the Wall, and before the need to import foreign labor, expensive because of its special needs. With long contracts, imperfect competition may hold down wages, and more competition would bid them up, as the wage drift which exists in Germany implies. In a competitive market in which labor maximized its short-run advantage, wages would have gone far higher.

The importance of labor docility is, of course, in holding down costs and maintaining the growth of exports. Beyond this, however, it has relevance for an implicit model in which income distribution plays a critical role in balance-of-payments adjustment. Robert Mundell once said[17] that a rising share of wages in national income is followed by a worsening of the balance of payments. We shall see later that this model does not apply to Germany. But what is impressive is that the share of wages in income rose so modestly – from 59.1 per cent in 1950 to only 60.9 per cent in 1960 – and since then to 64.8 per cent in 1963[18] after the exhaustion of labor reserves.

VI   Competition in German markets

Egon Sohmen believes that the big difference between the economic performances of Germany and other countries lies in the competitiveness of their markets. In one paper he emphasizes the importance of competition for German growth;[19] another focuses more narrowly on flexible exchange rates.[20] Between the lines in both papers, however, and explicitly in his new book,[21] he states that competition leads to lower goods prices, which, with high elasticities, lead to export surpluses.

---

[17]   In a seminar at Massachusetts Institute of Technology.

[18]   Germany, Statistisches Reichsamt, *Wirtschaft und Statistik*, XII, No. 5 (May, 1960), 258; XVI, No. 1 (January, 1964), 8.

[19]   "Competition and Growth: The Lessons of West Germany", *American Economic Review*, XLIX, No. 5 (December, 1959), 986-1003. See also the comments by K. W. Roskamp, A. I. MacBean and W. G. Shepherd, and R. G. Opie, and Professor Sohmen's reply, *op. cit.*, L, No. 5 (December, 1960), 1015-31.

[20]   "The Dollar and the Mark", *The Dollar in Crisis,* ed. S. E. Harris (New York: Harcourt, Brace and World, 1961), pp. 185-200.

[21]   *Internationale Währungsprobleme* (Frankfurt-am-Main: Fritz-Knapp Verlag, 1964).

In steel, he has a case that competition is stronger in Europe than in the United States. A decline in capacity utilization from 75 to 45 per cent in the United States failed to disturb the internal price structure, whereas the 1962 decline from 95 to 85 per cent utilization in Europe produced a substantial price decline.[22] But the implications of this for the balance of payments are unclear. Rising steel prices in the United States have doubtless helped to raise the export unit values above general prices, as already discussed. In Europe, however, the market is highly competitive within the European Coal and Steel Community area, but prices within the Community are detached from those without. In 1963, German orders for iron and steel showed a very small gain within the ECSC and a large drop outside.

Price differentiation between the home and foreign markets suggests that the home market is imperfectly rather than highly competitive. So does the widespread discussion in Germany of retail price maintenance. In his earliest paper, Sohmen worried lest growing cartelization in industry and banking weaken the basis for German growth.[23] Rationalization cartels which distribute production between firms by differentiated items and which are believed to have been formed across national lines in the Common Market may lead to lower costs and prices through internal economies of scale. These would increase competition in one sense and reduce it in another. On the other hand, France, Italy, and Austria all experienced export surpluses during substantial stretches of the postwar period without well-developed policies of improving competition. The relations between market organization and export surpluses are thus difficult to establish.

"Competitiveness" is used in a wider sense by Angus Maddison to refer merely to the maintenance of competitive prices in foreign trade. In his *Economic Growth in the West*,[24] Maddison states that the German authorities followed a vigorous line of action in each of three major aspects of growth policy: management of demand, maintenance of competitiveness, and fostering output potential by policies favoring high investment and foreign trade (p. 102). Maintenance of demand means promotion of expenditure for high utilization of capacity, and while

---

[22] *Ibid.*

[23] "Competition and Growth...", pp. 998-1000.

[24] *Economic Growth in the West: Comparative Experience in Europe and North America* (New York: The Twentieth Century Fund, 1964).

Maddison suggests that the German government may have fallen somewhat short of optimum policies in this respect during the early part of
the 1950's, he gives it high marks thereafter (*passim,* esp. pp. 151-52).
But it is not so clear what he means by competitiveness. On occasion,
this seems to imply holding demand down, rather than up, applying
restrictive monetary policies each time inflation threatened (p. 138). For
the rest, however, it refers to only vaguely described policies directed
specifically to prices and incomes in a world of high demand elasticities
(p. 187). Germany is said to have better domestic defenses against inflation than other countries (p. 180) and a more successful policy generally
(p. 185), although the measures to raise imports and reduce the surplus
are acknowledged to have been unsuccessful (p. 180). Maddison recog-
nizes that the problem of controlling inflation in Germany was more
easily resolved than elsewhere for a number of reasons – the psychological
shock of monetary reform, the weak position of the unions, and the rapid
rise of productivity (p. 138). But so intent is he on making the point of
the importance of policies to control demand that he makes little
allowance for the objective conditions of supply.

What seems to have been the case in Germany is that supply has been
highly elastic without regard to market organization or monetary and
fiscal policy. It is not only the authorities who are anxious to avoid inflation, but the entire population. Germany's Phillips curve, that is, is
virtually horizontal, with prices rising very little as unemployment moves
toward zero. Wide differences in Phillips curves between countries, if they
exist, are more important for balance-of-payments changes among competing countries, where the elasticities are high, than differences in policy
arising from differences in intelligence or political courage.

VII   The German propensities to save, or not to absorb

As is well known, and as we have recently been reminded by Harry
Johnson's trenchant review of the Brookings report,[25] it is not enough to
expand exports to enjoy an export surplus. A country must refrain from

---

[25]   Harry G. Johnson, "The International Competitive Position of the United
States and the Balance of Payments for 1968: A Review Article", *Review of Economics
and Statistics*, XVLI, No. 1 (February, 1964), 14-32.

importing in an equal amount; it must not spend and respend all the income earned from exports until it spills over into imports: that is, it must save. Export surplus equals net savings, or domestic savings minus domestic investment. So much is identity, but it is also possible to look at the savings as producing the export surplus, rather than the export surplus the savings. And, to repeat, no net savings, no export surplus.

In the early period after 1951, the large net savings came from a government surplus established by the Finance Minister, Dr. Schaeffer, who levied taxes for Germany's contribution to the European defense effort well in advance of the ultimate expenditure, building up a secret government reserve. This hoard, which grew to nearly DM 6 billion in 1953, became known as the "Julius Turm" after the tower in Spandau in which some of the gold received as part of the French indemnity of 1871 was covertly stored as a war chest.[26] It was easy, at this stage, to regard the export surplus as an inadvertent consequence of fiscal policy, and to anticipate that it would disappear when the government books were balanced again.

But when government savings declined, undivided corporate profits stepped into the breach. Later, with a profit squeeze, savings of private households took over. Savings climb each year, but the distribution of savings by sector varies widely, as Table 1 shows.

Table 1

The formation of savings in the Federal Republic of Germany, selected years (in percent of current domestic savings)

Year	Households	Enterprises (Undistributed profits)	Government (Surplus on current account)
1950	21	47	31
1953	25	26	49
1958	33	36	32
1960	27	34	41
1963 preliminary	37	21	43

SOURCES   Germany, Statistisches Reichsamt, *Wirtschaft und Statistik*, XII, No. 12 (December, 1960), 710; and *Monthly Report of the Deutsche Bundesbank*, XVI, No. 4 (April, 1960), 5. The two series joined may not be strictly comparable.

---

[26] See Frederick G. Reuss, *Fiscal Policy for Growth without Inflation: The German Experiment* (Baltimore: The Johns Hopkins Press, 1963), pp. 157-58.

The savings of households increase almost consistently, as does the ratio of private savings to disposable income, which has risen from 3 per cent in the early 1950's to $5\frac{1}{2}$ per cent in 1956, 8 per cent in 1957, $8\frac{1}{2}$ per cent in 1962, and $9\frac{1}{2}$ per cent in 1963. In 1963, disposable income rose by 6.7 per cent and savings by 20 per cent for an impressive income elasticity of 3. While the Deutsche Bundesbank believes that some of the savings may be due to transitional factors, such as hesitation in buying consumer durables, it finds the phenomenon remarkable.[27]

Recall that household savings are rising as a percentage of disposable income with a redistribution of income in favor of labor, not property-owners. Many reasons are adduced for the high marginal propensity to save of the German, but most of these apply to the middle-class household rather than the wage-earner: the Pigou effect, or trying to restore the asset position after the losses imposed by inflation, deflation, war, and expulsion or flight from the East; wealth illusion, arising from the absence of a national debt;[28] the postwar quest for a sense of identity, which sociologists believe deeply affects German thought and action. Or possibly the German worker merely is convinced that the gain in his level of living is too good to last, and, operating on a Friedman consumption function, he spends only his permanent income. If so, he differs remarkably from the French and Italian working classes, who want more income and are prepared to spend even more than these income gains.

The erratic behavior of government surplus and undistributed corporate profits, however, casts considerable doubt on the absorption approach to balance-of-payments equilibrium, at least in the short run. The balance-of-payments surplus equals net savings ex post, but there need be no automatic mechanism to bring them into equilibrium ex ante. In fact, if government, business, and households all fear inflation and react to rising prices by spending less, not more, the income mechanism which is supposed to adjust ex ante savings and ex ante investment in a closed economy will not function. A case might be made that the current-account deficit of 1962 was the result of the decline in undistributed corporate profits from DM 19.3 billion in 1960 and DM 16.5 billion in 1961 to DM

---

[27]   *Monthly Report...*, *loc. cit.*; and *Monthly Report...*, XVI, No. 2 (February, 1964), 6-8.

[28]   This could presumably be corrected by a capital subsidy. Note that losses through inflation and war typically are thought to make people save less, rather than more.

13.8 billion in 1962. But these profits go still lower in 1963, especially during the first half, and rebound only after the new export surge of the second half of 1963. Ex post nonabsorption equals ex post export surplus through some such mechanism as windfall profits and losses and unintended investment and disinvestment in inventories which bring savings and investment into line in a closed economy. In the short run, the absorption theory is no use. In the long, the high propensity to export and the high propensity to save are identical. Goods are produced which cannot be sold at home and therefore must be sold abroad. Or high exports threaten inflation, which produces the response of increased savings.

Note in passing the inapplicability of the Mundell model to Germany. With income redistribution nothing happens, because wage-earners save like capitalists.

VIII Deficiencies of the German capital market

Important opinion, ranging from the United States Treasury to members of the staff of the EEC and individual German economists, argues that the problem lies not in the German current-account surplus, which is a consequence of high productivity and high propensities to save, but in the inadequate capacity of the German capital market to fund this surplus in appropriate form. Private capital movements, in fact, have been inward, except in 1958 and 1959, requiring official capital exports to hold down increases in official reserves. In one view, the trouble lies in the high liquidity preference of the German saver, which holds rates on long-term securities at a high level where they are attractive to foreign investors. Savers want only demand or savings deposits; banks are therefore obliged to stay liquid and keep large deposits with the Bundesbank; the Bundesbank must in turn stay liquid with gold and foreign exchange. The liquid form of the savings means that they are in considerable part held in liquid claims on the world. Or, in the other version, the difficulty stems from the oligopolistic behavior of the banking system:[29] the banks like

---

[29] See U.S. Congress, Joint Economic Committee, Economic Practices and Policies, Paper No. 3, *A Description and Analysis of Certain European Capital Markets* (Washington, D. C.: Government Printing Office, 1964), esp. p. 130: "It would appear,

to have industrial corporations dependent on them, and issue securities only at high commissions. In addition, the land governments protect their access to the market by a $2\frac{1}{2}$ per cent tax on private issues.[30] Firms are financed through open-book credits from banks and undistributed profits. In 1963, for example, DM 60 billion of gross investment by enterprises outside of housing were financed with the issue of DM 2 billion of fixed-interest securities and DM 1.3 billion of shares. The major items (in billions of DM) were: depreciation (31); undistributed profits (16); medium- and long-term bank credit (9); short-term bank credit (3.3); capital transfers, largely from government (3.8); direct government credit (3.9). Against the bank loans, there was an increase of deposits with banks (6.9).[31] And the rates on bank loans ranged upward from 5 to 9 and 10 per cent, nominal.[32]

Government direct advances to industry (and housing) are necessary for lack of a capital market, and of tax advantages in depreciation. In the absence of a government debt, it is impossible to use government surpluses to retire securities which investors can replace with private issues. But the high long-term rate – on this showing, a product of oligopoly among the dominant banks – encourages capital inflows and discourages capital outflows in long-term securities, which make the Bundesbank hold in liquid reserves that part of the surplus which the government does not fund.

A wide range for debate exists between those who say that Germany still has a shortage of capital and should be borrowing from abroad, and those who regard the export surplus as "natural", in the state of savings and investment needs, and conclude that the fault lies in the capital items. Should capital adjust to the current account, or vice versa? The debate is an ancient one. If one looks beyond balance-of-payments theory and compares Germany with the United States, one can argue that German investment needs, especially in housing but also in infrastructure and in

---

therefore, that there is very little competition in issuing of bonds". And: "These arrangements for issuing bonds may contribute materially to the high cost of raising capital in Germany".

   30   Kurt Richebächer ("Germany's Unsought Surplus", *The Banker,* April, 1964, p. 225) argues that this should be immediately repealed.

   31   See the excellent article on "Wealth Form and its Financing in 1963", in *Monthly Report of the Bundesbank,* XVI, No. 4 (April, 1964), and the table on p. 14.

   32   *Ibid.,* Table 2, p. 70.

further modernization of production and especially distribution, may exceed German savings capacity. This view also supports government savings in excess both of the government's own investment and of the investment involved in the countercyclical behavior of social security funds. But if Germany is compared with the rest of the world – Europe, but especially the less developed countries – Germany should be a capital exporter, and the task is to find better instrumentalities for distributing gross savings inside the country and net savings abroad.

It takes two to tango, to be sure, and one should not forget Sohmen's warning that further capital exports by Germany might be matched by an addition to the current-account surplus, instead of funding it.[33]

It is hard to resolve the debate. Interest rates on long-term securities have been coming down very slowly, as compared with rates in the short-term market in Germany. Six per cent bonds of public authorities, which sold for 92.7 in 1957, went as high as 102.8 in May, 1962, when the lowest yield was reached, but have since gone back to 100. Some experts insist that moving the long-term rate toward 5 per cent would unleash heavy borrowing which would be inflationary, although it is hard to see any impact of the 1962 decline in the data for new issues. The interest rate may be high in Germany because of a high marginal efficiency of capital or because of high liquidity preference and/or oligopoly in banking, but the identification problem remains.

IX   German innovation and technical progress

Innovation is again subject to differences of opinion. According to Maddison, technical progress cannot be given any substantial independent role in explaining differences in economic growth in Europe (and presumably also in balance-of-payments behavior),[34] although at another point he observes that the productivity achievements of Germany, France, and Italy were due to special factors.[35] The Economic Commission for Europe, on the other hand, states that the contribution of technical progress and innovation to the high productivity of capital and labor,

---

[33]   Sohmen, "The Dollar and the Mark".

[34]   *Op. cit.*, p. 81.

[35]   *Ibid.*, p. 156.

which distinguishes German performance, must have been considerable.[36] As the remark implies, direct evidence is missing. Most data on productivity are derived by dividing indexes of output by indexes of input; the relation of the resultant time series to new products and new processes, apart from the gains from using factors more efficiently at higher capacity utilization, is obscure. The ECE study cites a series of specific reasons that might account for increased technical efficiency – technical assistance, joint ventures and licensing, encouragement of research, and, of course, the high rate of gross capital formation. The impact of high capacity utilization can be argued: a backlog of orders can produce real gains in efficiency if the entrepreneur is able to organize production in ways that minimize changing machinery settings, and hence reduce knockdown time. On the other hand, in some instances, a heavy order book disrupts production, as all customers are in a hurry, and the entrepreneur is forced by exigent demands to turn from one to another to equalize customer impatience at the margin, properly weighted for the importance of the buyer, thus raising costs.

The importance of the subject turns on the belief that the export-led model of growth has positive feedback built into it. Nothing exceeds like excess. Growth gives increasing returns to scale and lower costs, which lead to exports, which lead through savings and investment to more growth, lower prices, more exports, more growth.[37] As Balassa points out, however, this model requires something to hold down wages,[38] either unlimited supplies of labor, or perfect labor mobility, or that euphemism for wage stability – income policy. An economic journalist has extended the analysis to two sectors, one of which is efficient and exports, experiencing declining costs; the other is inefficient, with rising costs and low income elasticity of demand. To cut back demand, he suggests, raises prices by cutting output in the decreasing-cost industry, with highly

---

[36]   United Nations, Economic Commission for Europe, *Some Factors in Economic Growth in Europe during the 1950s* (Geneva, 1964), chap. vi, p. 6.

[37]   This model was set out by A. Lamfalussy, in *The United Kingdom and the Six: An Essay on Economic Growth in Western Europe* (Homewood, Ill.: Richard D. Irwin, 1963). The theme is also found in Sir Roy Harrod's *The British Economy* (New York: McGraw-Hill, 1963). See also W. Beckerman, "Projecting Europe's Growth", *Economic Journal*, LXXII, No. 288 (December, 1962), 912-25; and Bela Balassa, "Some Observations on Mr. Beckerman's 'Export-Propelled' Growth Model", and Mr. Beckerman's "Reply", *Economic Journal*, LXXIII, No. 292 (December, 1963), 781-87.

[38]   *Op. cit.*

Table 2

Balance of payments of the Federal Republic of Germany (in billions of DM)

	1950	1951	1952	1953	1954	1955	1956	1957	1958	1959	1960	1961	1962	1963
Current account:														
Exports	8.4	14.6	16.9	18.5	21.9	25.6	30.7	35.8	36.8	41.0	47.8	50.9	50.9	58.3
Imports	− 10.7	− 13.1	− 14.7	− 14.8	− 18.0	− 22.3	− 25.1	− 28.5	− 29.4	− 33.1	− 39.6	− 41.2	− 46.5	− 48.9
Net transactions in goods	− 2.3	+ 1.5	+ 2.2	+ 3.7	+ 3.9	+ 3.2	+ 5.7	+ 7.4	+ 7.5	+ 7.8	+ 8.6	+ 9.8	+ 6.4	+ 9.4
Net services	− 0.2	− 0.7	+ 0.2	+ 0.5	+ 0.1	− 0.3	− 0.1	+ 0.3	+ 0.4	− 0.4	− 0.6	− 2.6	− 3.5	− 3.6
Net transfers	+ 2.1	+ 1.5	+ 0.2	− 0.5	− 0.5	− 0.8	− 1.2	− 1.9	− 1.9	− 3.2	− 3.4	− 4.4	− 5.1	− 5.0
Net balance on current account	− 0.4	+ 2.3	+ 2.5	+ 3.8	+ 3.6	+ 2.1	+ 4.4	+ 5.8	+ 6.0	+ 4.1	+ 4.6	+ 2.8	− 2.2	+ 0.9
Capital account:														
German investment abroad	− 0.1	+ 0.1	− 1.7	…	− 0.2	− 0.3	− 0.6	− 1.0	− 1.7	− 4.9	− 2.4	− 3.0	− 2.5	− 2.2
Foreign investment in F. R. S.	+ 0.5	− 0.2	− 0.2	− 0.4	− 0.4	− 0.1	…	+ 0.4	+ 0.1	− 0.6	+ 2.1	− 1.3	+ 2.3	+ 4.2
Net long-term capital	+ 0.5	− 0.1	− 1.8	− 0.4	− 0.5	− 0.4	− 0.6	− 0.6	− 1.6	− 5.4	− 0.2	− 4.3	− 0.1	+ 2.0
Net short-term capital	− 0.3	+ 0.2	+ 1.8	+ 0.4	+ 0.1	− 0.1	+ 0.6	− 1.8	− 0.8	− 0.8	+ 2.0	− 0.9	+ 0.9	+ 0.3
Net balance on capital account	+ 0.2	+ 0.1	…	+ 0.1	− 0.4	− 0.5	+ 0.1	− 2.4	− 2.4	− 6.2	+ 1.7	− 5.1	+ 0.7	+ 2.2
Private	(− 0.3)	(+ 0.2)	(+ 0.5)	(+ 0.3)	(…)	(…)	(+ 1.0)	(+ 0.2)	(− 1.3)	(− 2.3)	(+ 3.9)	(+ 1.2)	(+ 1.3)	(+ 3.9)
Official	(+ 0.5)	(− 0.1)	(− 0.5)	(− 0.3)	(− 0.4)	(− 0.5)	(− 1.0)	(− 2.7)	(− 1.1)	(− 3.9)	(− 2.2)	(− 6.3)	(− 0.6)	(− 1.6)
Net movement of gold and exchange	+ 0.6	− 2.0	− 2.8	− 3.6	− 2.8	− 1.9	− 5.0	− 5.1	− 3.2	+ 2.2	− 8.0	+ 1.9	+ 0.6	− 2.6
Net errors and omissions	− 0.4	− 0.4	+ 0.3	− 0.2	− 0.4	+ 0.2	+ 0.6	+ 1.8	− 4.0	− 1.0	+ 1.7	+ 0.4	+ 0.9	− 0.5

… = less than DM 50 million.

SOURCE   *Monthly Report of the Deutsche Bundesbank*, XVI, No. 5 (May, 1964), 28-29.

elastic demand, without much cutting demand or output or reducing prices in the inefficient sector. Monopoly in factor and goods markets may even drive up prices in the archaic sector with demand cut. In his non-Euclidian, non-Keynesian, non-Phillipsian world, increased demand lowers prices (or at least rates of price increase), and decreased demand raises them.[39] There may be something to this picture. As Wells puts it, investment was higher in Germany; it was concentrated in the export industries; growth of demand led to rationalization of production and ultimately to lower costs; the secret of German success in exports lay in its rate of growth, and the secret of the rate of growth lay in exports.[40]

This brings us back, eleven years later, to Hicks's *Inaugural Lecture,* with export-biased growth (*cum* dumping), with the addition of Johnson's amendment for demand elasticities greater than one, such as apply, particularly, in the competitive situation of trade among industrial countries. This was, it will be remembered, a Keynesian underemployment model, in which supplies were infinitely elastic, and there was no problem of financing the surplus at home or abroad. With limited resources and full employment, it should behave differently; but, given the complexity of general equilibrium, it is difficult to say exactly how. The curious thing about the German economy is that it behaves as if it were a Keynesian economy, when all the world can see that it is at full employment with 660,000 unfilled jobs and 110,000 unemployed (June 30, 1964). It even eliminates the problem of financing the surplus at home – although unhappily the international problem remains. What remains baffling is, first, why labor is so restrained in putting up its price when the demand curve moves to the right, and, second, why it saves so much of its income.

Of the nine listed explanations with which we started, we exclude but one – beggar-thy-neighbor policies by Germany. The rest fit into a unified picture in which relative inflation abroad, if not absolute, is accounted for in part by high elasticities of supply in Germany, in the short run as in the long. The export structure is right, but German innovation and push make it more so. Labor turns out product without pushing up costs, and releases a large share of that product for export by refraining from consumption. Government saves, along with industry and labor.

Two points stand out in conclusion, both of which run counter to the

---

[39]   Norman Macrae, *Sunshades in October* (London: George Allen & Unwin, 1963).
[40]   *Op. cit.*, pp. 74-82.

strongly asserted conclusions of Maddison on growth. First, it is supply, rather than demand, that accounts for the German experience. To coin a phrase, demand is necessaiy, but not sufficient. Second, without disparaging the skill of the German authorities, it seems to have been not policy but the *force des choses* which produced the German results. Here is the critical asymmetry: policy directed to expand exports, hold down prices, curb domestic spending, and so on, works like a charm; policy to increase imports or improve the functioning of the capital market is unsuccessful. Like kisses and diamonds in the indifference curves of young ladies, policy is nice, but elastic supply is an economy's best friend.

COMPETITION AND GROWTH:
THE LESSON OF THE UNITED STATES BALANCE
OF PAYMENTS

Egon Sohmen

I Price flexibility and employment

Stripped of all superficial differences of treatment, the controversy
between "classical" and "Keynesian" economists in the years following
publication of the *General Theory* centered on the question of whether or
not flexibility of prices and wages, defined as the degree of responsiveness
of prices to a state of excess supply, would ensure the maintenance of full
employment.[1] Most investigations into the possible effects of price flexibility have been confined to the model of a closed economy. In the
General Theory, Keynes briefly mentioned the favorable employment
effects of a fall of prices (which he usually identified with a fall of wages)
through the induced rise in exports relative to imports,[2] but he subsequently restricted his argument to the case of a closed system.[3] He
concluded in the end that "there is, therefore, no ground for the belief that
a flexible wage policy is capable of maintaining a state of continuous full
employment. ...The economic system cannot be made self-adjusting along
these lines".[4] The reader is not warned again that this is not meant to be
a policy recommendation for the real world, but merely an assertion
about a theoretical model that excludes, among other things, all international trade.

---

[1] The most important literature references are Gottfried Haberler, *Prosperity and*
Depression (4th ed.; Cambridge, Mass.: Harvard University Press, 1958), esp. pp.
388-89 and Appendix II; Arthur C. Pigou, "The Classical Stationary State", *Economic*
Journal, LIII (December, 1943), 343-51; Don Patinkin, *Money, Interest and Prices*
(Evanston, Ill.: Row, Peterson, 1956), esp. chap. xiii.

[2] John M. Keynes, *The General Theory of Employment, Interest and Money*
(London: Macmillan and Co., 1936), pp. 262-63.

[3] *Ibid.*, pp. 264-65.

[4] *Ibid.*, p. 267.

The direct effect of a general fall of prices in one country on its export and import volumes is rather obvious. When exchange rates are fixed, more of that country's products will be bought in substitution for those of other countries. This cannot fail to raise business activity in it.[5] If doubts are expressed about the effectiveness of this factor, they can only rest on the possibility of indirect repercussions such as (*a*) the imposition of new trade restrictions by foreign governments or (*b*) monetary contraction abroad in response to losses of reserves by foreign central banks.[6] During a worldwide depression, when an increase of domestic employment through an improvement of the foreign balance is regarded as a "beggar-my-neighbor policy,"[7] the increased likelihood of protective action by other countries, and hence the reduced effectiveness of greater price flexibility as a means of assuring full employment, is beyond dispute.[8]

Considerations of this kind cannot have restrained policy recommendations in the more recent past. For more than six years, chronic stagnation in the United States has been accompanied by a more than adequate level of effective demand in the rest of the world. Many western European countries would, in fact, have been more than pleased if prices in the United States had responded more normally to a state of excess supply so that the inflationary impact of abnormally high trade surpluses in Europe might have been reduced.

II   United States export prices and the balance of payments

The question of the relative competitiveness of American industry on the world markets has received increasing attention in recent years in con-

---

[5]   The possibility that any country's exports may suffer from Giffen's paradox is so remote that I do not extend discussion of it beyond this footnote.

[6]   See Oskar Lange, *Price Flexibility and Employment* (Cowles Commission Monograph, No. 8 [Bloomington, Ind.: Principia Press, 1952], chap. viii.

[7]   Joan Robinson, "Beggar-my-neighbour Remedies for Unemployment", *Readings in the Theory of International Trade* (Philadelphia: The Blakiston Co., 1949), pp. 393-407.

[8]   Another possible objection can be disposed of very briefly. It might be argued that, with elastic price expectations, a fall of domestic prices might induce foreigners to defer purchases in that country so that its foreign balance (temporarily) worsens. This is a vaguely realistic possibility only if the country in question has a near-monopoly on the world market in all its exports. Otherwise, its sales will presumably still increase at the expense of its competitors. See Lange, *op. cit.*, p. 47.

nection with the balance-of-payments difficulties of the United States. The widespread view that the competitive position of the United States is basically satisfactory rests on the superficially impressive figures for her export surpluses: for the years 1958-63, there has been an average surplus of $3.7 billion (including services but excluding military aid shipments). This figure is already seen in better perspective when it is pointed out that it amounts to 0.7 per cent of the gross national product of the United States. By comparison, West Germany (including West Berlin) achieved an average export surplus of 2.1 per cent of GNP during this period.

With an average surplus on trade and service account of $3.7 billion for the period 1958-63, $2.6 billion were contributed by net earnings of dividends and interest. This component obviously does not reflect the competitiveness of American industry. It may, on the contrary, be negatively correlated with it: United States dividend earnings tend to increase because American companies find it profitable to transfer part of their production to foreign subsidiaries with lower production costs. Although the exact incidence of tying foreign aid is difficult to establish, exports certainly benefit from this practice. Approximately 80 per cent of United States aid, which amounted to about $4 billion during the first few years of the 1960's, is now tied to purchases in the United States. American export figures consequently do not correctly reflect the country's competitiveness. Finally, exports and imports would surely not be at their present levels if the economy were fully employed. Only the export surplus that would arise with full employment could serve as a legitimate criterion for a country's competitiveness.[9]

Apart from all this, it must be emphasized that the adequacy of a country's export surplus can never be judged by its absolute size or even by considerations of the kind just mentioned. The relevant question is whether the export surplus can adjust to the balance of autonomous (private as well as official) transfers on capital account and donations without the application of brute force in the form of artificial interference with international trade and payments or policies causing large-scale unemployment. By this criterion, the United States has failed unambiguously to generate a sufficient export surplus. The debate over whether the American balance-of-payments deficits are really caused by

---

[9] For readers who remain unconvinced, the reduced competitiveness of American industries on the world market is illustrated by both the price and the volume indicators

too high a domestic price level or rather by too high a level of aid and capital transfers to other countries in essence repeats the "bullion controversy" of one and a half centuries ago.[10]

One aspect of the American balance-of-payments deficits that deserves more attention is their smallness in relation to the size of the economy. Any one of the various possible definitions of a "balance-of-payments deficit" refers to a difference between payments to and receipts from the rest of the world. These payments, in turn, are only a fraction (in the case of the United States, a particularly small fraction) of the total volume of transactions in the country. It is most remarkable that a tiny hair should wag the modest tail which in turn wags a dog of rather impressive proportions. Using the Department of Commerce definition, the average United States balance-of-payments deficit for the years 1958 to 1962 amounted to 0.6 per cent of the gross national product; the percentage for the "basic balance" was 0.5 per cent for these same years.[11] Even with pegged exchange rates, the price changes required to direct such a small fraction of the country's resources toward production for export should never have presented any difficulty for a normally functioning economy.

in the following table:

	Per cent change of export unit values of manufactures, 1953-62	Country shares of exports of manufactures by 12 leading industrial countries	
		1953	1962
USA	22	26.2	19.9
Great Britain	17	20.9	15.2
West Germany	6	13.4	20.1
Japan	− 11	3.8	7.5
Italy	− 20	3.3	6.1

SOURCE   Walter S. Salant and Others, *The United States Balance of Paym entsin 1968* (Washington, D. C.: Brookings Institution, 1963), Tables III-1 and III-6.
See also Hang Sheng Cheng, "Relative Movements in the Prices of Exports of Manufactures", *International Monetary Fund Staff Papers*, IX (March, 1962), 81-106, and the reference in n. 15 below.

[10]   David Ricardo, *The High Price of Bullion* (London, 1810), reprinted in *The Works and Correspondence of David Ricardo*, ed. Piero Straffa, Vol. III (Cambridge, Eng.: Cambridge University Press, 1951).

[11]   Salant and Others, *op. cit.*, p. 6.

The failure of the United States to accomplish this minor reallocation appears all the more remarkable if it is remembered that it would not even have required a reduction of the quantity of resources devoted to domestic use. More than 5 per cent of the labor force has been out of work, and most industries have operated at levels substantially below capacity ever since balance-of-payments deficits became a problem for the United States. The task ought to have been particularly easy in view of the fact that prices were rising in most other countries. The extraordinary behavior of a few important industries was the principal obstacle that prevented both the elimination of the balance-of-payments deficits and a return to an acceptable employment level.

III   The high price of steel

The most instructive example is the performance of the American steel industry. Even a cursory examination reveals the striking contrast between its behavior and that of steel manufacturers in other countries. Figures 1, 2, and 3 show the evolution from 1955 to 1963 of average export prices per ton (in United States dollars) of finished steel products, estimated steel-producing capacity, and actual production of steel in the United States and in the six countries of the European Coal and Steel Community.[12]

---

[12]   There appears to be some confusion about the extent of the gap between American and European export prices for steel. In his testimony on steel prices before the Joint Economic Committee (Hearings before the Joint Economic Committee, 88th Cong., 1st Sess., *Steel Prices, Unit Costs, Profits, and Foreign Competition* [Washington D.C.: Government Printing Office, 1963], Walther Lederer expressed the view that export prices for open-hearth steel hardly differ at all (p. 481 and table on p. 479) and that the low European prices in another table he presented (p. 482) were only due to the fact that this table referred to the lower-quality Bessemer steel. The larger part of the difference between the two sets of prices in the two tables is not explained by quality differences (cf. the notes to Figure 1), but by the fact that the higher figures (p. 479) refer to *domestic list prices* in Europe. Domestic prices in Europe are less flexible than export prices to third countries, but they frequently deviate so much from quoted list prices as to make the latter almost meaningless. In recent years, actual prices on domestic sales have generally been closer to export prices than to published list prices as a result of intense competition from abroad (especially Japan). The *Annual Reports* of the European Coal and Steel Community have in recent years expressed increasing apprehension, in language vaguely resembling that of a conscientious cartel manager, about the mounting tendency to violate the open-price system incorporated in Article 60 of the ECSC treaty, and the consequent fall of steel prices in the European market. See esp. the *12th Annual Report* (for 1963), chap. iii, p. 2.

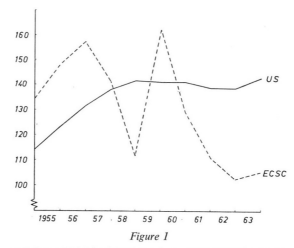

Figure 1

Average Export Prices of Finished Steel Products, 1955-1964 (beginning of year, U.S. $ per metric ton). Arithmetical averages of the export prices, F.O.B. ports of shipment, for five major finished steel products (merchant bars, wire-rod, plates, hot- and cold-rolled sheets).

SOURCES   European Coal and Steel Community, *Annual Reports*, 1955-1963. For western Europe, the *Annual Reports* only list export prices for Bessemer steel, whose quality is inferior to open-hearth steel. The latter is the only type of steel for which United States export prices are listed. To make the prices in Figure 1 comparable, the listed export prices for Europe have been increased by 10 per cent, the maximum price differential between the two qualities in Europe.

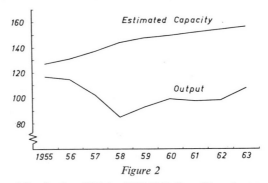

Figure 2

Steel Capacity and Production, U.S.A., 1955-1963 (in million short tons).

SOURCES   European Coal and Steel Community, *Annual Reports,* 1955-1963; and Hearings before the Joint Economic Committee, 88th Cong., 1st Sess., *Steel Prices, Unit Costs, Profits, and Foreign Competition* (Washington, D.C.: Government Printing Office, 1963), pp. 186, 339. 1956 and 1959 were years of major steel strikes in the United States.

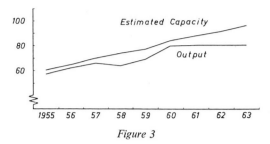

Figure 3

Steel Capacity and Production, European Coal and Steel Community, 1955-1963 (in million short tons).

SOURCES   European Coal and Steel Community, *Annual Reports,* 1955-1963; and Hearings before the Joint Economic Committee, 88th Cong., 1st Sess., *Steel Prices, Unit Costs, Profits, and Foreign Competition* (Washington, D.C.: Government Printing Office, 1963), pp. 186, 339. 1956 and 1959 were years of major steel strikes in the United States.

The pattern of steel prices provides an easy explanation for the divergent evolution of demand for American and for European steel. Its significance for the competitive positions of the United States and western Europe on the world markets is not, of course, limited to exports and imports of steel alone. The level of steel prices is a major factor influencing the export prices, and hence the export performance, of countries in which manufactures provide the bulk of export revenue.[13] It is well established, moreover, that pricing policies in many other oligopolistic sectors of the American economy, such as the automobile and machinery industries, are very similar to those found in the steel industry.[14] The observed losses in world market shares of the United States for these sectors over the past decade are not in the least surprising.[15]

---

[13]   Otto Eckstein and Gary Fromm have estimated that the wholesale price index for all items except farm and food products would only have risen by 5 per cent instead of the actual rise of 10.5 per cent from 1953 to 1958 if steel prices had risen at the average rate of increase of all other prices in the index. In other words, the excess of the increase in steel prices over the average price rise of all other commodities was responsible for about 55 per cent of the rise in the wholesale price index during that period. "Steel and the Postwar Inflation", Study Paper No. 2, Joint Economic Committee, 86th Cong., 1st Sess., *Study of Employment, Growth, and Price Levels* (Washington, D.C.: Government Printing Office, 1959), p. 12.

[14]   See Thomas A. Wilson, "An Analysis of the Inflation in Machinery Prices" Study Paper No. 3., *op. cit.*; and John M. Blair, "Administered Prices: A Phenomenon in Search of a Theory", *American Economic Review, Papers and Proceedings,* XLIX (May, 1959), 431-50.

[15]   See Bela Balassa, "Recent Developments in the Competitiveness of American

It is hardly necessary to devote much space to explaining that the pricing policies of American steelmakers cannot be even remotely close to what could be expected to occur in a reasonably competitive market. An industry in which prices do not fall and are even raised at frequent intervals while the average rate of plant utilization remains at about two-thirds of total capacity for many years must be devoid of even the weakest remnants of interfirm rivalry.

A rise in the price of a given commodity far exceeding the rate of increase of prices in general, at a time when demand for it is stagnating, may be the result of a relentless upward push of wages by a union exercising monopoly control over the labor supply, even though the industry may be highly competitive. While union behavior could also have been the dominant factor causing the rise of steel prices, the available evidence is, at best, rather mixed. This conclusion has been reached by Gardiner Means, among others.[16] It can be shown, to be sure, that wages in the steel industry have increased faster than in almost all other industries during the 1950's, and have done so in the face of widespread unemployment.[17] No indictment of monopoly power can bypass the harmful effects of its exploitation by labor unions. Whether union pressure has been the *cause* of the rise in steel prices is nevertheless an entirely separate issue. On the basis of the available evidence, it is difficult to reject the hypothesis that the role of the United Steelworkers Union was the more passive one of trying to cut what it considered to be its fair share out of rising profits as round after round of steel price increases followed each other. Most important as a symptom is the fact that a large part of steelmaking capacity lay idle for so many years. It is difficult to imagine that an industry in which profits are being eroded by rapidly rising wages would not do its best to use the existing plant as fully as possible, especially if economies of scale are as important as they are in steel.[18]

Industry and Prospects for the Future", Joint Economic Committee, 87th Cong., 2nd Sess., *Factors Affecting the United States Balance of Payments,* Part I (Washington, D.C.: Government Printing Office, 1963), pp. 51-54.

[16]   Gardiner C. Means, *Pricing Power and the Public Interest* (New York: Harper & Bros., 1962), esp. chaps. vi and vii.

[17]   See Eckstein and Fromm, *op. cit.,* pp. 14-21.

[18]   Gardiner Means argues that 1953 can be taken as a typical year in which the steel industry earned normal returns on its assets and operated close to full plant utilization. On the basis of the increases of labor and materials costs from 1953 to 1959, he estimates that steel prices would have had to increase by approximately 15 per cent

The relatively most convincing explanation of the inflation in steel may be that the industry has attempted to operate in tacit collusion in order to secure maximum profits. Even this interpretation, which Morris Adelman has defended most vigorously,[19] leaves many questions unanswered. Why, for example, did the steel industry continue to expand capacity at a time when only about two-thirds of the available plant was being used, if it was striving to maximize aggregate profits? Equally mysterious is the indifference of the industry to the obvious threat of foreign competition as the gap between its own export prices and those of its principal rivals widened. Roger M. Blough, Chairman of the Board of United States Steel, had this to say about the abortive attempt to raise steel prices in April, 1962:

> While the price rise might have appeared to intensify our competitive difficulties with cheaper foreign steel, that steel is usually priced in relation to ours anyway, and in the long run, the increase would have improved our competitive strength. By using the added

---

to guarantee an unchanged rate of return. Instead, steel prices increased by 36 per cent (*op. cit.*, pp. 148-49). Blair observed earlier that the rates of net return after taxes for given rates of operation rose markedly for the United States Steel Corporation in the years following 1955 when prices increased most rapidly (*op. cit.*, pp. 442-43). If employment costs had been the driving force causing the inflation in steel, a profit squeeze would presumably have occurred instead.

Cost comparisons with Europe are not easy. Labor costs are substantially lower in Europe than in the United States (in 1961, $1.25 per hour compared to $4). Their rates of increase have been about the same in the two regions (74 as compared to 72 per cent from 1952 to 1961). By contrast, coal has been more expensive in Europe by an average of about 50 per cent during the late 1950's and early 1960's. In evaluating comparative production costs, account must also be taken of the fact that steel plants are, on the whole, significantly smaller in Europe than in the United States in an industry in which economies of scale are reported to be very important. Hearings before the Joint Economic Committee, 88th Cong., 1st Sess., *Steel Prices, Unit Costs, Profits, and Foreign Competition* (Washington, D.C.: Government Printing Office, 1963), pp. 21 and 710; European Coal and Steel Community, *12th Annual Report* (Luxembourg, 1964), Statistical Appendix; OECD, *L'industrie sidérurgique en 1962* (Paris, 1964), Statistical Appendix, Table 10.

[19] "Steel, Administered Prices and Inflation", *Quarterly Journal of Economics*, LXXV (February, 1961), 16-40. One wonders, however, how Professor Adelman reconciles his judgment that "any individual steelmaker could have produced and sold more steel at a cost far below the current price" (p. 24) with the view that "what happened in steel had nothing to do with inflation" (p. 34).

profits produced by the price increase to help obtain the most modern and efficient tools of production, we could hope eventually to narrow the gap between American and foreign steel prices.[20]

United States Steel was thus planning to meet the competition of cheaper foreign steel by *raising* prices.

IV   Approaches to inflationary stagnation

Whatever may have been the motives for the policies of the American steel industry and the very similar behavior of other oligopolistic industries in the United States, there cannot be any doubt about the adverse effects of these policies on the economy. Without them, the balance-of-payments deficits of the United States might never have become serious enough to attract anybody's attention, nor would chronic stagnation in their wake have become the disturbing economic and social problem it has been for the past few years.[21] The fact that major American industries set their prices without any apparent regard to the state of the market should dampen the hopes of those who expect that devaluation of the dollar would cure America's difficulties. If carried sufficiently far, devaluation can undoubtedly raise effective demand to the full-employment level. Nobody who has carefully observed the American economy can take it for granted, however, that steel and other industries would fail to raise prices under these conditions, or that unions having the necessary market power would refrain from making the most of the opportunity. Price and wage increases might before long restore the present balance-of-payments and employment situation.

---

[20]   Roger M. Blough, ed. by Eleanor Harris, "My side of the Steel Price Story", *Look,* January 29, 1963, p. 23. Reprinted by permission.

[21]   'A staggering 25 per cent of the male Negro teen-agers who are in the labor force are out of work, according to normally unpublished Government statistics obtained yesterday. ...The jobless rate for the group ... has ranged between 21 per cent and 25 per cent since 1958" (*New York Times,* August 24, 1964, p. 1). The order of magnitude of the steel problem may be judged by the following rough calculation: production of steel at the rate of capacity utilization that prevailed in Europe, and the exportation of the additional steel at world market prices (assuming, rather too pessimistically, unit elasticity of world demand for steel), would alone have been sufficient to eliminate the American balance-of-payments deficits of the past seven years.

Many of those who accept this argument will conclude that the obvious remedy is to devalue the dollar not just once, but to unpeg it entirely and let it depreciate continuously. In the event that this course of action is ever adopted by the United States, it is easy to predict the most probable consequences. The Board of Governors of the Federal Reserve System might eventually want to arrest the accelerating inflation that would be likely to occur if the United States government seriously attempted to keep the economy fully employed with unchanged market structure. Stagnation would then be quickly restored. Unemployment might, in fact, be higher than it is now, because monetary policy might have to be very tight after a period of more rapid inflation in order to persuade a suspicious public that the attempt to restore stability would not break down again.

Another possibility is that the Federal Reserve would be unable to prevent inflation from accelerating. The most pessimistic predictions of the staunchest advocates of rigid exchange rates would then be likely to become true. The present American dilemma is not of a type for which flexibility of exchange rates can be safely recommended as an easy way out. Until a few years ago, many economists regarded permissive inflationary policy as an easy method of preserving full employment under conditions of sellers' inflation. It is now widely recognized that an economy plagued by oligopolistic commodity and labor markets of the kind found in the United States may not be able to pursue full-employment policies under a regime of currency convertibility and pegged exchange rates. It may prove to be another shocking disappointment for many economists to discover that full-employment policies cannot be followed under these circumstances without disastrous consequences even when exchange rates are free to move.[22] Little need be said about the fact that easier access to credit facilities for central banks, whether on a bilateral or a multilateral basis (an increase of "international liquidity") has to be ruled out as a solution to the American dilemma, whatever the merits of the proposal may be in other cases. Extended financing of rising deficits would only serve to camouflage temporarily the outward symptoms of a much more deep-seated malady.

---

[22] The reader will appreciate the fact that there are more legitimate if perhaps more subtle arguments for fluctuating rates than the one claiming that they provide an easy escape from sellers' inflation.

It ought not to be surprising that the difficulties caused by market imperfections cannot be adequately resolved by policies designed to cope with entirely different problems, but only by reforming market structure. Nobody will deny that such changes are politically among the most difficult measures to accomplish. I am not persuaded that it is entirely impossible to bring about a degree of price flexibility in the most important American industries that would rule out pathological developments such as those experienced by the United States over the past few years. It is too often accepted as inevitable that prices in highly concentrated industries are as inflexible as they turn out to be in the American steel industry. Figure 1 above showed that steel prices in the European Coal and Steel Community behaved very differently, making possible a much higher rate of utilization of plant at all times.

The phenomenon is certainly consistent with the hypothesis that competition has been more intense in western Europe than in the United States, at least in the steel industry. This is nevertheless a hypothesis which, whether it is applied to steel or to any other industry, is frequently regarded as so implausible that it hardly merits attention.[23] To some extent, the opposition is merely due to semantics, as when competition is taken to be synonymous with consumers' sovereignty, private enterprise, or absence of government activity.[24] It should also be obvious that the degree of competition cannot be judged by merely counting the number of sellers or measuring market shares of the biggest companies in a national

---

[23]   With reference to Germany, Henry C. Wallich wrote that "taking all measures together, one cannot help concluding that the effort of the United States to remake Germany in its own antitrust image has met with rather limited success" (*Mainsprings of the German Revival* [New Haven, Conn.: Yale University Press, 1955], p. 383). Similarly, Alvin H. Hansen stated that "Germany historically is par excellence the country of cartels, and while the American Military Government made some effort to weaken the hold of cartels, the effort has met with relatively little success" (*The American Economy* [New York: McGraw-Hill Book Co, 1957], pp. 12-13). In his contribution to this volume, Charles P. Kindleberger discusses nine possible factors that may have contributed to West Germany's persistent balance-of-payments surpluses. On reflection, it will be seen that almost all of them can be most easily explained as symptoms of a higher degree of competition in Germany's commodity and labor markets.

[24]   Cf. "Comment" by Karl W. Roskamp on my article "Competition and Growth; The Lesson of West Germany", *American Economic Review*, L (December, 1960), 1015. Although its measurement in practice is obviously exceedingly difficult, the percentage excess of price over marginal cost, as proposed by Abba P. Lerner, may still be the

market. Such rough-hewn criteria take account neither of the degree to which domestic companies are exposed to competition from abroad nor of the extent to which they find it possible to enter into overt or tacit agreements with each other. The degree of price flexibility may still be the best indicator of competition that can be verified by an outside observer. Although monopoly is, in theory, quite compatible with price flexibility, this does not seem to hold in practice, especially and for rather obvious reasons in the case of tacit collusion in an oligopolistic industry.

Can the difficulties be overcome by price and wage controls? This proposal still appears to have more support than active antitrust policy. Apart from political or ideological objections, on which tastes may differ, the practical workability of this approach is rather doubtful. What is really needed are not merely lower, but more flexible prices. There is no assurance that rigidity will be less pronounced if prices are administered publicly rather than privately. If price and wage controls were operating ideally, the control agency would presumably have to imitate as closely as possible what a competitive market would accomplish. If strong antitrust policy is considered politically infeasible, it is difficult to see why price controls should be politically feasible if they lead to exactly the same pattern of prices and output.

The pricing policies of the American steel industry also constitute a counterexample to the otherwise plausible view that liberal trade policies are already a fully adequate antitrust policy. Although landed prices of foreign steel have for several years been appreciably below domestic American prices, foreign competition has so far not become a really important factor on the American market.

If the development of American export prices is not merely an exercise in monopoly power in a few strategically important industries, and if the different behavior of their European counterparts in industries such as steel is not to be explained by a greater (though by no means wholly satisfactory) awareness of competition, it would be of paramount importance that other hypotheses be furnished and tested. If the relatively higher rate of increase of industrial prices in the United States is not, in turn, the principal cause of the Great Stagnation from which the country

---

relatively most suitable theoretical yardstick of competition in an industry. See his "The Concept of Monopoly and the Measurement of Monopoly Power", *Review of Economic Studies*, I (June, 1934), 157-75.

has been suffering for so many years, it would be equally urgent to present convincing alternative explanations. Many attempts at explaining the divergence between American and foreign rates of growth have concentrated on factors determining supply rather than effective demand. There is certainly no doubt that the availability of skilled manpower, the growth of the capital stock, or the extent to which technological innovations are introduced will materially affect the maximum *potential* rate at which output can grow. At a time when most American industries operate below their full capacities, however, there is not much point in attributing differences in growth rates to differences between rates of increase of capacity. In evaluating the latter aspect, it is also fairly obvious that European industries have been more willing to invest because, among other things, swiftly rising demand tended continually to push production beyond available capacities.

One currently popular view is that the ability to avoid inflation in the export industries in spite of rapid wage increases is indeed the explanation both of the export surpluses of many western European countries and of the prosperity they have enjoyed, but that price stability is largely due to the fact that these countries have achieved much faster progress in labor productivity.

This argument seems to reverse the chain of causation that was presumably at work in recent years. All measures of labor productivity are calculated by dividing an index of output by some index of input. When the increasingly forceful exploitation of monopoly power pushes up prices and thus – through the foreign-trade and other effects – reduces business activity, output will be rising more slowly than in other countries that are not plagued by these ills. Empirical studies have shown that employment usually falls less than in proportion to the fall of output during times of recession.[25] As a natural consequence of all this, any measure of labor productivity will normally show a slower rate of increase in a country suffering from a lack of effective demand. It is also

---

[25]   See especially Arthur M. Okun, "Potential GNP: Its Measurement and Significance", reprinted from the 1962 *Proceedings of the Business and Economic Statistics Section* of the American Statistical Association as Cowles Foundation Paper No. 190 (New Haven, Conn., 1963). Okun concludes that an increase of unemployment by 1 per cent of the labor force has, on the average and for unemployment levels above 4 per cent, resulted in a reduction of the real gross national product of the United States by about 3 per cent over the past two decades.

evident that high business activity favors investment, and that a rapidly growing capital stock will bring about rapidly rising marginal returns to labor even without any special tricks. Slower progress in labor productivity may thus frequently arise as a *consequence* of sellers' inflation and its depressive effects rather than the reverse.[26]

V Conclusions

I have argued that the effectiveness of price flexibility in maintaining full employment is assured for an open economy, and that the institutional considerations which prompted doubts about it during the Great Depression are hardly relevant today. The relative flexibility of steel prices in the United States and in Europe was used to demonstrate this proposition. Steel prices are a convenient example not only because they affect foreign trade and production of an important industry, but also because they exercise a strong influence on the general price level, the export performance, and the level of activity of the economy as a whole. The empirical evidence on trade flows, output, and employment, of which only a small sample could be offered here, shows that these variables respond in very "classical" fashion to price changes. I ventured the hypothesis that greater flexibility of European steel prices was due to more intense competition, and concluded that the only policy measure that promises enduring success in the effort to assure full employment without balance-of-payments difficulties for the United States is a determined attempt to intensify competition in the American economy. Although there is little doubt that America owes much of its present worries to the monopoly power of labor unions, the performance of the steel industry suggests that imperfections in the commodity markets are an additional and very important element that deserves a great deal more attention.

---

[26] This is the most probable sequence of events in the short and medium run as an economy is faced with a contraction of aggregate demand. Over the long run, the economy may adjust to a lower level of production in which all relevant growth rates are about the same as at full employment.

INDEX